internet cool guide

Contents

22	Arts & Culture
27	Books
29	Business
33	Careers
36	Cars
42	Chat
43	Computers & Internet
50	Dating, Mating, & Relating
54	Directories & People Finders
56	Education
62	Entertainment
67	Fashion & Beauty
70	Film & Television
78	Finance & Investing
85	Food & Drink
91	Games & Gambling
96	Health
103	Home & Living
107	Kids & Teens
112	Law
114	Music
120	News & E-Zines
129	Parenting
132	Politics & Issues
138	Reference
143	Religion
145	Science & Nature
149	Seniors
150	Shopping
170	Sports
176	Travel
183	Wacky
184	Women

Ratings

- *outstanding content*
- *originality*
- *cool design*

Digital Culture 101

Number of Internet users worldwide: **195** million

Percentage living in Europe and North America: **95**

Percentage living in the United States: **52**

Number of households in the United States joining the Internet, per hour: **760**

Percentage of whites who have Internet access: **21**

Percentage of blacks who do: **7.7**

First head of state to send an e-mail message: Queen Elizabeth II

Number of e-mail messages sent per day: **2** billion

Number of instant messages sent per day: **403** million

Number of first-class letters mailed per day: 293 million

Portion of the Web indexed by search engines: **1/6**

#2 most popular search term: sex

#1 most popular search term: MP3

Percentage of Internet users who have bought something online this year: 53

Percentage who bought books and publications: 52

Percentage of retail stock trades now taking place on the Internet: 25

Percentage of car buyers in the United States who shop online: 40
Number of households expected to bank online by the year 2003: 32 million

Number of Internet consumers in the United States who have been the victims of credit card fraud: 6 million

Number of people the FBI has arrested for stalking children online, since 1995: 270

Percentage of American men who are likely to click on sex sites: 86

Percentage of American women who are: 14

Percentage of those who access sex sites that are married or living with a partner: 81

Number of people who downloaded the Starr Report from CNN Interactive in the first two days it was available: 1,700,000

Nothing But Net

So you're on the Web. You're surfing. You're chatting. You're scoping out shopping deals. Want to get more out of your experience online? Read on. These simple tips will make your Web journey faster, easier, and way more fun.

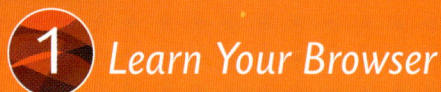

1 Learn Your Browser

Did you know that you can view a list of every Web site you've ever seen? Or that you can view Web pages in different languages? Whether you're using Netscape or Internet Explorer, you'll be amazed at what your browser can do. Spend some time getting to know what all those little buttons and menus are for—and take these tips for a test drive:

• Organize your bookmarks. Bookmarks (called favorites in Internet Explorer) let you save the addresses of your favorite sites for quick access. To keep your bookmarks folder in check, try dividing your bookmarks into subfolders—keep search engines in one folder, for example, or use one for each of your hobbies. You might create a different bookmarks folder for each member of your family.

• Speed up your browsing. Your browser will let you view Web pages without the images—you'll miss out on the cool graphics, but you'll be amazed at how much faster you can surf. Also try using keyboard shortcuts instead of your mouse. For example, instead of clicking the Back button when you want to view a previous page, simply type Command-left arrow on a Macintosh keyboard, or Alt-left arrow on a PC keyboard.

• Make searching simple. We all know how difficult it can be to find the information you need on the Internet. Your browser can help. In Netscape, you can enter a search directly into the Location field (that's the one where you type in the Web address). Simply type a question mark followed by your search term, like this: *?politics*. Netscape runs a search query for you and returns results in seconds.

2 Boost Your Bandwidth

So your Internet connection is slower than . . . If you're serious about surfing the Web, a faster Internet connection will make your time online a lot less frustrating. Plus, you'll be able to view Web pages with cool animations, movies, and sounds. Interested? You have a number of options: buy a faster modem (56k), check whether your cable company provides superfast cable access, or consider investing in an ISDN or DSL line. Be sure to find out whether your Internet service provider (ISP) supports such connections before taking the plunge.

3) Get Personal

Everywhere you look on the Web these days, sites are letting you personalize their content, whether it's custom-tailored news reports, online financial portfolios with the latest on your investments, or even your own day planner online. Our favorites? Sites that let you customize your home page to suit your own tastes and interests. Check out My Yahoo (my.yahoo.com), where you can personalize the content and layout of your start page. You choose the news that interests you, get the latest weather report for your home town, or view stock prices, lottery results, even new music releases. Very cool.

4) Build a Net Community

Your neighborhood just got bigger—way bigger. With chat, newsgroups, and thousands of Web communities, it's easy to meet and greet with anyone from China (7 million are online right now) to Iceland (120,000 surfers so far). To join a newsgroup or chat discussion, check out Deja (www.deja.com), where you can eavesdrop on 45,000 discussion groups. Learn the trade secrets of chefs or rate the candidates in your local election. Or download free ICQ software (www.icq.com) and chat with hundreds of thousands of people around the globe. Trust us—you won't know how you ever got along without it.

5) Take Control of Your Inbox

Ever feel overwhelmed by all the e-mails you get? It's no wonder: Americans send over two billion e-mail messages a day. Add up those annoying spam (junk e-mail) messages and the forwards from Grandma and . . . (surprise) you've got inbox overload. What to do?

• Get a second, free e-mail account (try www.hotmail.com) and use it for mailing lists or whenever you fill out a form on the Web. That way, you control who has access to your primary e-mail address.

• Take full advantage of your e-mail reader. Many programs can automatically sort incoming mail into various folders. If you use America Online, you can set your mail controls to block e-mail from specific addresses and domains.

• Consider using a filtering program that blocks spam messages, such as Spam Buster. For other options, check out the Junkbusters site at www.junkbusters.com.

6 · Learn Two Search Engines Well

There are more search engines popping up these days than you can shake a stick at, and they've each got their own quirks: one only searches highly trafficked Web sites, another organizes your results into folders, yet another can find the nearest movie theater and your long lost college roommate. Our advice? Think about what you search for most, determine what engines work for you, and learn how to use two of them. That's right, just two. Your best bets? For general Web searches, try Yahoo, Alta Vista, or HotBot. For human-picked site recommendations in a variety of categories, check out Magellan, About.com, or (of course!) the Internet Cool Guide. See our Search Engine Savvy page for details on how to master your search engine of choice.

7 · Become a Savvy e-Consumer

Just imagine: you and your credit card turned loose in the largest consumer playground since the Mall of America. Gucci, Prada, caviar, fresh Maine lobster, secondhand couture dresses, samurai swords, Thighmasters, Matisse masterworks and Beanie Babies—all a click away, 24 hours a day, 7 days a week, direct to you or your small-town Kansas cousin. Pretty amazing, eh? Net shopping is for the most part safer, smarter, and simpler than the way you shop right now. But be careful: six million Internet consumers in the United States have been the victims of credit card fraud, and that number is sure to grow as more of us buy stuff online. Taking a few precautions never hurts.

• Always pay with plastic. That way you can get a refund from your credit card company if you buy from a deadbeat vendor.

• Never send your credit card number to anyone over e-mail. When you fill out an order form on the Web, your credit card information gets encrypted—that is, scrambled—so that no one can swipe your number. Encryption works so well, it's probably safer than handing your credit card to a waiter in a restaurant. But if you send your credit card number in an e-mail message, you make your info vulnerable to all kinds of snoops. Don't do it!

• Be sure that you're shopping on a secure site. Look for the padlock icon at the bottom left corner of your browser window—if it's locked, you're on a secure site. If you don't see a padlock, check the URL (site address): if it begins with https:// instead of http:// (notice the extra "s"), the page uses encryption to safeguard your information.

• Do your homework. Is the site endorsed by the Better Business Bureau Online or a similar organization? Have any claims been filed against it with the Federal Trade Commission? Is it part of a larger shopping network like Yahoo! or Excite? Are the street address and phone number of the company listed on the site?

8. Make It Safe For Kids

A new generation of kids is being weaned on the Web, and that's a challenge for parents, who are often less techno-savvy than their little ones. We all know that e-mail, chat rooms, and the Internet can be dangerous territory for kids. Access to pornography and offensive material is just the beginning: kids can have all sorts of encounters with strangers online, in chat rooms and over e-mail. They may not understand the ramifications of giving out personal information on a Web site. And they often lack the intellectual and emotional tools necessary to navigate the cyber world—it is a jungle out there. Still, it's important to let them explore—after all, the Internet can be a phenomenal learning tool. The best thing parents can do is get involved with their child's online life, and set some basic ground rules for the family. A few suggestions:

• To block access to offensive Web sites, use your browser controls (or software like NetNanny or CyberPatrol).

• Remind your kids never to give out personal information to anyone online—on a Web site, in an e-mail message, or in a chat room or newsgroup. That means their name, age, e-mail and home address, school name, or pictures of themselves.

• Find out if your child is listed in any e-mail directories, and check out your Internet Service Provider's privacy policy. They could be selling your child's personal information.

• Never allow your child to meet an online friend without your consent, and accompany them the first time they meet this person.

9. Explore!

Did you know that you can do your taxes online? Watch South Park or a Bob Dylan concert? View your credit report? Get tickets to a movie or Broadway show? Read *Newsweek* or *Rolling Stone* for free? Find a doctor, lawyer, personal astrologer, or garden guru? Log on and explore, or start with the recommendations here. It's a wide, wide Web out there. What are you waiting for?

Online Privacy:
What You Should Know

The government, industry, and consumer advocacy groups are in the midst of a bitter battle over your personal information. Every Web site you visit, every purchase you make online, even your name, profession, income, e-mail and postal address—all this information can be automatically tracked, stored, or sold to other companies for marketing purposes without your knowledge or consent. As if you didn't have enough to worry about.

And there's more: while marketers want to track your surfing and purchasing habits, the government (or the company you work for) may be monitoring your e-mail. That's right: e-mail is never private. In fact, some courts have ruled that the e-mail messages you send from your office are owned by your boss.

So what's being done about all this? As far as the buying and selling of personal information goes, the government has basically allowed companies to regulate themselves. But this makes consumer advocates nervous—they want the U.S. government to enact tough online privacy standards, as European governments have. While many companies have begun posting privacy policies on their sites, a recent study found that only 33% of the most trafficked Web sites have a privacy statement that lets you know how your information will be used. That means you never know who your information might be sold to—or for what purpose.

There's also been much controversy over encryption, a technology that scrambles information (such as your credit card number or an e-mail message) so that it can't be snooped on en route to its destination. Some want to outlaw public access to encryption programs, so that criminals can't outmaneuver law enforcement officials by sending encrypted messages. But recent rulings have mandated that encryption software remain legal—even for you and me.

In a perfect world, we would control who has access to our personal information and correspondence—and we'd control what it's being used for. But with new data collection and storage methods being developed every day, it's important to be aware of your privacy, every time you log on.

Is it safe to submit my name, address, and other personal information to a Web site?
Many sites require you to register before allowing you access to their services—and that usually means filling out a form with your name, address, and consumer preferences. Before you fill out these forms, be sure to check if the site has a privacy policy. Will they disclose or sell your information to others? If you're not sure, or if you're uncomfortable giving out your info, you can always fake it.

Is it safe to enter my credit card number on a Web site?
Check to see if you're on a secure site by looking for the padlock symbol at the lower corner of your browser window. If it's locked, the site is secure, and your information is safe. If you're still concerned, you can strengthen the level of encryption of your browser, making it even harder to unscramble your data. Software such as Fortify is available for download at www.zdnet.com.

Should I be worried about cookies?
Cookies make it possible for a Web site to "recognize" you—they record information about you such as your registration name and password, your comings and goings to a site, or what's in your online shopping cart. Cookies aren't all bad—they actually allow Web sites to serve you better. But do be aware of them: set your browser to notify you before accepting a cookie from a site. You can also block cookies altogether in your browser preferences.

How can I surf the Web anonymously?
Check out the old standard: www.anonymizer.com. The site lets you surf the Web anonymously, but it may slow you down. Also stay informed: initiatives like AT&T's Crowds project (www.research.att.com/projects/crowds) are devising new ways to let users troll the Web under cover. With Crowds, users are pooled together in groups, and their identities are shuffled around. That way no one can tell who's actually accessing the site at any particular time.

How can I be sure my e-mail remains private?
It's true: e-mail is about as private as a gym shower. Not only do you and the recipient have copies of your message, but your server probably keeps a copy as well. There are also a number of points along the electronic mail route where your e-mail can be snatched. If you're concerned, you can encrypt your e-mail using a program like Pretty Good Privacy— that way only those who have an electronic "key" can unlock your e-mail message. You can also send free, encrypted e-mail over the Web at sites like www.ziplip.com and www.hushmail.com.

For more information on privacy, see www.epic.org.

Search Engine Savvy

With hundreds of millions of Web pages out there, searching the Web can be a daunting task. No fear—even a novice can become a search guru by following these three simple steps.

step 1 Choose Your Weapon

Because each search engine excels at a different type of search, figuring out which to use is crucial. Directory searchers (such as Yahoo!) divide the Web into user-friendly categories (such as sports, shopping, and travel), not unlike the table of contents of a book. Search engines on the other hand (examples are Alta Vista and Google) search the entire text of Web pages for specific words or phrases—and often return thousands of results. These engines are more like a book's index. So, if you're looking for a general topic, like music sites—or Elvis sites for example—use Yahoo! If you're looking for Web pages that describe the rhinestone-studded leisure suits that Elvis wore on stage in Las Vegas, use Alta Vista.

step 2 Learn the Language

Knowing how to narrow down a search and learning a few terms (called search operators) will greatly improve your results. Rule #1: Be as specific as possible. If you want to find the Prince William fan page, don't enter "royal family" in the search field. Rule #2: Use search operators (sometimes called Boolean operators) to format your request. They're not that complicated—really! Here are the most basic ones:

+   When you want to be sure that a certain word appears in your search results, use a plus sign before the word. If you type *"elvis graceland"* into a search field, most search engines will return all pages with the word "elvis" on them, and all pages with the word "graceland" on them, but not necessarily pages with both words.

      If you want to find pages with BOTH "elvis" and "graceland" on them, type: *+elvis +graceland*. This is a good way to narrow down a search.

- Similarly, if you put a minus sign before a word, the search engine will skip pages that contain that word. Say you want to find information on Elvis, but avoid anything on his later days as a Vegas star. Type: *elvis-vegas.*

" " Use quotation marks to search for consecutive words—if you want to find pages that mention the song "Love Me Tender," enter the name of the song in quotes: *"love me tender."*

Otherwise, the search will return pages with "love," pages with "me," and pages with "tender," but not necessarily the three words together.

* The *, or wildcard character, is used when you don't know how to spell a word, or if you want to find different forms of a word. For example, if you want to find pages on Elvis impersonators, you can include pages with "impersonation" and "impersonate" by typing: *+elvis +imperson**

AND See + above. as in *elvis and graceland*

NOT See - above. as in *elvis not graceland*

OR Finds documents containing at least one of the specified words or phrases: *"hound dog" or "love me tender"*

NEAR Finds documents containing both specified words or phrases within ten words of each other: *elvis near death*

NOTE: Using different search engines is like driving different cars—each one has its own quirks. Some won't understand all of the above search terms, and others will use their own. See below for a tutorial on four popular engines—if in doubt, take a look at the search engine's help page.

step 3 *And You're Off!*

Once you've entered your search request, you'll see the results page. The results (called "hits") are ranked—at the top are the Web sites that the search engine thinks are closest to what you are looking for. These rankings can be hit and miss—after all, the computer can't read your mind! Chances are you'll find some useful starting points, though. Your Web journey is just beginning . . .

Best Directory

Yahoo! www.yahoo.com
That's right—one of the most popular search engines around is also one of the best. According to the *The San Jose Mercury News*, "Yahoo is closest in spirit to the work of Linnaeus, the 18th-century botanist whose classification system organized the natural world." Raves aside, Yahoo! does a good job organizing half a million sites into 25,000 categories, and is ideal for searching general topics such as jazz music or computer games. Its well-designed interface and logical structure make it perfect for beginners. And Yahoo! is a terrific homepage, with useful extras such as e-mail, newsfeeds, and links to shopping, stock quotes, and personals. One caveat: if you're searching for specific terms, or want to use complex search commands, skip Yahoo! and go right to AltaVista or Northern Light.

Yahoo! Tutorial
Yahoo! supports the following commands:
- **+** The word must be found in all of the search results:
  +elvis +graceland
- **-** The word cannot be in any of the search results: *elvis -vegas*
- **t:** Restricts searches to the titles of Web pages only:
  joe boxer vs. *t:joe boxer*
- **u:** Restricts searches to document URLs (or addresses): *intel* vs. *u:intel*
- **" "** Searches for consecutive words: *"love me tender"*
- ***** Wildcard matching: *imperson** would return impersonate, impersonator, etc.

Tip: When using multiple search operators in Yahoo, the syntax must be combined in the following order: + - t: u: " " and *
Correct: +elvis -graceland +"love me tender"
Incorrect: "love me tender" -graceland +elvis

Also: From the Search Options page you can restrict your search by date (search only Web pages in the last 6 months, for example), or customize the number of results per page.

Try Yahoo!
Imagine you love James Brown, and want to see a list of other soul musicians. No problem. Type *"james brown"* in the search field (in quotes, to weed out the zillions of pages with either "james" or "brown" in them). At the top of your screen, under the Yahoo! logo, you'll see this:
Entertainment > Music > Artists > By Genre > Soul and R&B > Brown, James
These are Yahoo categories, each one more specific than the one before. To find a list of music types (country, rock, soul, etc.), click on *By Genre*. To see a list of soul and R&B artists, click on the *Soul and R&B* link.

Smartest Newcomer

Google www.google.com
Its founders say they chose the name Google because a googol is a gigantic number—ten to the 1000th power to be exact. Luckily, the Web doesn't have that many pages (yet), but at 320 million and growing, a new crop of search engines has emerged promising better ways to sift through the information morass. The quirkiest and smartest of these is Google, which judges the quality of a site based on how many sites link to it. (The theory is the more links, the better the Web site. Since so many sites link to the New York Times site, for example, its probably a better resource than the Podunk Times, which very few pages would connect to.) Google's ultra-clean main page skips the bells and whistles and displays just a search field and two buttons—simple. Coolest of all is Google's "I Feel Lucky" button. Simply enter a search term and click on "I Feel Lucky"—Google skips the search results and takes you straight to the top-ranked site. Pretty great, but note that Google doesn't support complex searches.

Google Tutorial
- **+**   The word must be found in all of the search results: *+elvis +graceland*
- **-**   The word cannot be in any of the search results: *elvis -vegas*
- **" "** Searches for consecutive words: *"love me tender"*

Beware! Google removes such words as "and" and "or," so if you want them, be sure to put plus signs next to them: if you enter "Lord of the Flies" in Google's search field, it will return all documents containing the words "lord" and "flies." Instead, type "Lord +of +the Flies." Also, Google does not "stem"—that is, it doesn't pick up slight variants on a word. For instance, if you enter "cats" in the search field, Google will only look for pages with the exact spelling "cats," but not those with "cat."

Try Google!
Looking for the Bloomingdale's home page but not sure of the address? Google's your best bet. Enter *bloomingdale's* in the search field and click the "I Feel Lucky" button. Faster than you can say "Jean Paul Gaultier"— there you are.

Best Overall Engine

Alta Vista www.altavista.com
Alta Vista doesn't have the fun and flavor of Yahoo!, but what it lacks in personality, it makes up for in sheer power. With a massive index (the full text of 125 million Web pages) and loads of search features, Alta Vista excels at finding the needle in the virtual haystack. The possibilities are endless—Alta Vista lets you ask questions in plain language, and search the Web for URLs, titles, text, even images. You can limit your search to Web pages in Spanish (or Russian, or Chinese), or instantly translate an entire Web site into any of ten different languages. *C'est superbe!* One tip: always use lowercase letters in Alta Vista's search field.

Alta Vista Tutorial
- **+** The word must be found in all of the search results:
  +elvis +graceland
- **-** The word cannot be in any of the search results: *elvis -vegas*
- **" "** Phrase words in exact sequence: *"love me tender"*
- ***** Wildcard matching: *imperson** would return impersonate, impersonator, etc.
- **AND** Finds only documents containing all of the specified words or phrases.
- **OR** Finds documents containing at least one of the specified words.
- **NOT** Excludes documents containing the specified word or phrase.
- **NEAR** Finds documents containing both specified words or phrases within ten words of each other.

Try Alta Vista!
Want to see Alta Vista really flex its muscles? Try these advanced search commands:

text: Finds pages that contain the specified text in any part of the page other than the title or URL (address). For example: *text:leisure suit*.

url: Finds pages with a specific word or phrase in the URL.
domain: Limits search to a specified domain. To limit your search to web sites in Germany's domain, for example, type *domain:de* in the search field.

image: Searched Web pages for images of a certain file name. Type *image:elvis*, for example, to find pages with images of Elvis.

link: Use it to find all the pages that link to a certain site. For example, to find all the Web sites that link to Alta Vista's site, type *link:altavista.com*.

(For true search junkies: check out Alta Vista's Refine tool and advanced help page for even more options.)

Best Metasearch

MetaCrawler www.metacrawler.com
Metasearchers take your search request and run it on a gaggle of search engines simultaneously, saving you the work of figuring out which one best fits your needs. An inspired idea, but with a few flaws. For one thing, metasearchers don't return every result from each engine—only a small selection from each—and their rankings are sometimes unhelpful, jumbling the best sites with lesser sources. Metacrawler, however, is definitely worth a look—it searches Yahoo!, Lycos, Infoseek, WebCrawler, Excite, AltaVista, Thunderstone, and Looksmart simultaneously. A big plus: with MetaCrawler you can skip learning the different commands for each engine—it formats for you.

MetaCrawler Tutorial
- **+**   The word must be found in all of the search results: *+elvis +graceland*
- **-**   The word cannot be in any of the search results: *elvis -vegas*
- **" "** Phrase words in exact sequence: *"love me tender"*
- ***** Wildcard matching: *imperson** would return impersonate, impersonator, etc.

Try MetaCrawler!
Check out search voyeurs MetaSpy and MetaSpy Exposed, which let you peek in on what other people are searching for at any given time of day; MetaSpy is the G-rated version, and MetaSpy Exposed is no-holds-barred, for adults only.

geek speak guide

New words for a new world: since when did spam blocking, nested boolean queries, and the future of e-commerce become fodder for cocktail-party conversation? A crash course in techspeak for the uninitiated:

attachment
A file that is "attached" (or added on) to an e-mail message.

bookmark
To save favorite Web addresses in your browser, you can bookmark the site.

bounce message
Also referred to as barfmail, it's an automatic notification you get when an e-mail message doesn't go through.

cookie
A text file that a Web site puts on your hard drive so that the site can "recognize" you at a later time.

cybercitizen
A citizen of the Internet, or a member of the cybercommunity.

egosurfing
is searching to see how many places on the Web your name appears. Try it! At Alta Vista, simply enter your name surrounded by double quotes in the search field, like this: *"Your Name"*

bandwidth
Bandwidth refers to the size of the data pipeline. To have higher bandwidth is to have a faster Internet connection which carries more information.

boolean operators
Boolean operators are words (such as and, not, and near) used to format sophisticated queries when using a search engine such as Yahoo! or Alta Vista.

bulletin board system (bbs)
A message database where people can log in and leave broadcast messages for others, usually grouped into topics. These include biggies like Compuserve and thousands of little local bulletin boards run by amateurs out of their homes. *(See also newsgroup.)*

browser
A program that allows you to view the Web, such as Netscape or Internet Explorer.

cybercafe / cyberburger joint
A cafe or fast-food joint that provides Internet access to customers. Thousands have cropped up around the world, from Alaska to Sao Paulo to Laos.

dead link
A hypertext link that no longer points to the intended Web page, usually because the page was moved or deleted.

e-zine
The upstart Web counterpart of print magazines. Thousands of e-zines now dot the cyber landscape, on every topic from news and opinion to sex and snowboarding.

e-commerce
(electronic commerce) is the buying and selling of retail goods on the Internet. Also called e-business or e-tailing (or electronic retailing).

faq
A frequently asked question, or a list of frequently asked questions posted on a newsgroup or Web site. Consult the faq page when you have questions about the newsgroup or site.

flaming
is posting an obnoxious message on a public newsgroup or chat room, or sending an intentionally nasty e-mail. (FYI, flaming is poor netiquette!).

html
(Hyper Text Markup Language) The computer language used to create Web pages.

irc
(Internet Relay Chat) Any system that lets you communicate with others in text or audio in real time—that is, live.

MP3
A file format that lets you download music from the Internet. You can play MP3s with an MP3 player, downloadable from www.mp3.com.

newbie
A Web freshman—new to the Internet and obviously so.

plug-in
An application that works in conjunction with your browser. Examples are Real Audio, which lets you listen to streaming music on the Internet, and Macromedia's Shockwave, which lets you view Shockwave animations and games.

geek
According to cyberlorist Eric Raymond: "One who fulfills all the dreariest negative stereotypes about hackers: an asocial, malodorous, pasty-faced monomaniac with all the personality of a cheese grater." But watch out—geeks, also called hackers, turbo nerds, propeller heads, terminal junkies, girl geeks, and spods—may yet inherit the earth.

geekosphere
Assuming you're a full- or part-time geek, the geekosphere is the physical ambiance around you and your computer during a marathon night of Web surfing: post-its, inspirational quotes, family photos, coffee cup, mouse pad, and half-empty cans of Jolt cola...

handle
Your handle is your cyber identity—either your e-mail name, or the alias you use in chat rooms.

isp
(Internet Service Provider) A company that sells access to the Internet—examples are AOL and Compuserve. Some (but not all) ISPs come equipped with a browser (see above).

jolt
Sometimes described as "the fuel on which the Internet is run," a typical can of Jolt cola contains about twice the amount of caffeine as Coke or coffee—a boon to late-night Web surfers.

netiquette
is etiquette on the Internet.

newsgroup
An Internet discussion group, or Usenet group, organized by subject, where you can post messages and see responses from others. Examples are alt.music.punk or rec.gardening.tulips.

snail mail
Good old-fashioned mail that's delivered by the post office. You remember—the kind that needs stamps.

spam
Spam is unsolicited junk e-mail. Your e-mail provider may offer spam-blocking, which filters out these annoying messages.

webcam
A video camera, usually attached directly to a computer, whose latest image can be viewed on a Web site. A live cam is one that shows live streaming video—like the infamously weird Jennicam, a 24-hour live broadcast of college student Jennifer Ringley's dorm room.

arts & culture

CultureFinder www.culturefinder.com

An incredible resource for theater, music, and art events nationwide, CultureFinder combs 300,000 art exhibits and performances in 1,300 cities to provide you with the perfect plans for this evening or next Christmas. Tickets for most listings can be ordered online from CultureFinder's Ticket Butler. You'll also find reviews, celebrity chat, and the fabulous Culture Briefs section, which gives plot summaries of popular musicals like *Grease* and *Rent*.

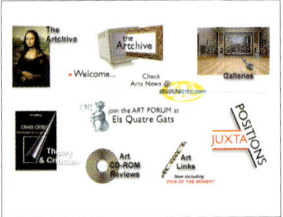

The Artchive

www.artchive.com

Just what the name implies: the Artchive is a catalog of over 2,000 scanned works of art from more than 200 artists, the likes of Picasso, Brancusi, Goya, and de Kooning. View the works by artist or browse the online galleries with such exhibits as "The First Impressionist Exhibition, 1874," complete with criticism and catalog entries. The Artchive also includes selected articles of art theory and criticism; but the high-quality scans and selection alone justify a trip to this site.

ArtMuseum.net www.artmuseum.net

Bringing art into the digital age. ArtMuseum.net has joined forces with museums like the Whitney to create multimedia exhibitions specifically geared for online participation. The exhibitions require plug-ins like Shockwave and Flash, which can be downloaded from the site—they're worth it for the viewing experience.

Internet Art Resources www.artresources.com

Bursting with listings of museums, galleries, artists, and art schools throughout the United States, Art Resources is a stellar source for famous and not-so-famous artists and galleries. A database of nearly 3,000 images plus reviews and features bring you up to date on the current scene.

LA County Museum of Art www.lacma.org

From Peruvian burial mantles and copper Thai Buddhas to paintings by Rembrandt and Gauguin, LACMA online proves that high culture has indeed survived in the city of traffic jams and movie stars. Browse through LACMA's 11 curatorial departments to view examples of some of the finest Asian and Islamic art in the Western world, as well as the extensive collections of American and European painting, sculpture, decorative arts, photography, and costume and textile samples.

Whitney Museum of American Art www.whitney.org
You could fly to New York to see great art—or save your money and dial up the Whitney online. You'll find a virtual slide show of works by Edward Hopper, Jasper Johns, and other greats from the museum's permanent collection. Special exhibitions from the Whitney Annual and Biennial programs, complete with calendars, event information, and an overview of the Whitney's 12,000 classic artworks make the site a must-see.

 **The Museum of Modern Art**
www.moma.org
Elegant and tech-savvy, just as you'd expect, the MOMA online lets you view selected works from its permanent collection complete with audio commentary. Highlights of temporary exhibitions, past, present and future, as well as special online projects like Art Safari for kids and the Time Capsule AIDS project let users interact with art.

The Metropolitan Museum of Art www.metmuseum.org
Take a virtual tour of the 200,000-square-foot, 125-year-old art museum without leaving your chair. Floor plans of the Met's dozens of galleries allow visitors to view selections from the three million works in the permanent collection spanning 5,000 years of cultural history. Medieval armor, marble reliefs from ancient Greece, and Kandinsky paintings—it's all here. Visit the museum shop for gift ideas and online shopping.

 **Guggenheim Museums**
www.guggenheim.org
A soaring flash video intro is your first peek at this modern art extravaganza online. The five international Guggenheim sites host sophisticated retrospectives of artists like Rauschenberg and Serra. Check out the cool, kitschy gifts available at the site's store.

The Louvre www.mistral.culture.fr/louvre
The virtual Louvre beats its real-world counterpart in the fact that you won't have to correctly pronounce the museum's name to enjoy its contents. One of the most visitor-friendly museums online, the Louvre's Web site will wow you with Quicktime virtual tours, extensive information on the artworks, and a fascinating history of the much-loved museum. No worries—you can get a tour in English.

The Jewish Museum New York www.jewishmuseum.org
The online galleries of New York's Jewish Museum are beautifully presented and highly informative: browse topic areas like "Forging an Identity" and "Realizing a Future" for a visual history of Jewish identity and culture. You can also listen to contemporary artists speak about their work.

arts & culture

American Ballet Theatre www.abt.org
With full biographies of the dancers and notes on the hundreds of composers, choreographers, and ballets included in the repertory of the company's 60-year history, ABT's Web site is a complete ballet directory. The best part of the site is the Quicktime-animated ballet dictionary, which lets you view video clips of company dancers illustrating steps and terms.

The Ballroom Dance Resource www.ballroomdancers.com
Want to learn the hustle, the waltz, or the merengue without embarassing yourself in a dance class? Now you can learn to dance without leaving your seat! The Ballroom Dance Resource is packed with step-by-step instructions and videos of dancers in action, plus information on how to find a partner or a class and even where to find costumes.

Dancebot www.dancebot.com
Sleek and light on graphics, Dancebot is a fast, extensive search engine for world dance resources from folk dance newsgroups to samba studios. Dozens of categories to browse and three search methods link dancers and dance lovers to hundreds of sites and communities, fulfilling Dancebot's mission to help dancers connect, pool their knowledge, and enhance the world of dance.

Playbill Online www.playbill.com
The ubiquitous theater magazine and program boosts its informative content to a new degree online, providing news, features, and interviews for Broadway, off-Broadway, London, and regional performances. Browse or search current show times and venues, buy tickets, even book hotel rooms and restaurant reservations. Playbill Online's memorabilia boutique and links to Amazon.com's theater bookshop come to the rescue for anything you may have forgotten to pick up at the show.

New York Times Current Theater
www.nytimes.com/library/theater
Settled comfortably in the heart of Times Square, the prestigious newspaper has a front row seat to all of Broadway—literally. No wonder its reviews are the quintessence of theater criticism. This site is nothing more than a simple archive of reviews for all current productions on and off Broadway, but the quality of the writing (and links to the rest of the online paper) make it worth a look.

The Phantom of the Opera www.thephantomoftheopera.com
With gossamer images of floating dancers and shattered masks sunk in a black background, the official site for *The Phantom of the Opera* is as illusory and extravagant as the long-running musical. Fans will have as much fun making the phantom appear and disappear by running the mouse across the screen as they will downloading video clips and browsing the photo gallery. Tour and ticket info, historical framework, and production credits are here, too.

arts & culture

Architecture www.architecturemag.com
An industry journal and art publication in one, Architecture deserves kudos for its amazing translation from print magazine to Web presence, maintaining all the gloss and finesse one expects of a refined design review. With lucid writing on surprisingly practical issues of modern architecture across the globe, this site appeals to design professionals and the rest of us.

 Culturekiosque.com
www.culturekiosque.com
This award-winning European pavilion of classical music, cinema, technology, and art provides a decidedly continental commentary on the latest in international culture. Log on for insider news and views on jazz, art, archaeology, and opera—as well as reviews of popular TV shows, bands, and movies, in French. *Viva les X-Files!*

Guerrilla Girls www.guerrillagirls.com
The self-proclaimed "conscience of culture," the Guerilla Girls are an underground band of feminist Robin Hoods aiming to overturn the universal historical "dead white male" trend in literature, art, and the humanities. View their witty, provocative posters, chart their travels to and from various protest rallies and university lectures, and read interviews and articles explaining and exploring the Guerrilla Girls' mission and progress.

DoubleTake Magazine www.doubletakemagazine.org
Beautiful and innovative, DoubleTake incorporates a fine selection of photography, fiction, nonfiction, and poetry—documenting everything from landmark social movements to the nuances of everyday existence. The Web site includes a fabulous teachers' classroom companion that encourages inquiry and exploration of topics such as identity and place.

Artnet.com www.artnet.com
The premiere virtual art fair, Artnet.com is an enormous resource for buying, selling, finding, and appraising fine art. Search or browse hundreds of listings for galleries, artists, fairs, and museums to find everything from tribal art to antiques to design and furniture. Online auctions with over 1.8 million lots from over 500 auction houses, complete with e-mail auction updates, are available to registered members. In addition, the Artnet.com online magazine keeps users up to date on the latest news and views of the art world.

Photography in New York International www.photography-guide.com
A slick and comprehensive guide to photography galleries and exhibitions in New York, across the United States, and worldwide. The extensive contact information and cross-referenced photographer listings are the best available on the Web. Find Brassaï or Ansel Adams in your city or across the globe, or search for the latest photo exhibits in a specific area.

alt.culture www.altculture.com
Any doubt about the coolness of this site will be swept away with one spin through its exhaustive list of awards and two-thumbs-up reviews. Alt.culture has almost 1,000 pithy dictionary descriptions of '90s cultural trivia: Mentos and *Twin Peaks*, nitrous oxide and No Fear, MTV, Queer Nation, the Unabomber, and hip-hop. The entries are terse, wry, informative, and totally addictive: set the autopilot to deliver a random entry every 10 seconds and entertain yourself for hours.

ReVue www.revue.com
Fabulous design and organization turns this online bilingual photo magazine into a beautiful virtual gallery. Special themes like "wind," photojournalism essays on youth in Cuba and ethnic Albanians, and other themed exhibits are presented in sections that give the feeling of the different rooms in a museum. The hundreds of photographs are clear and can be enlarged, and the magazine is updated regularly with new work.

Adbusters Culture Jammer's Headquarters www.adbusters.org
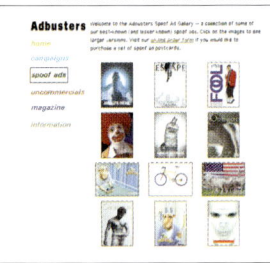
Aiming to turn your computer (aka your "drab number cruncher") into the most versatile activist tool ever reckoned with, Adbusters has taken its infamous spoof ad campaigns online. View Quicktime versions of the their "uncommercials," complete with explanations of Adbusters' mission to combat consumer culture, and find out how to participate in Adbusters' campaigns nationwide.

disinformation www.disinfo.com
There's information ... and then there's information from the front. Disinformation is the counterculture center of the Web, with info on Zapatistas, underground comics censorship, and other antiestablishment rants. The site features Real Video interviews and cartoon clips and a continuously updated talk show, as well as chats, forums, and a shop stocked with Timothy Leary-esque books, videos, and gear.

24 Hour Museum www.24hourmuseum.org.uk
With art, news, and views from the United Kingdom, the 24 Hour Museum is a solid example of the direction art education and information are taking online. Check the oft-updated news stories to find out what Britain's art insiders are talking about, or peruse British museum and exhibition information from archaeology to world cultures. The "My First Museum" section for children is particularly well done, with a click-and-point painting exercise and an animated virtual tour.

Smithsonian Institution www.si.edu
America's encyclopedia of history, culture, technology, and art. This vast resource would take weeks to view from end to end. View online exhibits on everything from Aeronautics & Space History and African American History to Entomology, Inventors, Political History, and Zoology. A gold mine of culture and historical information on the Web.

Whatsonstage.com www.whatsonstage.com
When you need to know what's on in the West End and beyond, surf over to What's On Stage, London's theater guide. Keep posted on upcoming festivals and tours, reviews of current productions, and news stories on the scene in London and beyond, or use the search engine to find specific shows, dates, and locations.

books

Amazon.com www.amazon.com
Unless you've been living under a rock for the past decade, you probably know that there's an incredible electronic bookstore on the Internet called Amazon.com. It's got great deals on books, a superb customer service department, really neat contests, and insightful customer reviews. Amazon.com really goes out of the way to treat its customers well, and although it's no substitute for your cozy neighborhood book shop (if you still have one, that is), it will win your loyalty with free gifts and browsable pages. Shop elsewhere for out-of-print books, though; you'll find much better prices at other sites.

BarnesandNoble.com www.barnesandnoble.com
This online megastore probably has every in-print book known to man, but its main attraction may be the links to *The New York Times Book Review* and NPR's Selected Shorts. Enormous content, great prices, but unfortunately, no comfy chairs for book browsing.

The Internet Bookshop www.bookshop.co.uk
If you'd like a different cultural perspective on books, then head for The Internet Bookshop, which offers savings of up to 50% on British and American books. You can submit information about your reading preferences and it will send you an e-mail on new publications that may interest you.

Powell's Books www.powells.com
Featuring new, used, and out-of-print books, Powell's has some fabulous deals on great reads. There's a rare book room, a list of staff picks, a best-seller room, and a weekly contest to win free books. Articles about poets and writers make this a joy for fans of the written word.

Wordsworth Books www.wordsworth.com
In addition to hundreds of thousands of books, Wordsworth Books rounds up exclusive interviews with authors, a weekly contest, a list of author events, recommendations that are just for kids, and title compilations of various literary award winners. Kids will absolutely love the Curious George section (and you will, too).

American Booksellers Association www.bookweb.org
ABA is a not-for-profit trade organization that supports
the needs and concerns of independently owned bookstores. If you dis-
like patronizing big chain stores, simply enter your zip code in the search
mode and the site will spit out a list of indies where you can shop without bruising your conscience.

A Common Reader www.commonreader.com
Anybody who loves books simply must visit A Common Reader. Each and
every selection is championed by the extremely well-read staff, whose
tantalizing plot descriptions will make you want to toss the whole collection into your shopping cart. Intriguing categories include
"Real/Imagined Lives," "Uncommon Pleasures," and "The Presence of
the Past." A jewel.

Advanced Book Exchange www.abebooks.com
Ever look for a treasured book only to be told by a smarmy salesclerk,
"Sorry, that's out of print"? Well, unclench your fists, because the
Advanced Book Exchange is here. This free service allows you to enter a
book by title or author into the search mode and get a list of used book-
sellers from all over the world who have what you want.

Online Books

www.cs.cmu.edu/afs/cs/misc/mosaic/common/omega/web/
books.html
Read any of over 9,000 full-text books on this site, which includes
works by Nathaniel Hawthorne, Edith Wharton, Honoré de Balzac,
and hundreds more. The site houses only books that are free of charge
and not copyrighted, so your favorite may not be available, but the vast
listings contain something for everybody including many award-winners,
banned books, a tribute to female authors, and a number of foreign-
language links.

New York Review of Books www.nybooks.com/nyrev
Intellectual nirvana with Joan Didion, John Updike, and other heavy-hit-
ter thinkers. Book lovers will find the site hard to pass up. A searchable
database of reviews from the last 35 years lets readers in on a virtual
conversation with some of the most notable writers and thinkers of
modern literature.

n. b. www.readcat.nybooks.com
Sister site to the New York Review and Granta, n. b. offers
an alternative selection of eclectic new books from the *Reader's Catalog*.
Annotated listings, selected reviews, and features on new releases in
memoir, criticism, and politics are articulate and analytical. All the listings
are available for online or mail-order sale at a discount.

Washington Post Chapter One
www.washingtonpost.com/wp-srv/style/books/features/chapone.htm
Saving book lovers a trip to the bookstore, Washington Post Chapter One offers one incredible feature even Amazon.com doesn't: it posts entire first chapters of fiction and nonfiction works along with reviews to let the readers decide for themselves what they think. A link to online shopping lets you compare prices at various online booksellers, too.

The Pulitzer Prizes www.pulitzer.org
A complete, searchable list of current and archived winners of the prestigious prizes in journalism, literature, drama, and music since their inception in 1917. Interesting tidbits: the 1973 winner for Public Service in Journalism (the Washington Post for its investigation of the Watergate scandal), the 1948 drama winner (Tennessee Williams for *A Streetcar Named Desire*), and the "No Award" listing for the novel category in 1941, the year Hemingway submitted *For Whom the Bell Tolls*.

BoldType www.boldtype.com
An online literary salon, BoldType shines with stellar book reviews, author essays (very cool), and book excerpts. Check out Bold Type Audio to hear authors reading their works—you'll find John Updike, Vikram Seth, Bret Easton Ellis, Chitra Divakaruni, and many more.

Mississippi Review www.sushi.st.usm.edu/mrw
A funny, wonderful quarterly literary review of new poetry and fiction by famous and emerging writers across the nation. MR has published such literary luminaries as Jamaica Kinkaid and Margaret Atwood, plus a host of lesser-knowns. The impressive archives date back to the Review's online debut in 1995.

business

Microsoft Smallbiz
www.microsoft.com/smallbiz
Just because they're called "small" businesses doesn't mean they don't face responsibilities and challenges like larger enterprises—they're just different responsibilities and challenges. MSN's Smallbiz site offers resources specially tailored to the small business owner. Create your own Web site with assistance from the technology guides, find tech consultants with the buyer's guide, or just peruse the features, worldwide affiliate sites, and chat areas for more information geared toward small business needs.

Yahoo! Store www.store.yahoo.com
Create your own online store in minutes ... sound too good to be true? Read the How It Works section and you'll find that, yes, it does cost money ($100/month for stores selling 50 items, $300/month for up to 1,000 items, etc.), but it's also perfectly real. For the HTML illiterate, fear not—your store, which can even be www.yourname.com, can be as bare bones as product names and prices or, with a few graphics, can be as fancy as the Rolling Stone store (a participating member of Yahoo! Store). Read carefully and take a "test drive" to make sure it's right for your business needs, but with a cancel anytime offer, it's hard to go too wrong with this unusual commerce opportunity.

Buy.co.uk www.buy.co.uk
A virtual sticky note service for personal and business cost cutting in the United Kingdom. Buy.co.uk offers cost comparisons to help you find the lowest prices available for utilities such as electric and gas, mobile telephones, and water. In the spirit of good deals, they also offer the "e-lephant" reminder service—register for free to be notified of when special deals, at stores and in travel, arise, or just check back often to browse the specials sections when the urge strikes.

BusinessWeek Online www.businessweek.com
More resources than would ever fit in one print magazine, BW Online offers multiple tiers of access, from free to full subscription, and a broad array of services. The weekly e-mail newsletter, the comprehensive Daily Briefing section of business news and analysis, plus select sections with resources for small business, entrepreneurs, technology, and investing are open to the general public. The real meat of the magazine costs, but those seriously interested in business will likely find it well worth it.

Fortune.com www.fortune.com
The who's who in business won't miss a beat: *Fortune* magazine's full print content is online—and then some. Browse categories on careers, technology, business life, and the key to Fortune: lists of the top 500 companies across the globe. Additional resources online include a fairly comprehensive assortment of buying guides—business books via Barnes and Noble, computers at Outpost, and office products from Office Depot to name a few.

Fast Company www.fastcompany.com

A *Wired* for the business world, Fast Company dives into technology with grace and style. All the wit and wisdom of the print version is here, including business advice and tips on life and sanity maintenance in the workplace. The only difference between the Web site and the print version seems to be that there's more of it on the Web—searchable archives, expanded resources, community polls and events, and the delectably efficient convenience of the Internet.

SmartMoney.com www.smartmoney.com
The *Wall Street Journal*'s foray into personal business management moves from the racks to the little screen with everything from the print mag plus the kitchen sink. There seems to be no limit to the resources offered at this one-stop portfolio/market/investor/features hub. Hourly stock updates and cool visual "market maps" are searchable and neatly organized. Smart Money is as compact and useful as a site can get—and it's personalized.

Dow Jones Business Directory
www.businessdirectory.dowjones.com
The business Yellow Pages straight from the source. Search by site name, category, or keyword for the best business sites, complete with ratings and reviews based on content, design, speed, and navigation. A great jumping-off point for business and financial resources on the Web.

Jump! www.jump.com
Palm Pilot ... Outlook ... Intranet... . Keeping your organizers organized can be a daunting task. Jump! attempts to consolidate timekeepers and planners both personal and public with a free online subscription. Just imagine—the e-mail personal address book plus the database contacts plus the calendar tasks all in one place. The only disadvantage is that you have to be online to access it, but we're betting that you'll be able to check it from your cell phone soon enough. How many organizers do you want? If the answer is one, check out Jump!

When.com www.when.com
Setting up meetings can take dozens of phone calls and e-mails—simplify simplify simplify with When.com. Get started by filling out the free registration form, specify type (group or personal), and the scheduling process is begun! Options include notification on book releases, concert dates, Web events, and special interests from sports to wine, trade shows to television.

Direct FX www.foreign-currency.com
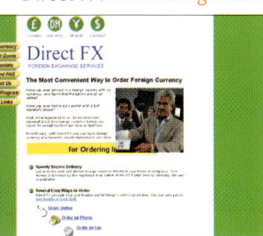
The travel agent booked a flight that lands at 2 a.m. local time. You can hope that the cab driver understands what traveler's checks are, or get foreign currency before your trip. At Direct FX, order foreign currency online, by phone, or fax, and have it delivered to your door before you go. There is a suggested minimum of $200 and a maximum of $2,950 (USD), but the convenient process and peace of mind offered for the busy traveler makes the service a worthy one.

Visa-ATM Locator www.visa.com/atms
Putting your money at your fingertips at all times, Visa's ATM Locator knows where those elfin cash machines lie across the globe. Particularly useful for the traveler who isn't keen on carrying wads of cash around. Find out how close the ATM is to your hotel in Bangkok, the terminal at Narita, or your new office before you head out of the house.

United States Postal Service www.usps.gov

The home page's beautiful introduction says it all: "No crowds. No Lines. 7 days a week, 24 hours a day." The USPO online can't pick up your packages, but it can provide rate information, stamp catalogs, package tracking, zip code directories, and change of address applications. Additional services are local post office locators, downloadable passport applications, and for the Cliff Clavens of the world, T-shirts, hats, and other postal paraphernalia.

FedEx www.fedex.com
The first name in shipping, FedEx brings all its convenient services to the Web. Select your location and enter the package weight to have the cost calculated, or search for the nearest FedEx office and drop-off locations to speak with human beings. For the virtually inclined, FedEx offers the whole shebang without ever leaving the house: have boxes and envelopes dropped off and picked up within hours and enjoy the comforts of your favorite chair at all times.

The Internet Shipping Center www.intershipper.net

Comparing costs can be a tedious process. InterShipper simplifies shipping with a rate comparison search engine. Just type in the zip codes for point of origin and destination, and the approximate weight in pounds—within 20 seconds, a startlingly comprehensive list of shipping method and carrier, expected arrival date, and price are revealed. Convenient and efficient.

StampsOnline www.stampsonline.com

Collect them, mail them, wallpaper the bathroom with them—while the uses vary, stamps are undeniably useful. Browse the gallery of stamp images, spice up your utility bill with "Victorian Love" or "Tropical Flowers," or make that five-year-old nephew's day with the colorful cartoon cache at the Just for Kids section. Collectors, novice and seasoned, might want to check out Collector's Corner, and regular mail folks can just bask in the convenience and variety of purchasing stamps online.

Fundsnet www.fundsnetservices.com
Whether you're a student or an artist, a nonprofit organization, fundraiser, grantmaker, or philanthropist, FundsNet has a place for you! With featured funding sites updated daily and hundreds of links to advice, writing and application tips, guideline interpretations, and links to actual resources, FundsNet is a good orientation point in that search for financial support.

United States Department of Labor www.dol.gov
Often people have a general understanding of what should and should not happen in the workplace—but better to be certain. The U.S. Department of Labor provides guides that explain the rules and regulations regarding small businesses, retirement, health benefits, safety standards, and wage requirements to name a few. The Statistics & Data section offers a particularly engaging window into the state of employment in the country today.

AFL-CIO www.aflcio.org
"Economic justice to the workplace—social justice to the nation" is the mission statement for this official Web site of the American Federation of Labor-Congress of Industrial Organizations. People interested in learning more about unions and related topics owe it to themselves to become familiar with this valuable resource on the issues that concern labor organizations today.

U.S. Patent & Trademark Office www.uspto.gov
There is something to be said for going to firsthand information. The USPTO does its best to make it easy for anyone interested in learning about patent and trademark application procedures, archives, and detailed FAQs on the process of obtaining patents and trademarks from submission to acceptance.

CareerPath.com www.careerpath.com
To find a job anywhere in the country, CareerPath.com is the place to start. Search for company profiles, recruiting fairs, and employment listings by keyword or job title; with nearly 400,000 jobs available, it's a whole lot better than combing the Sunday paper. But with so many possibilities, search returns can be overwhelming; be specific for best results.

Monster.com www.monster.com
The undisputed champion of online job hunting. The job listings alone make Monster.com a must see—not to mention the "My Monster" start page, which lets you store your resume, cover letter, and job prospects online. Special features include company profiles, advice guides, personalized job search agents, and chat boards.

CareerMosaic www.careermosaic.com
Though CareerMosaic's job search feature is not as strong as others, the nifty company profile section provides direct links to employment listings at hundreds of hot company home pages. Also useful is *Fortune* magazine's online career section, with dozens of articles on job searching, employee hiring and retention, and ratings of the best companies to work for.

Jobtrak.com www.jobtrak.com

If you're nowhere near the college or university you attended, Jobtrak.com can put you back in touch with the job-hunting resources of your alma mater. Having contracted with over 900 college career centers across the country, Jobtrack.com manages and posts job opportunities for alumni and students. In the tough arena of job hunting, any little connection counts; it's definitely worth a look to see what your college may have posted here.

Cool Works www.coolworks.com
For those short-term summer or winter jobs, why not make it something adventuresome? Cool Works links job seekers with positions at national parks, resorts, amusement parks, ski resorts, and the like. Over 70,000 job opportunities searchable by state, type, and lifestyle (RVers, elderly, labor-intensive) put Alaska, the Grand Canyon, and Yellowstone at your fingertips.

JobWeb www.jobweb.org
Sponsored by the National Association of Colleges and Employers, JobWeb hosts an exhaustive list of career resources for the college student or anyone who has ever been one. From career counseling to headhunters and salary information, this site's got practical, no-nonsense advice that would make a mom proud.

Overseas Jobs Express www.overseasjobs.com
Stuck in a rut? Get the heck out of Dodge and try a job overseas! OJE makes no attempt to hide the fact that it's selling information, from country guides to employment books, but the site also offers a healthy supply of free information and links for finding employment overseas. Wander around to see what the other side offers, or order the print version of their newsletter to keep informed.

EscapeArtist www.escapeartist.com

Living overseas is a way of life for a surprisingly large number of Americans—find out how to make it happen at EscapeArtist. The quintessential site for "international job seekers, expatriates, tax exiles and adventure seekers," this site has info about countries, living abroad, offshore investment, as well as links to several important resources any expat should know about. Truly unique.

careers

Virtual Job Fair www.vjf.com
Jobs for techies. Westech, one of the leading high-tech career resource centers, connects professionals and employers in the industry through résumé postings and specified search capabilities, claiming successful placement of over two million since its founding in 1982. With those figures, employers and job seekers in the tech industry owe it to themselves to take a look.

Manpower www.manpower.com
Its 3,200 offices in 50 countries make Manpower the largest temp placement and staffing agency in the world, and thanks to the Internet, it expands its reach to over 250,000 businesses worldwide, from Ecuador to Australia. Submit your résumé, search job databases, or find the nearest Manpower staffing office.

Headhunter.net www.headhunter.net
A recruitment site that takes its statistics seriously. View the daily updates on the number of résumés, job postings, and daily users, all of which combined total somewhere over 200,000. Employers can control the priority of their job postings by "upgrading" their listing, or invest in the "VIP Résumé Reserve" to check out the newest and most attractive résumés before they're put in the batch with the rest. A great site for the passive job seeker or recruiter.

The Wall Street Journal's Careers careers.wsj.com
Career advice from the people who know business. The Wall Street Journal's online career magazine maintains the topical and writing quality of the print publication for free. Useful information, engaging features, updated daily.

VaultReports.com www.vaultreports.com

Taking insider journalism to the job market, Vault Reports profiles hundreds of companies and industries (such as consulting and high tech) with alarming insight, making this a treasure trove for the job seeker. Get the skinny on top i-banking firms and internships, or read about the players on the Silicon Valley scene. The job search form lets job seekers select criteria, then sit back and relax while VR e-mails reports on positions that match their skills and experience. One of the most innovative, comprehensive job sites on the Web.

Tripod Resume Builder
www.tripod.com/explore/jobs_career/resume
Writing a résumé can be an art—or a program online. At Tripod, respond to eight questions about your education or employment background, and voila! The completed resume is constructed and viewable online. While the Resume Builder is very useful in setting up the initial structure, be sure to edit the finished product to personalize as far as possible. A good starting point to construct a résumé from scratch or just get a sense of the way it's done.

CareerBuilder www.careerbuilder.com
Career advice abounds at this interactive recruitment station online, from finding the ideal job to writing the perfect cover letter, negotiating job offers, and balancing a personal life while still getting ahead, all presented in clear, concise, and practical terms. The site even offers free e-mail for those on the job who are searching on the sly—just one more feature that shows they know what's really going on in the workplace.

PlanetRecruit International www.planetrecruit.com
Search for jobs overseas in the language you're used to. With PlanetRecruit, jobs across the globe are only a click away. Whether the job is in a foreign metropolis or small town, Planet Recruit probably has a link to it.

FreeAgent.com www.freeagent.com
Love the freedom of freelancing but hate the hassle of insurance, invoicing, and the rest? Become a member of Free Agent.com and you can have a personal assistant take care of all that nasty paperwork for you. Need health insurance? No problem. Help with tax payments? A breeze. You do your work, and Free Agent takes care of the rest—for a fee, of course.

cars

F1Racing.net www.f1racing.net
F1Racing.net features daily updated news on—what else?—car racing. In addition to headline stories, this Web site also profiles teams, drivers, and their cars. Cartoons, standings, stats, and screen savers are also available. Simply designed and easy to search, F1 is an excellent bookmark candidate for any racing enthusiast.

NASCAR Online www.nascar.com
The official site of the National Association of Stock Car Racing, NASCAR Online has everything you want to know in the way of news, qualifying results, the Winston Cup series, racing teams, and schedules. There's also a "garage" where fans can get a look at the mechanical side of racing. Browsing through the photo gallery is the next best thing to suiting up in the pit.

goracing.com www.goracing.com
In addition to the latest news on teams, tracks, statistics, and standings, goracing.com lets you look up the points and racing results of over 15 series. An all-star lineup of drivers make the rounds of this site's chat room, giving fans an opportunity to talk with their heroes. It takes a few seconds to browse from room to room, but goracing.com is content-rich enough to withstand the wait.

Hemmings Motor News www.hmn.com
Whether you're a serious buyer or just browsing, Hemmings Motor News affords a great opportunity to check out collectible autos online. There are over 800 advertisements for antique, classic, vintage, and muscle cars updated each month, so you may want to bookmark this site for repeated visits. You'll also find a page of price guide books and links to several dealer showrooms here.

Autoshop-Online www.autoshop-online.com
Don't have the first idea about how a car works? Check out Autoshop-Online, which offers an (anti) crash course in Automotive 101, plus tips on maintenance, fuel conservation, and the safe operation of motor vehicles. Best of all, it's got an interactive service department to deal with specific problems—it will answer any question you've got within a day for a very reasonable fee. Great for folks who are still unsure about which side their gas tank is on.

Weekend Mechanics Club www.weekendmechanicsclub.com
Not interested in buying the local mechanic a summer home? Then dial up this site, which can help you locate hard-to-find parts, track down stores in your area, search for coupons and rebates, and discover ways to make your car live longer. Check out the feature articles to learn why good batteries go bad and what you can do about those nasty fuel injector deposits.

CSK Auto www.cskauto.com
Mechanics and amateur tinkerers alike will love CSK Auto, where you can purchase items from CSK Auto's wholesale or retail stores. This Web site also has helpful maintenance tips so you can spend more time in your car instead of under it. If the advice you need isn't on the Car Care page, check out the archives.

Cars.com www.cars.com
If you're in the market for a used car, drop by Cars.com. It's got listings of over 50 different models of both new and used cars that are up for sale across the country. You can search by model, make, year, price, dealer, or town—it's up to you. This comprehensive Web site also features consumer reports outlining prices, safety, and specifics so you'll be well armed with knowledge when it does come time to make an offer. There's even a page that outlines the benefits of getting a loan versus leasing a car. An excellent resource.

Car Talk www.cartalk.cars.com
A subdivision of Cars.com, Car Talk is a Web site "starring" Tom and Ray Magliozzi, whose addictive weekly show can be heard on National Public Radio. They'll tell you all you need to know about insurance, lemon laws, and repairs in a few clicks of the mouse. The content is both informative and hilarious, and the user-friendly design will encourage online waders to dive right in and join the fun.

Autobytel.com www.autobytel.com
Whether you want to buy, finance, or lease a new or used car, this Web site can probably set you up. Search the invoice pricing, safety characteristics, and vehicle reviews if you've got cold feet; there are no high-pressure sales tactics in this electronic showroom. You can also take out a free subscription to "My Service," a personalized electronic newsletter that features an Expert Mechanic to answer all of your automotive questions.

CarsDirect.com www.carsdirect.com
CarsDirect.com is an "all-you-need-to-know" site devoted to purchasing automobiles. It allows you to research particular models, compare them with other cars, and learn about various savings options available to you. Once you've decided which car you'd like, you can go ahead and customize it. Then, when everything is just the way you want it, CarsDirect.com will move you to the checkout line, where you can review financing information and even apply for a loan. Easy as pie!

Edmund's Automobile Buyer's Guide www.edmunds.com

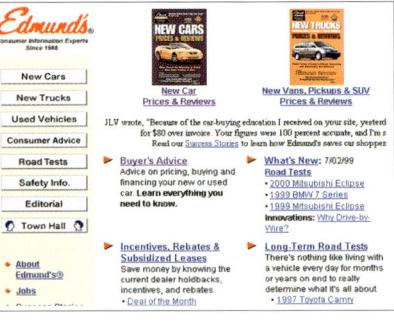

Whether you have no idea about cars or need a quick overview of a particular model, Edmund's can help you. It's got consumer info on new and used cars and trucks, as well as road test results, safety reports, buying incentives, rebates, and subsidized leases. Bargain hunters will appreciate the Deal of the Month page, and comparison shoppers will want to check out the Most Wanted lists.

Kelley Blue Book www.kbb.com
Kelley Blue Book has free used-car value reports, trade-in and retail values for motorcycles, information on new-car pricing, and quotes on financing and insurance. It's also got a Lemon Check feature, a list of the 50 hottest cars on the market, and a comprehensive FAQ page. Low key but informative and useful, this site is a great way to browse for cars on your own terms.

Microsoft CarPoint www.carpoint.msn.com
Coupling an exhaustive amount of consumer information with a fresh, open design, Microsoft CarPoint is one of the most surfable auto sites on the Web. In addition to the requisite advice on choosing, financing, and buying new or used cars, this site also features a virtual auto show, a surround video gallery, and several window-shopping lists. Clever and comprehensive, CarPoint makes you think that the world could stand to be dominated by a guy like Bill Gates.

Auto.com www.auto.com
You'll find consumer, industry, and racing news at Auto.com, as well as information on car shows and services. This site is definitely geared toward people who know something about cars, but the articles aren't so technical that they're unreadable.

All Things Automotive www.autodirectory.com
Whether your needs are very general or real specific, you can find what you need at All Things Automotive. It can direct you to sites devoted to motor sports, auto enthusiasts, buying cars, and finding parts and service. ATA can also show you where to read up on such miscellaneous topics as recreational vehicles, electric cars, and careers in the automotive industry.

Supercars—Past and Present www.supercars.net
If you dream of zooming down a deserted highway in a '63 Corvette Stingray or taking the '99 Bentley for a spin, dial up this site. It's got all the information you want on the most beautiful and/or powerful automobiles in the world. A great site for people who appreciate fine cars. The message boards are divided into five categories: Web page discussion, car comparisons, and Japanese, American, and European models.

Car And Driver Online www.caranddriver.com
This site is for folks who really love to drive; grumpy commuters need not drop by. Virtually every aspect of automobiling is covered here, from concept cars to road tests to car shows. The real attraction is the in-depth articles; if the topic you're interested in isn't featured this week, then search the generous archives.

Road & Track Online www.roadandtrack.com
People who get sweaty palms from driving in the center lane won't appreciate this site, but everyone else who gets hauled into traffic court will. It's got the lowdown on the fastest, sleekest, and hottest cars around. There's a terrific section devoted to road trips, profiles of cool travel destinations that are "off the beaten path," and beautiful photos. Attractive layout and well-written articles give this site a place of distinction on the Web.

LeaseSource www.leasesource.com
An excellent resource for anyone thinking about leasing a car. It's got pricing data, contract summaries, information on finding a dealer, an instant credit report, free insurance quotes, and much, much more. Anyone armed with this knowledge is bound to negotiate a great deal.

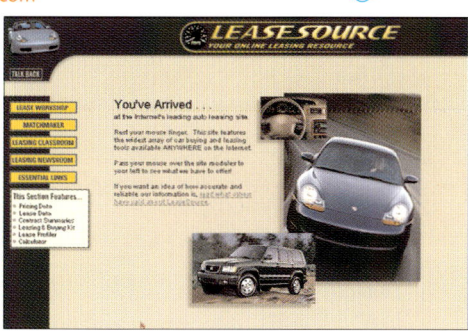

Giggo.com www.giggo.com

Giggo.com will tell you everything you need to know about finding the perfect car, applying for a loan, and negotiating a great financing deal. Subjects are broken down into small categories so you won't have to sort through reams of material to get the information you want.

Budget Rent A Car www.drivebudget.com
Need to make a quick getaway? Dial up Budget Rent A Car, which can set you up with a sturdy set of wheels that won't break your bank account. If you're dissatisfied with the prices you see here, you can even submit a lower bid and receive an e-mailed response within 24 hours.

BreezeNet's Guide to Rental Cars www.bnm.com

Featuring over 90 major auto rental companies at over 100 airports in the United States and abroad, BreezeNet is a great way to reserve a set of wheels at a reasonable price from the comfort of your own home. Rates are a delightful surprise for a New Yorker headed to Omaha, but a dreadful shock for folks going the opposite route.

CarPoolers.com www.carpoolers.com
People who are faced with biking or crawling long distances will be delighted to find CarPoolers.com, a national registration service for ride sharing. Sign on and save money, protect the environment, reduce stress, and make friends (or enemies, as the case may be). Go ahead and fill up those carpool lanes that single drivers are always cursing.

Rides Online www.rides.org
Hats off to this Web site dedicated to giving San Francisco residents cheaper, faster, and more ecological ways to travel around the city. There are pages devoted to ride services, commuting options, and carpooling incentives. There's also a match list of car, van, and bike partners. If only every city had a site like this!

WWW Speedtrap Registry www.speedtrap.com
When you absolutely, positively have to get there in three minutes flat...or you just want to thumb your nose at the establishment, there's always WWW Speedtrap Registry. It's a databank for all those nasty speedtraps honeycombing this and 36 other countries. If you just recently got a ticket and want to save fellow drivers the same aggravation, be sure to add your speedtrap to the ever-growing list posted here.

MotoDirectory.com www.moto-directory.com
Motorcycle lovers are in luck ... there is indeed a Web site that's designed just for them. MotoDirectory.com is a set of links to literally hundreds of motorcycle pages. Nearly every topic imaginable is covered: apparel and clothing, brand-specific merchandise, clubs and associations, events and rallies, scooters & mopeds, touring and travel, and women riders, to name a few. This site is updated five days a week, so it's very current, as well as comprehensive.

4freequotes.com www.4freequotes.com
Want to find the best car insurance rate possible? Look up 4freequotes.com, which enables you to submit a quote form to up to 10 companies at one time. Simply list your state and the kind of policy you're interested in, and 4freequotes will give you up to 10 quotes listed in your area. This site also has a FAQ page about auto insurance, links to top insurance companies, a list of company ratings, and the results of a consumer poll.

Gas-Money.com www.gasmoney.com
If you want to make your money stretch further, Gas-Money.com is for you. It will tell you where to find the best prices and when rates go up or down. Allows you to make informed choices about where to spend your hard-earned money. Great for folks who are on a fixed income or do lots of driving.

Off-road.com www.off-road.com
In the market for a sport utility vehicle? Then you'd be wise to dial up Off-road.com, which has information not only on SUVs, but dirt bikes and 4x4s as well. There are product reviews, technical help files, trail and race reports, articles on land use, and stories from experienced riders about their favorite trails. The content here is very impressive, as is the massive archive of past issues.

Ferrari North America www.ferrari.com
Fans of these beautiful cars will get hours of surfing pleasure out of this Web site. It will help you buy a pre-owned or new Ferrari, tour the engines of various models, take advantage of spare parts specials, and even paint a car to your very own specifications. Despite its cool visuals and features, the search engine leaves something to be desired ... everything takes a really long time to load.

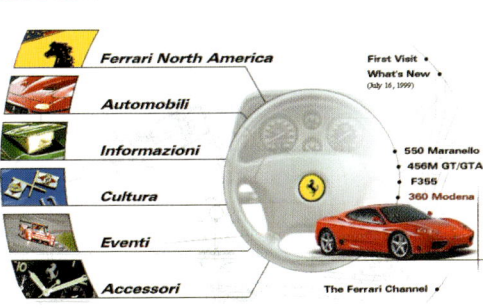

Harley-Davidson www.harley-davidson.com
This Web site's gorgeous design lives up to Harley-Davidson's respected name. Sleek, understated, and fun to surf, it invites you to check out its products, read up on the riding experience, and learn about the history of Harley-Davidson. You can also sign up for motorcycle camp or make plans to visit the newest fleet!

Toyota USA www.toyota.com
Whether you want to buy a new Toyota or maintain a used one, this Web site will be of use. It features profiles of each and every model, as well as information on financing and insurance. There's also a dealer locator to make your shopping experience more convenient. Be sure to check out the Motor Sports section of this site.

Blackhawk Automotive Museum www.blackhawkauto.org

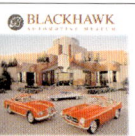
Located in Danville, California, the Blackhawk Automotive Museum houses some of the most historically significant and beautifully designed cars in the world. Paintings, photos, and sculptures are also on display at the museum; check out its Web site to see which exhibits are being featured this month.

Electric Vehicle Association of the Americas www.evaa.org
Now you won't have to get all your information on electric cars from Ed Begley Jr.! That's because EVAA can tell you where to buy them, how to charge them, what they cost, and why you should get them. There's also an events calendar and a directory of EV charging sites. EVAA could stand to offer a lot more content, but it's a good place to begin research on the Car of the Future.

AAA.com www.aaa.com
The official Web site of The American Automobile Association can set you up with a membership (which does, indeed, have its privileges: discounts on hotels, theme parks, and car rentals, to name a few). It's got road reports and travel tips, too. The search engine is a little slow, but be patient.

Europcar www.europcar.com
Europe doesn't have the most famous highways in the world for nothing—drive them! And rent the car ahead of time at Europcar. Browse the 96 country listings (which reach well beyond Europe to Africa, the Middle East, India, and Mexico) for no-pressure travel planning in English. The online rate-checking and reservation service requires filling out a few forms, but it is faster and cheaper than calling or faxing the different locations in the destination country.

chat

Deja www.deja.com
Haven't joined a newsgroup yet? Deja makes it easy with 45,000 discussion forums on everything from buying a car to traveling in Africa. Deja pools the comments and opinions of its users in a remarkable ratings section; you can check out your cyberpeers' rankings and reviews of an exhaustive list of movies, books, vacations, cigars, or virtually any other product and service available. Join a discussion on Julia Roberts' new film or new haircut, or just browse the book reviews. An awesome resource.

Talk City www.talkcity.com
With 20 topical categories of chat and bulletin boards and thousands of user-generated chat rooms, it's no wonder Talk City hosts as many as 18,000 users at a time. There's something for everyone here—art, entertainment, health, spirituality, and hundreds of other topics are discussed in forums that adhere to the firm "city standards" of conduct. Talk City also hosts free home pages and personals.

Yahoo! Chat www.chat.yahoo.com
Is there any service that Yahoo! doesn't provide? The site hosts a mind-boggling list of chat rooms—including almost 20 on specific TV shows alone—not to mention the scores of group- and interest-specific rooms in four languages. But what really sets Yahoo! Chat apart are its customizable features; you can create your own chat home page that lists your favorite rooms and chat buddies. The easy-to-grasp format makes Yahoo! a great hub for newbies.

WBS www.chat.go.com
One of the oldest and largest communities on the Web, WBS is a virtual café, post office, newsstand, and white pages all in one place. Chat with some of the site's 3.4 million members, check your personal free e-mail account, look up a member, browse hosted home pages, or check out the member-created newsletters.

The Ultimate Chatlist www.chatlist.com
The name says it all. The site is an extensive, searchable list of chat sites and bulletin boards all across the Web. Ultimate Chatlist has chat room and message boards of its own as well, and lets users add URLs to its database. First-timers should check out the glossary of frequently used chat acronyms and emoticons (chat smiley faces)—chatting has a language all its own!

ICQ www.icq.com
A unique tool that lets you know when friends are logged on, ICQ (I Seek You) is by far the most popular way to personalize the Internet. Download ICQ software and create a network of friends to chat with in real time (no matter what ISP they have)—a great way to connect with Grandma or far-flung friends. Be careful, though—ICQ is definitely addictive!

computers & internet

Outpost www.outpost.com
Whether you're dying for a Darth Maul Mouse Mat or are in need of a serious scanner, Outpost.com has
the cure. This site is a great bet for buying PC and Mac software, hardware, accessories, and nearly everything else for your computer. The site's True Price function shows you the cost of your items including shipping and other hidden charges, so checking out won't be a nasty surprise.

Dell www.dell.com

One of the industry leaders in computer systems, Dell makes computer shopping more personal than ever—browse by system use (small business, large business, education, personal, etc.) and find out what the experts recommend. Laptops, desktops, and accessories can be ordered on the spot, or you can custom-design your system. For the less technically inclined, tech support reps at Dell are both human and humane.

PalmGear HQ www.palmpilotgear.com
The fastest-selling invention since the slinky, the Palm Pilot will change your life, guaranteed. Now, with accessories and programs cropping up like bunnies, it is easier than ever to expand your personal organizational power. Search products by type (hardware, software, etc.), phrase, and popularity, or just browse "the essentials" to ensure maximum organization.

ZDNet www.zdnet.com
The godfather of computing online. ZDNet is home to PC Magazine, MacWorld, and Yahoo! Internet Life, to name a few, and is by far the most comprehensive resource directory for technology news, products, investing, and developments. Be sure to take a look at the frequently updated ZDNet Feature Links for free downloads and other handy resources.

NECX Global Electronics Exchange www.necx.com

This massive electronics and computer products exchange site is a definite first stop for anyone looking to buy or sell such products online. Categories range from audio/video to graphic accelerators, LCD projectors, modems, monitors, and motherboards for sale, accompanied by useful price comparators, feature summaries, and similar-product searches. Not for the first-time computer buyer, but very useful for the decently versed.

whatis.com www.whatis.com
The only thing that develops faster than technology is the lingo that describes it. Keep on top of the most commonly used or obscure terminology at whatis.com. The Top Twenty section ranks the most frequently requested words of the week and compares last week's rankings. An invaluable reference guide—bookmark immediately!

Internet Shopping Outlet www.shoplet.com
Same idea as the factory outlet but you'll find no hot dog stands in here! This hub offers links to BookBuyers, Internet Software, Hardware, Games, and Download Outlets online. While the prices are at times no great stretch from prices at the multitude of sale sites, it's a good resource for accessing an array of products, all at sale prices all the time.

DaveCentral
www.davecentral.com
The independent computer user's dreamland for freeware, shareware, demos, and betas. Featured categories include new Windows and Linux software, plus the ever-changing "Dave's Pick" replete with catchy, user-friendly reviews that share the need-to-know info without all the confusing lingo. Web developers are in for the real treat with an exhaustive collection of online tools from button makers to font mappers and more.

Insight www.insight.com
Rock bottom prices on computers for the working world. When that super-fast PC featured in *PC World* is way more power than you need for e-mail and Word, go to Insight for incredible deals on solid, standard computers (as low as $400), monitors, printers, and accessories. Great deals, no frills.

Pricewatch www.pricewatch.com
Practical information for comparison shopping. Pricewatch's clean design makes it easy to browse through the different kinds of products ranging from handhelds to memory, software, and consumer electronics. Type in what you're looking for and in surprisingly little time a chart comparing brand, product description, price, and shipping information appears. Technology costs, but at least you'll have the peace of mind that you got the best deal out there.

Beyond.com www.beyond.com
Hardware, software ... and hardware and software! Beyond.com is a well-kept clearinghouse for great deals on software, with games, business utilities, kids' tools, graphics, reference, programming and operating systems, and basic hardware, such as printers, scanners, and handheld devices. The software section is a bit more comprehensive, but the site as a whole is worth a wander for deals and downloads.

Micro Warehouse www.warehouse.com
PC, Mac, supplies, networking—for starters. Micro Warehouse links to the major manufacturer stores such as Adobe, HP, IBM, Novell, and Toshiba, in case the deals they offer here don't include the desired products. Search by product name, manufacturer, or—for the truly together—item number, specifications, or manufacturer part number.

The Industry Standard www.thestandard.net
Perhaps the first in Web news standards, this magazine of the "Internet Economy" fills in the blanks of today's Web headlines, analysis of current tech events, features, and profiles. Additional resources include sections on finance, marketing, e-commerce, and recruitment, to name a few.

PBS Technology www.pbs.org/technology

America's educators tame the beast that is technology for the educated and curious, teachers, parents, regular folk, and kids. Articles focus on the ways technology affects culture, learning, and living, with links to additional resources on historical, scientific and technical information on the subject. Scroll down to browse PBS Tech's sibling sites, including A Science Odyssey, Netlearning, and NOVA.

Egghead www.egghead.com

The computer lover's headquarters. Though there's no shortage of hardware and software purchasing sites online, Egghead pulls the best of the bunch together in one easily navigable location. Check daily for featured deals, or search under the computer, software, surplus direct liquidation, or auction sections for specific products. The computer novice may be a bit lost, but techies should have a ball at this comprehensive clearing-house for computer-related technology.

Onsale www.onsale.com

One of the Web's first auction sites, Onsale runs the gambit with auction offers on computer technology, sports equipment, electronics, and travel deals. The process is simple—browse the categories to check what's being offered, make your bid, and within hours find out if your bid made the cut. Delivery to your door at rock-bottom prices makes this site a first stop in online auctioning.

CNET www.cnet.com

Hands down the best portal for techies or anyone else who wants to keep up. Set up as a Yahoo!-style guide to technology, CNET offers extensive directories for hardware, software, handheld organizers, and games, plus Web building tools, free downloads, and price comparison guides. For the tech-savvy only.

Learn the Net www.learnthenet.com

So you had to know a little bit to get to this site, but for the world-wide curious, education awaits right here. Tutorials offered in English, Spanish, French, Italian, and German are available for kids and adults in Web navigation, e-mail, newsgroups, conferencing, research, and making the most of multimedia. For beginning and moderately fluent Internet users.

Jumbo! Download Network www.jumbo.com
The 300,000 freeware and shareware programs at this site are actually not its only appealing feature. The basic design offers easy navigation through dozens of categories from games to developers, multimedia tools, and utilities. Worth a daily peek to find out if their "Program of the Day" is the one that will make yours. The tech-savvy could walk blind through the site, but fear not if you're easily confused—Jumbo! will show the way with comprehensive subject guides.

Homestead www.homestead.com
Stake out your spot on the Web with Homestead. While not the only free Web page hosting service online, the absence of pop-up advertisements here is a welcome relief. Plus, Homestead's simple Web publishing tools make it easy to drag and click your page into perfection—without knowing a word of HTML. A great beginner-friendly tool.

SupportHelp.com www.supporthelp.com
Your browser keeps crashing. Your printer is a lost cause. You can't bother with the manuals. Where do you turn for help? SupportHelp.com. The site gives tech support information for over 4,500 manufacturers and products (hardware and software). Just type in a keyword, company name, or product, and you'll see a list of helpful resources in seconds. Useful links to tech trouble-shooting discussions round out the offerings here.

Pointcast www.pointcast.com
Wouldn't it be nice to have information come to you, instead of having to go out and find it? Poincast lets you select the news you want (from sites like the New York Times, CNN, and the Wall Street Journal) and streams the news (customized!) directly to a screen saver on your desktop. It's free and fairly simple to download-one of the coolest tools on the market.

GeoCities www.geocities.com
No need to get caught up in HTML when Yahoo! GeoCities will walk you through every step of creating your own Web page. Set up a free account and they'll give you clip art, Java applets, and interactive add-ons (like guest books and hit counters) to go along with your own pictures, sounds and text. If only they would get rid of those pop-up advertisements . . .

Chumbo.com www.chumbo.com
The Amazon.com of the software world. Chumbo.com's simply designed and locatable categories include education, business, multimedia, entertainment, programming and operating systems, and utilities software. Click on a category, browse through products by name, type, or popularity, read about the features and customer reviews, and shop away. Straightforward, easy shopping for software.

search engines & internet guides

Northern Light www.northernlight.com
The engine that's well known for returning consistent and accurate search results, all organized into handy folders. Northern Light really shines with its Special Collection search, with thousands of text sources (including magazine and journal articles) accessible online for a modest fee. Additional features include the usgov search (a clearinghouse for United States government publications), Investext stock market research, plus business, news, computing, and reference resources. A winner.

HotBot www.hotbot.com

As the Web grows faster and faster, many search engines are having a hard time keeping up. But with 34% of the Web indexed to date, HotBot tops the list. The Wired search engine certainly pulls up the goods—though sometimes too many of them. One word search can often return thousands of hit-or-miss results. But no other engine beats HotBot in user-friendliness and elegance; the site's pull-down menus make complex searches a breeze. You'll also find well organized and vastly subdivided guides to the most popular sites on the Net.

Excite www.excite.com
Personalized startup pages for the news junkie are what make Excite so ... well, exciting. Spend a few minutes selecting any or all of Excite's news features—top stories, stock quotes, weather, horoscopes, sports, chat—you can even customize colors and layout! Just click to make it your start page—all the news and search features you'll ever need are there, right when you log on.

4anything www.4anything.com
User-friendly guides to (almost) everything on the Web. Search by keyword for listings of the best of 4anything's topics, which run the gamut of just about anyone's research, entertainment, or informational needs. 4general information, browse through the main guide section, or go straight to the local directories, chats, and city sections. Tip: if you know you're looking for car sites, for example, just key in www.4cars.com—you don't have to go through the main page. Intrepid Web wanderers can forgo the selective guides for an "All Sites" list extraordinaire.

Britannica Internet Guide www.britannica.com
Hand-picked site recommendations from the trusted authority. Britannica's Internet Guide features high quality sites with superior content; a sure bet if you're doing research on the Internet. Look elsewhere for fun lifestyle sites—the picks here are usually fairly serious. The front page has top headlines and rankings of the Web's most popular sites, plus multimedia tours of various topics.

Magellan www.magellan.excite.com
With human-picked Web guides like Magellan, it's a wonder anyone uses search engines anymore. Look here to find top-notch sites in whatever category you like—autos, horoscopes, shopping, you name it. Read Magellan's review or just click through to the site. It's best to stick with the directory here; go elsewhere for Web-wide searches.

About.com www.about.com
Looking for news, views, and site recommendations on any topic? Head to About.com, where a (human!) guide maintains the page on the topic of your choice. Love sci fi? About.com's guide gives you links to all the news, sites, and chat you need. The guide sites are fantastically vast, sophisticated, frequently updated, and addictive to explore. A great bet for a home page.

eTour www.etour.com
"Surfing without searching" is the promise, and eTour delivers. Just make eTour your start page, enter your personal interests (pick from choices like gardening, football, or current events), and you'll see a new site (catered to your tastes) every time you log onto the Web. A good way to find sites you may never have heard about. Fun and well-executed.

Web100 www.web100.com
Yes, the spirit of democracy lives online. Web100 maintains a vast collection of site reviews contributed by users. Here's how it works: check out a suggested site, rate it on a scale from one to ten, and check back  the next hour to see how your choice fares on their "Site of the Hour." Current and archived picks are arranged by category and rating, making Web100 one of the most comprehensive, and hands down most frequently updated cool sites lists around.

Cool Site of the Day www.coolsiteoftheday.com
Screaming with fluorescent text and Java-flashing ads, it's not the most pleasant site to look at, but what it lacks in aesthetics it makes up for in breadth. The "original" cool site list (self-proclaimed—but they do have the URL) leaves no category unturned. From activism to free stuff, if it's cool, you'll find it as either a pick of the day or in the neatly organized topic list of archives.

glassdog.net www.glassdog.net

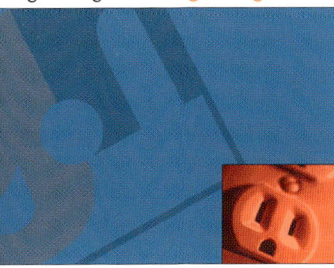

Surf over to glassdog.net to explore the edgier side of the Internet; you'll find arty and experimental sites submitted by their creators. Collaborative fiction, poetry, and art sites abound, most of which don't accept advertising. Check it out—or submit your own site. The offerings are updated daily.

dating, mating, relating

Swoon www.swoon.com
The catch-all site for "dating, mating, and relating" covers all the bases with everything from makeout music and dream interpretation, to advice columns and cheap date suggestions. Find answers on love, seduction, and the "quickie vs. marathon" debate in one of Swoon's many quizzes, articles, and surveys. If you can't find it here, click through to one of Condé Nast's additional offspring which include Glamour, GQ, Details, and Mademoiselle.

flirt.com www.flirt.com
As one might guess, flirt.com is all about the song and dance of searching, finding, and landing the mate of your dreams. Through any one on its four advice columnists (featuring one courageous male), the database of personals, and a variety of chats, forums and horoscopes, flirt's pros of precommitment rites and rituals are here to help—for a fee. They do offer five days free, so check out their teaser before plunging into a long-term relationship.

Breakup Girl www.breakupgirl.com
Self-pity's best friend. Breakup Girl is the broken woman's first aid in wallowing like a pro, with a few revenge strategies thrown in for good measure. Practical suggestions for post-boy blues include movie picks (10 Things I Hate About You), comfort books (Amy Sedaris!), and some quality time with yourself, Ben & Jerry's. If happily attached, Breakup Girl might recommend some reevaluation pointers, or jog a laugh or two in the advice column's archives of hapless and hopeful romantics. Better yet, sit back and watch cool Breakup Girl animations.

Match.com www.match.com
Having a tough time finding that special someone? The Internet is teeming with potential mates. Match.com has almost two million members. Search for specific qualities in appearance, lifestyle, education, and location or just browse. The free trial offers a peek at the millions (did I say millions?) of personals. Post your own personal statement with no length limit to see who's looking for you. Be sure to take a look at their monthly e-zine Mix 'n' Match at www.mixnmatch.com/match/pub for dating anecdotes, success stories, funny flops, and advice.

SecretAdmirer.com www.secretadmirer.com
In the old days, lovestruck souls had to rely on the local matchmaker or a mutual friend to reveal their crush. Now there's SecretAdmirer.com, a site that lets you send an anonymous e-mail message to the object of your infatuation. Your crush responds with an e-mail to the person they like—if it's you, SecretAdmirer.com reveals the match! Great fun.

iVillage.com Relationships www.ivillage.com/relationships

Being in a relationship doesn't mean that love is any easier than it is for singles—iVillage.com Relationships awaits for troubled twosomes. Check in with the "Couples Counselor" for Q & A's ranging from the decision to start a sexual relationship through marriage advice and remaining intimate with a houseful of kids. When all is smooth sailing again, pick up tips from the bedroom to the living room with the "Sex Coach" and "Ms. Demeanor" (in that order!).

Webpersonals www.webpersonals.com

Webpersonals.com is one of those rare places where the die-hard or simply curious can browse through ads for men + men, women + women, or men + women. Registration is free, and no one ever asks for any declaration of preference—explore, e-mail, engage, enjoy.

CyberMatch Worldwide www.cmww.com
Personals sites often involve some guesswork—Cybermatch tries to eliminate some of the mystery by requiring a photo for each ad posted, in addition to the standard bios listing education, personal interests, career information, and desired partner qualities. The site offers thousands of personals from across the globe, is confidential, and best of all, free. Listings include men seeking women and the reverse, as well as men-to-men and women-to-women searches.

CollegeDates.com www.collegedates.com
If you're a college kid who spends Saturday nights cuddling up to a cup of Ramen, put down your fork and head to CollegeDates.com. Designed to set you up with another student at your university, the site matches you based on a personalized profile that describes you and your potential mate right down to their eyewear. Just be careful—a search for that perfect curly-haired, gray-eyed love interest might bring up your professor's name!

dating, mating, relating 51

Nerve.com www.nerve.com
The self-billed magazine of "literate smut," Nerve is tasteful tidbits, pictures, articles, and stories for the sexually enlightened. Occupying a cool middle ground, Nerve is careful not to offend passersby with flashes of flesh, but covers its bases in an extensive links and library section to meet any need—from delicate to dominatrix. Check out Nerve's boutique, which carries sheepskin rugs, Twister sets, and other gifts for "the thoughtful hedonist."

World Museum of Erotic Art www.opkamer.nl/amea/index.shtml
As the name suggests, this online museum reaches beyond modern Western civilization in its collection of erotic art. Starting with the classic Kama Sutra, the museum's exhibits include the Japanese masters, ancient Rome, the first daguerreotypes, and Incan ceramics. Check back daily for their picture of the day or just pick up some postcards for your own collection.

Body Politic the.arc.co.uk/body/home.html
As much as an erotica magazine can hold to the p.c. ideal, nobody is left out at this witty, bawdy magazine for sexuality. All orientations, men and women, of all shapes, sizes, and colors are covered in clever and entertaining articles on sex, identity, beauty, and sensuality. For adults only.

Dr. Ruth cgi.pathfinder.com/drruth

Dr. Ruth may well be the dictionary definition of sex therapy (there might even be a picture of her!). The only accent that is better loved in America than Julia Child's is the only thing that's missing on this comprehensive site of advice, how-to's (yes, that's right), and Q & A 's, all searchably archived for the truly curious mind. It's free. It's Dr. Ruth. Need we say more?

Herotica www.her-erotica.com
The Internet can turn into quicksand for the unsuspecting woman in search of quality erotica without the triple-X photos. Herotica is for women, by women, presenting stories and photo spreads. Tasteful design and sleek black-and-white support categories in Vintage Erotica, Photo Spreads, Erotic Fictions, and the Boutique of products and supplies.

Partners Task Force for Gay & Lesbian Couples
www.buddybuddy.com/toc.html
It's illegal for gays and lesbians to marry their chosen ones. The Partners Task Force Web site gives you the scoop on the movement to change the law, including arguments for the legal right to marry, churches that perform gay ceremonies, and relationship tips for domestic partners and couples with kids.

Coalition for Positive Sexuality www.positive.org
For a sex ed site that specializes in "just the facts," point your browser toward the Coalition for Positive Sexuality. The site aims to arm teens with simple, accurate information on sex and sexuality so they can keep themselves safe. Check out the Just Say Yes link, an online tour that takes you through the basics, and the resource page, which gives you sites to contact if you need more info, or help.

weddings

The Knot www.theknot.com

The quintessential wedding site. This truly comprehensive portal site for nuptial planning, shopping, browsing and just about everything else is informative and totally fun. Create your own interactive wedding planning checklist, post a wedding Web page, browse wedding gowns, or register for gifts online. A must-see for anyone thinking about or committed to the big M.

Modern Bride www.modernbride.com
The name speaks for itself. Everything the print magazine offers in wedding planning with the convenience of the Web, including online registries for couples and their guests, honeymoon hot spots, fashion tips, and general advice on how to make this much-anticipated day go as smoothly as possible.

Bliss! www.blissezine.com
A support site of sorts for all participating in the big event. Bliss! offers the standard fare of advice, shopping links, and features on planning issues, but also spotlights scores of ideas for bridal showers, games, and an extensive review of books with tips to make planning as fun as the day itself.

Ucopia www.ucopia.com
The official wedding registry online for Modern Bride magazine, Ucopia makes it easy to forget how stressful gift buying can be. Select from lists of household items for the kitchen, bedroom, and family area, or just browse the "unique gift" collection with links to health spas, symphony subscriptions, and adventures (mostly linked to West Coast sites, but the ideas are helpful nonetheless). You can order your gift and have it wrapped and mailed in minutes.

Nearly-Wed Handbook www.nearlywed.com
The definitive guide on "How to Survive the Happiest Day of Your Life," the Nearly-Wed Handbook takes a refreshingly funny look at how to enjoy the event to come without taking everything so seriously. This practical, no-holds-barred site for wedding planning provides useful information on finding the right photographer, dress, caterer, and registry, with a wry sense of humor. Check it out—learn how to make the event of a lifetime fun to plan, too.

UnGroomed www.ungroomed.com

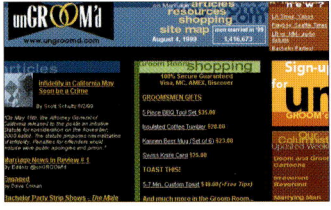 Weddings can be so bride-oriented—the grooms always seem to get left out. Ever feel that the groom could use some advice too? UnGroomed to the rescue. Read articles from the male perspective on commitment, gifts, furniture consolidation, and bachelor party expectations and etiquette.

The Wedding Channel www.weddingchannel.com
The bride and groom are not the only people in the wedding—what's a bridesmaid to do? The Wedding Channel serves the little people who make that ceremony so special, from flower girls and ring bearers to mothers and mothers-in-law and whay they will wear. This site offers hundreds of color photos to choose from—just click to order or find out more info!

Macy's Bridal www.macysbridal.com
The simplest registry service on the Web. For wedding guests planning ahead for that perfect gift, Macy's makes it easy with zillions of possibilities: throw pillows, blenders, ice-cream machines, or the ever-popular gravy boat are just a click away.

directories & people finders

InfoSpace www.infospace.com
Directory assistance at InfoSpace covers the territory. The Yellow Pages and White Pages here are standard fare, but more consistent than not in returning results. An added bonus is the Public Records section—this pay service provides users access to driver's license records and info on family members, neighbors, and even summary assets. Find someone else, or just check to see where you stand in public information.

US Public Info www.uspublicinfo.com
There are times when a telephone number isn't enough. This site specializes in people location and background checks. While many of the services it offers cost money, the No Find-No Fee policy makes the bill easy to justify. Check the free summary searches on investigative people searches and criminal records.

InfoUSA www.infousa.com
Though directed toward small business needs, InfoUSA offers a broad range of directory search features that could prove useful to anyone seeking quick, free information. Special features include the Reverse Lookup by Phone—just type in the 10-digit number and find the name and address. No individual registration required!

SearchShark www.search-shark.com
This powerhouse of a people finder leaves no stone unturned. The categories alone distinguish SearchShark from the other directories: in addition to the standard fare, you can search military directories, Social Security numbers, death indexes, or an array of public records. Even if these areas don't yield ideal results, SearchShark's breadth and scope should provide some leads on where to look to find just about anyone in the United States.

AnyWho www.anywho.com
Unlike the others, AnyWho, sponsored by phone know-it-all AT&T, offers an easily navigable toll-free directory that allows searches by category, city, and keyword. Scroll down to check out how they organized the categories to browse click by click to the numbers you need. Offers people, business, and Web site searches.

Switchboard.com www.switchboard.com
Let your mouse do the walking: Switchboard is as useful as the Yellow Pages, and a whole lot smarter. Switchboard's excellent business finder offers search options by name, type, and proximity to your location—simply type in your address to get business listings displayed with address, phone number, distance in miles, and an optional map, directions, and information on additional shops nearby.

Phone Numbers.net www.phonenumbers.net
Calling overseas to find phone numbers and addresses can get expensive. The solution? Phone numbers.net. The site provides access to phone directories around the globe without the cost or language barriers of telephone inquiries. Organized by country, this site offers business and residence phone numbers, e-mail addresses, and fax numbers for nearly any country, from Brunei to Australia. The results generally retrieve at least one English language directory, in addition to native language books.

WhoWhere www.whowhere.lycos.com
The process is simple: you type in the who, and they look, well, not everywhere, but through an impressive list of directories including government pages, phone directories, public records, and around the Internet. Self-registry is encouraged to ensure foolproof accuracy, but even without it, turnaround is quick and accurate.

directories & people finders

KnowX Public Records www.time.knowx.com
Great things are free ... or is it the other way around? But for serious people searchers, there will be times when money has to change hands for information, especially when it comes to accessing public records. KnowX takes the sting out of the fee by charging per database, per detailed record. The option to back out is there till the information you want is in sight, so there are no tricky click-through charges. Test out the free demo to see if it's for you.

555-1212.com www.555-1212.com
The number has long been synonymous with information—it's even more useful online! Well-organized categories of Yellow and White Pages, government and finance directories, and the unique international country code and phone listings. For identification of *69 numbers, check Reverse Lookup section by area code or full number.

FamilyTreeMaker www.familytreemaker.com
No more dusty records ... tracing family lineage is available online with more resources in one location than ever before. FamilyTreeMaker's Web site has the listings, the links, the databases, and over 340 million names in its records ... but FamilyTreeMaker is also a reasonably priced CD Rom that includes the Web site amenities plus self-publishing kits, family tree tools, and several other must-haves for anyone interested in creating a family tree. For the casual browser, the Web site should have enough to get you started.

Ancestry.com www.ancestry.com

With over 240 million names in 1,638 searchable databases, it's not difficult to understand why Ancestry.com should be your first stop in tracing family roots. Helpful guides on how to begin your genealogical search are here, with extensive lists of databases, magazines, books, and message boards. To find out where your family history began, start searching here.

education

The History Channel www.historychannel.com
On any of the 365 days a year, something of historical significance happened, guaranteed. Find out what at "This Day In History," from the Web's authority on historical information and events. Search the site, select a decade, or browse features on Wall Street, Automotive, and Civil War histories.

Education World www.education-world.com
The teaching professional's resource for lesson planning, curriculum, employment, and news and reviews on what's going on in the schools today. Browse the subject database for quick links to useful sites in fields ranging from liberal arts to K-12, continuing, special, and vocational education. A definite first stop for reference to quality education sites on the Web.

Learn2.com www.learn2.com
Sometimes it's hard to ask for help—at Learn2, often there's no asking required! With hundreds of "2torials" featured and in searchable archives, learning how to tie a tie, fix a running toilet, or repair a scratched CD (is this possible?) is cost and embarrassment free.

Hyper History www.hyperhistory.com
Only on the Web could the history of the world, with all its dates, facts, figures, and events manageably unfold in one panoramic chart. Search by name (keyword), event, or map to access 1,400 files spanning the past 3,000 years of civilization. Amazingly easy to navigate considering the massive amount of educational and entertaining information at this impressive undertaking.

The History Net www.thehistorynet.com
The National Historical Society's reservoir of facts and figures from the past makes even the most obscure areas of American history come to life. From the standard selections, such as the Civil War, World War II, and Vietnam, to special coverage on Aviation History, Early American Homes, and Women's History, THN presents the stories with fervor and style, making the process of learning history a joy.

Terraserver www.terraserver.microsoft.com
The earth, in pictures. The Terraserver provides digitized aerial photographs of the Earth from the U.S. Geological Survey and high-resolution satellite images courtesy of a joint Russian-American project. Simply click on a location on the world map (green areas are zoomable), click again to zoom in closer, and keep going until the actual streets are visible through somewhat grainy aerial imaging. Look for your hometown, check population density, or just wander through the Famous Places features to find out what the bird's-eye view of our world might look like.

Discovery Channel Online www.discovery.com
TV's most educational station has packed its sharply designed Web site with the standards—feature stories, people profiles, global expeditions—and then some. Additional amenities include interactive "Mind Games" trivia contests, "Live Cams!" files of nature's best from cheetahs to hurricanes, and searchable guides of ancient civilizations, planet Earth, and the space beyond.

Biography.com www.biography.com
Somebody famous was born today—Biography.com knows who, and plenty of intriguing tidbits and tales about their lives. In addition to the searchable database of names, the site offers topical features—Country Legends, Women's History, and '60's Sweethearts for instance—and minute-long RealVideo documentaries.

education 57

Educational Resources Information Center

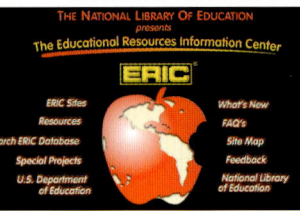

www.accesseric.org
Sponsored by the U.S. Department of Education, ERIC is the clearinghouse for education-related literature. If the over 900,000 abstracts of journal articles and other documents on educational research and programs seem a bit overwhelming, check out the ERIC Digests, which cover the most popular topics.

The Gateway to Educational Materials Project
www.thegateway.org
A special program of the ERIC Clearinghouse, The Gateway is just that. Browse the alphabetical list of subjects and keywords, or type in a specific request for straightforward links to the resources you need. This truly vast collection of resources arranged in quick-to-load, no-frills layout makes The Gateway the master key to educational resources on the Internet.

The English Server www.eserver.org
Created and maintained by the English department at Carnegie Mellon University, this immense collection of writings and resources in the arts and humanities is perhaps the most multifunctional academic site on the Web. With over 11,000 Web documents treating every imaginable topic from Marxist theory to psychoacoustics, The English Server is a remarkable source for research and information. Because it's a member-run cooperative, all of its features are completely interactive, providing an outstanding community for scholars or anyone curious about the humanities.

Thomas Historical Documents
www.lcweb2.loc.gov/const/consthome.html
For quick searches of the landmark U.S. documents, take a look at the Library of Congress's Historical Documents room. From the Declaration of Independence to the Federalist Papers and the Constitution, this site is a valuable resource for the student of American History.

Family Education Network www.familyeducation.com
This all-in-one family resource site has done its homework. The network offers articles on what to do when the kids sneak into R-rated films, suggested games, and a comprehensive Ask an Expert section with pediatricians, family therapists, teachers, and learning disabilities specialists on call. The site is navigable by age group and user location, and you can browse the weekly updated articles, polls, and quizzes.

National Parent Teacher Association www.pta.org
The largest and oldest volunteer organization in the United States is going stronger than ever with a Web site chock full of information and links for parents and teachers who

want to connect. The Internet checkpoint for the organization offers virtual conferences and special programs on such topics as violence prevention, TV ratings, and the environment.

Teachers.net www.teachers.net
Whether the topic is field trips for third graders, lesson plans for high school English, or administrative issues, Teachers.net has it covered. These topics and plenty more can be found at this extensive and clearly organized chat board for educators and school administrators. With an eye to utilizing live discussion options on the Internet, this simply designed site offers an impressive collection of live meetings and chat forums.

EDSITEment
www.edsitement.neh.fed.us
Sponsored in part by the National Endowment for the Humanities, it's not hard to believe EDSITEment's claim that they present the "best of the humanities on the Web." Curiously useful links include the American Memory Project, with archives of U.S. cultural history, Documents of African-American and Civil War Women, and Native Web, featuring links on indigenous people around the world. The site also includes lesson plans and suggestions for including the resources found here in the classroom.

Busy Teacher's Website K-12 www.ceismc.gatech.edu/busyt
Designed with efficiency in mind, the Busy Teacher's Website is cleanly organized with all those topics that teachers may need resources for, from art and English, to recess, guidance counseling, and interactive Web projects for students. The streamlined, no-frills design also means few clicks from topic headers to actual resources, freeing up precious time in any active teacher's schedule.

The Virtual SchoolHouse www.metalab.unc.edu/cisco/schoolhouse
The principal's office, the playground, the teacher's lounge ... sounds like a schoolhouse. But instead of people, the rooms at UNC's Virtual Schoolhouse house summaries and links to educational resources for teachers and administrators of all grades and subjects. The clearly organized, useful information that fills the halls of this schoolhouse online should appeal to any educator.

Back2College www.back2college.com
The portal for continuing education. Back2College is for anyone who has taken time off school, recently completed a degree looking to take a few additional classes, or just curious about what's going on in higher education. Check out the categories, which include financial aid, degrees online, gaining credit for life experience, tutoring, and discount textbooks, or peruse the daily updated articles on topics and trends in college education.

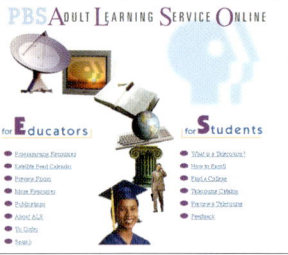

PBS Adult Learning Service Online
www.pbs.org/adultlearning/als
PBS's distance-learning courses are not yet available online, but their Web site does provide useful information on "telecourses"—videotaped classes that can be taken at home. With links to fully accredited colleges and universities across the country, and catalogs for business, science and math, education, and liberal arts courses, PBS, television's leader in learning through technology, is a good first stop for anyone interested in distance education.

Peterson's www.petersons.com

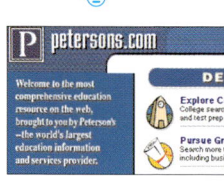

Peterson's almost begs you to save your pennies and forgo the book, as the online version offers so much more. The familiar college and university profiles are right there, with added information on graduate programs, distance learning, executive education, study abroad, summer camps, and private schools.

Kaplan www.kaplan.com

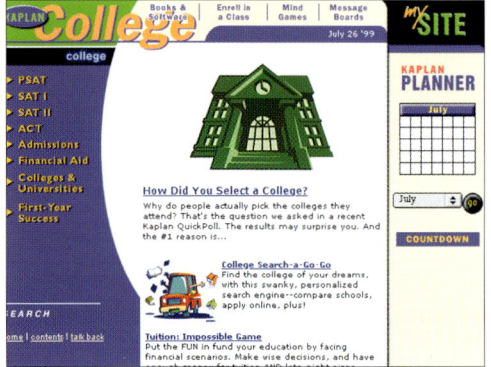

While Kaplan's Web site aims to get you to register for its courses, the amount of information it offers in the process makes this site a must-see for college, grad, law, or medical school preparation. If the feature articles on current issues in test prep don't pique your interest, click through the categories for detailed information on planning, tests, admissions, financial aid, school selection, getting in, and getting through the first year.

CollegeNET www.collegenet.com
Apply to college online? That's technology! CollegeNET boasts over 250 colleges and universities as part of its network of schools who accept applications online, including Virginia Tech, Ohio State, and Stanford. Find a school by region, tuition, sports, or majors offered, and figure out how to finance it with the NET's Mach25 free scholarship search.

US News.edu www.usnews.com/usnews/edu
The leader in school rankings upgrades its offerings with this expansive and potent Web site. Advanced search features allow the user to specify

criteria for personalized rankings, making the online version much more personable. Each section includes a vast listing of articles discussing student issues and the current buzz in the field.

Educational Testing Service www.ets.org
Standardized tests are a fact of higher learning—get the official scoop at ETS. Online you'll find information on the SAT, GRE, TOEFL, and more; practice test questions; college search tips; and links to registration procedures. You can't take the tests online, though—not yet at least.

Campus Tours www.campustours.com
Your perfect college could be anywhere from Miami to Honolulu—either start saving those frequent flier miles, or check out Campus Tours. Search by institution or state to take virtual college tours. Webcams, interactive maps, and occasionally video and Shockwave movies show you the campus up-close. Not every school is listed just yet, but it looks like the process is underway.

LearnPlus Online Language www.learnplus.com

Free language courses online? What's the catch? It seems the only one is that the site is still being developed, but as it currently offers free comprehensive courses in Spanish and German, it's already on its way to being one of those hidden treasures of the Web. Courses to be added in 2000 include level selection from beginner to advanced in Italian, French, Japanese, and English.

Berlitz www.berlitz.com
For years the household catchword for language learning, Berlitz is bigger than ever online, putting the world in reach within seconds. The site does offer a free tips section for useful phrases in other languages, but full conversational fluency costs either the price of the instructional books or registration at a language training center. Find the language you speak, the language you want to learn, pull out the credit card, and lesson one is underway.

FinAid www.finaid.org

The first stop in figuring out how to pay for your education. Sections are focused on answering questions about the different kinds of aid and scholarships available, how to qualify, where to look, and how to get them. The site also offers guides and FAQs specially tailored to the needs of parents, students, and educators. It's good to know that while college costs are soaring, quality scholarship information can still be had for free.

FreSch! www.freschinfo.com
Despite the jumbled design, FreSch! has just about everything there is on financial aid, scholarships, loans, and grants searchable by need, age, degree, ethnicity, state, and dozens of other criteria. With hundreds of pages offering tips and tricks on getting the funding you need, FreSch! is a must-see for anyone thinking of taking out student loans, or just looking for opportunities to ease education's financial burden.

education

Globewide Network Academy www.gnacademy.org
If there's a degree to be had, GNA's Distance Learning Catalog has it covered. Wander through the listings or search by course, program, or educational level to get in line for education from afar. Browse the categories for a sense of just how deep this site goes—whether perusing courses for a degree or just seeking inspiration, chances are there'll be something up your alley.

StudyAbroad.com
www.studyabroad.com
The information depot for educational opportunities overseas. While the design is a bit heavy on the eyes, the content is undeniably full and useful. Search by program, country, semester, subject, and level at this extensive, organized clearinghouse for study abroad research.

Youth for Understanding www.yfu.org
Finally, a site that takes the World Wide part of the Web seriously. YFU offers opportunities for study, living, or volunteering abroad with home pages for residents of almost 40 countries around the globe. Find out how to become an exchange student or host family for high school students, or how college students can enroll for semesters and years abroad.

American School Directory www.asd.com
The Internet gateway to 108,000 K-12 schools in the United States. The American School Directory is a great resource for anyone seeking information on public or private schools in their area. Provides links to school information, alumni directories, and even online yearbooks. An online payment center is available where parents can pay for everything from school meals to tickets to the prom. (Check if yours is a participating school.)

UCAS www.ucas.ac.uk
A meeting point for prospective students and the schools they may attend, the University and Colleges Admissions Service for the United Kingdom enables users to search by course, program, or academic institution. UCAS has introduced a pilot service where applicants can track the status of their applications for the Completion of Offers period.

entertainment

Disney Internet Guide www.disney.go.com/dig
It was either the World Wide Web, or a small country in South America—Disney went digital, and the results are in! The folks at Disney have picked some of their favorite Disney sites neatly organized in categories, such as Shopping, Fun for Families, Vacations, Music, Travel, and Animals. Scroll down to peruse additional Disney resources in radio, television, clothing, and (of course) animation.

Mr. Showbiz www.mrshowbiz.com
If you've got a hankering for entertainment news, look no further than Mr. Showbiz. Not only does he have the skinny on your favorite celebrities, he's also got the inside scoop on television, movies, music, and books. Plus, Mr. Showbiz has a wicked sense of humor—check out the Plastic Surgery Lab, where you can rearrange the stars' looks any way you choose. The "Romantically Linked" page should come with a warning from the Surgeon General ... following this maze of Hollywood romances is definitely addictive.

Hollywood Stock Exchange www.hsx.com
When the bottom finally falls out of the stock market, here's the first place to drown your sorrows. Yes, it's the Hollywood Stock Exchange, where you can sink "virtual millions" into "MovieStocks" and "StarBonds." Of course, since the money you're playing with isn't really your own, there's no harm putting a little wager on the next Kevin Costner movie, is there?

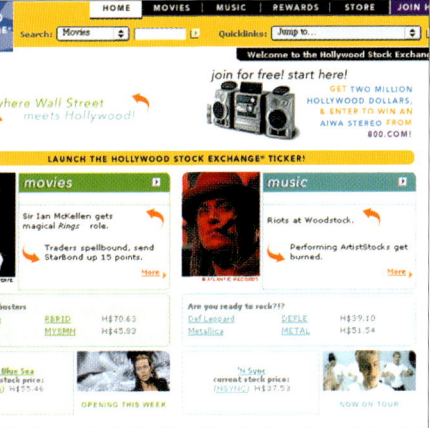

Feelin' Groovy
www.vallee.simplenet.com/feelingroovy/feelingroovy.html
Maudlin "Behind the Music Specials" got you down? Here's a place where you can feast your eyes on your favorite teen idols pre-rehab, hairlines intact. Not only does Feelin' Groovy feature dreamy beefcake shots of David Cassidy, and the New Kids, it's also got sound clips from albums still mouldering away in mom's basement. Sigh!

Who2 www.who2.com
This irreverent look at celebrity offers hundreds and hundreds of bios on famous people, be they movie stars, criminals, writers, or athletes. It also provides links to the best sites devoted to these folks, as well as a group of curious articles with titles like "Celebs with Missing Fingers" (Boris Yeltsin, Jerry Garcia) and "Famous Disappearances" (Agatha Christie, Jimmy Hoffa). Humorous, informative, and eminently browsable.

Variety.com www.variety.com
The most time-honored entertainment trade paper makes for great reading online. Find all about which projects are getting axed, which directors are over budget, and who's slated to star in the next blockbuster action picture. And don't forget those ads for open auditions; this could be your lucky break!

E! Online
www.eonline.com
A few clicks through this site will tell you what's hot and what's not in the world of entertainment. The coverage is extensive and unabashadly gushing; you won't find the sarcastic digs of Mr. Showbiz here, but you will find plenty of colorful photographs and in-depth interviews, as well as those infamous fashion reviews.

Starbuzz www.starbuzz.com
Starbuzz offers links to your favorite celebrity fan sites, as well as the latest entertainment news. This site features perhaps the most complete, up-to-date listings of celebrities on the Net, though it lacks the humor of Who2. It even offers a service where you can send an electric celebrity postcard to pals via e-mail, complete with a personalized message. You talkin' to me?

Entertainment Weekly www.ew.com

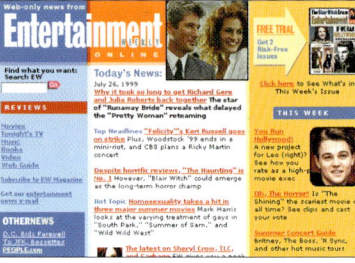

Read up on all the doings in Tinseltown and add your own two cents about the latest stinker you had the displeasure of seeing at your local cineplex. This site offers an above-average bulletin board that allows surfers to weigh in with their opinions on everything from movies to music to—yes—Web sites.

Famous Birthdays www.famousbirthdays.com
It takes a while to load and is none too easy on the eyes, but this site does provide the most extensive list of famous birthdays ever compiled on the Web. Best of all, the listings are arranged by date, year, and last name. Nobody is too old, young, or obscure to be included on Famous Birthdays, so you'll find a real range of celebrities here.

The National Enquirer www.nationalenquirer.com
Let's face it: we all want to know! Every bit as wacky and entertaining as its newsstand version, this virtual tabloid has one minor drawback: it offers most of the headline stories featured in the print version, but holds a few grisly little gems to keep you panting for the real thing. Hey, the reduced price of a subscription is but a click away!

DC Comics www.dccomics.com
The folks at DC Comics really knew what they were doing when they put together this visually stunning site. Old fans get a sneak peek at what their favorite superheroes will be up to in future editions, while new ones can read "Secret Files" on Captain Marvel, Batman, Lois Lane, and Superman. You can also subscribe to a free online weekly newsletter here.

Marvel Comics www.marvel.com
You'll find comic previews, news of upcoming movie and television projects, and most importantly, lots and lots of gorgeous artwork on this site, which is also the home of such luminaries as Spiderman, Hulk, and The Fantastic Four. There's even a listing of times when fans can chat online with the creators of their favorite comics.

WebComics www.webcomics.com
WebComics features over 80 strips online for your reading and viewing pleasure, many of which can't be found in your local newspaper, but are often more entertaining. You can also try your hand at Electronic Madlibs or drop in for a cyberchat with fellow cartoon lovers. Updated daily and weekly, depending on the strip.

Comics.com www.unitedmedia.com
Hang out with Snoopy in the Peanuts' Club House or turn your cursor into Dilbert; Comics.com offers a variety of amusements, all of which involve famous comic strips. The offerings are more traditional than those found on WebComics (featured strips include Momma and For Better or For Worse), but the content is more colorful and informative.

Pop Culture Corn www.pccmag.com
Edgier than Debbie Gibson pop culture, but more fun than most alternative underground 'zines, Pop Culture Corn is a literate review of the latest movies, music, television, literature, and technology. Features and reviews cover fluffy and grungy pop alike with as sincere a tone as appropriate for the subject matter, and the commentary is always intelligent and entertaining. Read reviews of this week's new film releases, comics, and video games, interviews with entertainment gurus and indie musicians, and features on professional wrestling or the future of the Internet.

Pop History Now www.pophistorynow.com
It's June 12, 1968. Elvis tops the pop charts, the Beatles just debuted their newest film, and the U.S. Navy is in Saigon. At Pop History Now, every day is a different day in pop history, complete with news, top TV, film, and music charts, and other snippets of trivia. The information is addictive; once you uncover the best songs and new consumer releases for June 22, 1957 (Elvis's "Teddy Bear" and Campbell's Soup extralarge 19 oz. cans), you'll want to explore the archives for other pop history profiles. Real Audio allows users to listen to the reports in "radio-minute" format.

Giant Sponge www.giantsponge.com
Eerily intelligent analysis of the very fluffiest of Gen-X pop culture, Giant Sponge is the equivalent of a marvelous, smile-inducing inside joke to anyone whose consciousness grazed the icons and idols of the 1980s. Articles on teen-movie lessons, Buffy the Vampire Slayer's role as a feminist hero, and the aging of the X generation ("geriatric X") are a witty window into the cultural mindframe of those who grew up on Cyndi Lauper and Atari.

iVillage Astrology www.astrology.net
You probably know what your sign is, but what about your Karmic sign?
iVillage Astrology gives you much more than your basic horoscope--it tells you what planets rule your love life, your finances, and even your summer vacation. Click on free charts to get a full work-up of your personality, or have your horoscope e-mailed to you daily.

Collector's Universe www.collectorsuniverse.com
What's the difference between Browny the Brown Bear and Bruno the Terrier? About $3,000, acording to Collector's Universe, a site that caters to people who collect everything from Beanies to Bank Notes. Use their price guides to find out how much your collection is worth, or the online auctions to make it larger. And keep up to the minute on your collectibles with their news and articles—it's a site no collector should be without.

The Astrology Zone www.astrologyzone.go.com
Nationally renowned Susan Miller is the Internet's first superstar astrologer. The secret to Miller's success are incredibly detailed horoscopes that manage to be substantive without putting you to sleep. In fact, her forecasts are nothing short of fascinating, highlighting opportunities, themes, and potential obstacles for each sign on a month-by-month basis. Her site's also got great information on the basic tenets of astrology, as well as matchmaking, travel, and fitness tips. Be sure to check out her "Books by Sign" column, too!

The Daily .WAV www.dailywav.com
Check in here for a daily dose of sound clip hilarity—every personality from William Shatner to Mike Myers ("Now is the time on Sprockets when we dance!") and every film from *Mommy Dearest* to *The Breakfast Club* has a five-second wav for your listening pleasure. *Simpsons* fans will be disappointed though—the site had to remove all Bart and Homer wavs. Doh!

Comedy.com comedy.com
Stand-up comedy, comic strips, jokes, movies—if it's funny, you can probably find it on Comedy.com. The coolest features here are video clips of stand-up superstars (Adam Sandler, Chris Rock) and links to film and TV sites (everything from *Animal House* to *South Park*). The Jokes section is amusingly categorized by type of joke—blonde jokes, sex jokes, office jokes ... even golf jokes. Read the ones they've got or submit your own.

Seeing Ear Theater www.scifi.com/set
One of the best entertainment sites on the entire Net, the Seeing Ear Theater is the "premiere site for Science Fiction Audio Trauma." Tune in to classic dramas like The House on Cypress Hill or Isaac Asimov's Nightfall. Who says the great days of radio are over? For a Web site devoted to radio, this features some awfully fetching artwork, too. Brought to you by the Sci Fi Network.

Hecklers Online www.hecklers.com

A wicked look at popular culture, Hecklers Online provides daily comedic updates designed to purify the soul from the unyielding torture of celebrity culture. Take a whack at the Celebrity Pinata, then feast your eyes on photos of Bill Gates as a child. (You think he's going through an awkward stage now?) Don't forget to consult the Magic-4 ball for a cynical glimpse into the future.

fashion & beauty

Style Experts www.stylexperts.com

Expertise in the true sense of the word. This site's fashion experts feature the leaders of the industry, with Niki Taylor answering questions on modeling, Todd Oldham on color, Kate Spade on accessories, and Vera Wang on weddings, to name a few. Ask your own questions, review the archives, and be in the know with a little help from those who really are.

Fashion Angel www.fashionangel.com

Just can't get enough of those fashion sites? Fashion Angel is sure to list some you haven't seen yet. A Yahoo!-ish directory of fashion on the Web, Angel's got links to shopping sites, hall of fames, 'zines, designers, alternative fashion, and more. Best of all, you can surf the site in sweats and no one will ever know!

Fashion Net www.fashion.net

Every field has one all-encompassing be-all end-all directory. Fashion.net aspires to be this. Though currently a little lean on content, this site is a good resource for finding links on trends and styles, beauty, modeling, shopping and the industry. Highlights include fashion-related technology, the top 10 fashion schools, modeling agency links, and shopping guides.

About.com www.fashion.about.com

At About.com, fashion is a many-tiered subject. This site organizes, comments on, ranks, and raves about every possible fashion issue under the sun, all neatly subdivided with articles that touch on everything from style and shopping to body issues and fashion theory. Talk about depth: start with accessories, which is subdivided into belts and earrings (to start), which are then subdivided into leather, cloth, clip-on, hoop ... the possibilities are endless. Why wade through men's ties when you're really just undie-hunting?

Fashion Live www.worldmedia.fr/fashion
A site for truly cosmopolitan fashion connoisseurs. Click through Fashion Live's ìcatwalk coverageî for detailed listings of current and upcoming fashion shows in New York, London, Milan, and Paris, or read the site's designer profiles, reviews, and play by plays of the worlds' best-dressed runways.

Models.com models.com
Unfortunately for the rest of us, models can't share their good looks. At Models.com, they share stories about where their looks have gotten them. Find out who's hot on Models.com's Top 50 Countdown, complete with images, commentary, agency, and nationality. The site offers insights into the lives of the famous and the not-so, with interviews, favorite night spots, style guides, and advice on how to break into the biz.

7thonsixth www.7thonsixth.com
We know the clothes matter—ever stop to think about the designers that make fashion happen? 7th on Sixth is all about the magicians who transform mere cloth and thread to a way of being. Read about upcoming shows, see the designers on display, read bios and photos, and check out lists of stores selling their wares.

Lumiere www.lumiere.com
Fashion news changes daily. So why are so many fashion magazines printed once a month? Thanks to modern technology, style devotees can get their fix every single day with Lumiere's ever-changing updates on the world of style. Check the site or sign up for e-mail updates detailing the trials and tribulations of fashion's foremost luminaries.

Stylin' www.papermag.com/stylin/stylin.html

Paper is style and fashion news that can laugh with, and at, itself. You'll find no "accessories" section here—just a close approximation with a sense of humor at the "Tchotcke of the Week." Search back issues to find out more about the Viagra Booklight (with magnifying glass) or the Mickey Mouse Hard Hat, learn what Monica Lewinsky should have worn to the Senate trial hearings, or just pipe up at the Fashion Schmashion commentator's conference.

Elle Online www.ellemag.com
Beauty and fashion heavy hitter *Elle* wasted no time delving into the digital with Elle Online. Look for the old standbys—beauty guides, trends, health and fitness, and astrology—or wander through their Model Gallery, which features a slide show of Elle's 20 top-selling models.

Bazaar www.bazaar411.com/fyi/viabazaar_frameset.html
Perhaps it's too much to ask to find the elegant and thoughtful magazine online in full. Bazaar's pro staff does offer extensive guidance on where the finds are in fashion, beauty, home, entertainment, cars, and design both online and in stores. Check the not-so-subtle pop-up window for what's featured in the current month's issue—you'll have to pay for that but, count your stars, the style guide is free.

Electra.com www.electra.com/swarchiv.html
Advertising may revolve around size two models, but the real world cuts women's bodies a little more slack. Electra.com offers lifestyle articles, style guides, advice, and shopping resources for plus-sized women, all encouraging acceptance and celebration of the female form in its many shapes and sizes.

British Vogue www.vogue.co.uk
Vogue has long been a classic for personalities, models, collections, and news. What's so great about British Vogue online? It's searchable! Find back issue articles on designers and celebrities, or try the collections search by item, designer, color, and price range. It's almost like playing dress-up … almost.

BeautyNet www.beautynet.com

Beautification is work—every detail needs attention. BeautyNet offers the latest tips and trends with a large selection of archived articles with the inside dirt on hair (microfringe bangs a must for this season), face (make-your-own facial), nails (innovative polishing techniques!) … you name it.

Style Wire www.women.msn.com/women/style
Microsoft strikes again! Style Wire has it all, with frequently updated features on the latest trends and how to master them. The Web Guide focuses on a new link weekly in addition to its favorites in fashion, tips, and plus sizes.

Costume Site www.milieux.com/costume
If the need should arise for a costume of any kind, this is where it will be. Featuring hundreds of links to costume resources for historical, theatrical, or ethnic dress as well as museum collections, this is the site for costume research, rental, or recreational information.

CNN Style www.cnn.com/style
Elsa Klench's ever-popular weekend show on CNN delivers dispatches from the fashion front; its Web site does the same, with breaking trends, couture show gossip, and interior design news. The content is limited but quite good; for anyone seeking a quick dose of style news, this is the spot.

fashion & beauty

FASHION PLANET

Fashion Planet www.fashion-planet.com
The world of fashion knows no bounds. Fashion Planet covers seasons, styles, and shopping, but extends its discriminating taste to other areas of life that afford such selectivity—travel, architecture, design, the arts, books, and fine dining, which make the image as much as fabrics and jewels. Fashion Planet is not a just list of links; it shapes a way of being—depending on the season, of course.

Fashion Dish www.fashiondish.com
Who better to dish on all things fashionable than a former *People* magazine editor? Anne-Marie Otey's sweet little site has gossip, advice on what to wear, and the always titillating best and worst dressed pages. Be careful—you just might land here sooner or later!

film & television

Movieline Online www.movielinemag.com
Cinema buffs will love Movieline Online, which includes such tantalizing features as "The 100 Greatest Movies Ever Made," "Bad Movies We Love," "Greatish Performances," "Celeb Speak," and "The Movie That Changed My Life." Articles are delightfully dishy, with tidbits like "Just how hated is that icy, terrifyingly ambitious, marginally attractive young lady? So hated that many likely male co-stars have practically told their agents they'd rather do Sally Struthers infomercials than go near her." Ouch! Who could it be?

eXposure www.exposure.co.uk
Touting itself as "the Internet resource for young film-makers," eXposure's main attraction is its "Complete Eejit's Guide to Film Making," which includes tips on how to storyboard movies, light a low-budget film, and use a home computer to edit your masterpiece. There's also a recipe for fake blood here. This site is what the Internet is all about: a free, easy, and useful exchange of information.

AtomFilms www.atomfilms.com
Atom Films showcases the world's best short films—chosen for their visual grace, style, beauty, or impact. This is a terrific site for budding filmmakers to seek inspiration and check out the competition. There are also film reviews and an impressive catalog of archived short movies.

Movie Juice www.moviejuice.com
Irreverent is too mild a word for Movie Juice, which seeks to "deconstruct the b.s. that is Hollywood." Dial up this site for scathing reviews of movies your office buddies praise to the heavens while you quietly retch into your wastebasket. Actually, Movie Juice is surprisingly fair when it comes to giving credit for a movie's strengths. Still, the site certainly isn't doing Robin Williams's career any favors.

Drew's Script-o-Rama www.script-o-rama
This site features the full scripts of over 600 movies, including drafts, which can differ greatly from the final version of a film. Intriguing offerings include the first draft of *Young Frankenstein* and the shooting script of *Blue Velvet*. Very impressive content, especially considering that everything here is free.

Dinner and a Movie www.dinnerandamovie.com
Dinner and a Movie is a godsend for folks who have had their eardrums blown out by the sound clips on 777-FILM. Enter your zip code and this Web site spits out all of the theaters in your area, which movies are being offered, and what times they are being shown. Not only that, Dinner and a Movie has restaurant reviews of eateries in the surrounding area of a given movie theater. If you live in an urban area, you can search movies by the name of your city. Ingenious!

Film 100 www.film100.com
Anyone interested in the history of cinema would do well to visit this site, which is a list of the 100 most influential people in film. Click on a name and you'll get a biography and portrait of the person in question. Names fall into 10 categories, including director, performer, screenwriter, technical innovator, and critic. You can even search by decade of influence. The biographies are really impressive—looks like somebody's been doing their homework.

Greatest Films www.greatestfilms.org

Everyone who loves movies should bookmark this site, which features film genres and recommendations, cinematic history through the decades, an overview of the Academy Awards, and a film quotes quiz, in addition to "favorite lists" published by various organizations and magazines. There are also compilations of great film star roles and memorable scenes.

BBC Online www.bbc.co.uk/home/today
Reruns of *The Nanny* make your teeth hurt? Then make your way over to BBC Online, where intelligent television programming is the watchword. Get updates on *East Enders*, peruse nifty finds at the Antiques Road Show, learn about the secret life of pets, or check out TV listings for your favorite BBC shows. Could be a bit flashier, but this is British broadcasting, after all!

film & television

Nick at Nite & TV Land www.nick-at-nite.com
Leave it to Nick at Nite to design this ultra-cool, super-fun Web site. Surf synopses of your favorite childhood shows, read up on TV luminaries of the past, win arcade prizes, buy television collectibles, or try your luck at Marcia Brady's Football Toss ("Oh my nose!"). Perhaps the only site that can get couch potatoes to switch seats.

Comedy Central.com
www.comedycentral.com
The bulk of this site is devoted to *The Daily Show* with Jon Stewart, but it also gives devotees of *South Park*, *Absolutely Fabulous*, and *Dr. Katz* something to sink their teeth into. There are schedules of shows and games to play (Mr. Hanky's Construction Set, Match Wits with Ben Stein, and Dr. Katz's Road to Sanity, among others), as well as tons of good ol' fashioned promotional material. Great for Comedy Central fans seeking a respite from those god awful *Mannequin 2* screenings run between the good stuff.

The Hollywood Reporter www.hollywoodreporter.com
If you want the latest buzz on the entertainment biz, look no further than The Hollywood Reporter. It's got the scoop on who's slated to star in the next blockbuster, which hotshot director is slated to lens this week's bestseller, and whose careers are on the rise. Access to articles is limited unless you're a subscriber, but you will be given a tantalizing taste of headline stories on a daily basis.

EpisodeGuides www.episodeguides.com
This Web site features episode synopses of nearly 30 television programs. Yes, the list includes *Seinfield*, *The Simpsons*, and all three incarnations of *Star Trek*, but there are a lot of odd choices here, too. (How many folks want a show-by-show account of *Veronica's Closet*? Still, there are good picture galleries, a respectable search engine, and a weekly trivia game that offers a prize. Fun but limited.

Screen It! Entertainment Reviews for Parents www.screenit.com
Screen It! offers parents the lowdown on "objectionable material" in movies. Unlike other guides, which use such vague terms as "profanity" or "adult situations," Screen It! delivers detailed descriptions of each and every titillating (or stomach-churning) cinematic moment. The only danger is that the reports will prove just as offensive as the movies they describe.

Trailerpage.com www.trailerpage.com
Trailers, otherwise known as movie previews, are arguably an art form unto themselves. If you'd like to see what's on the horizon in movieland, check in at Trailerpage.com. Most of the films listed also have a link to the movie's official site. This is an especially good place for cinema purists who get enraged by the gabfest that usually ensues during sneak previews.

The Motion Picture Association of America www.mpaa.org
As "advocate of the American motion picture, home video and television industries," the Motion Picture Association of America tries its darndest to warn folks in advance about any objectionable material contained in these mediums. It's the organization that came up with the movie rating system, and governs copyright and antipiracy laws, too. If you want to know what a particular movie is rated or need the specifics on film copyright infringement, stop here first.

Television Ticket Co. www.freetvshows.com
Heading out to Los Angeles? Then drop by Television Ticket Co., which can set you up with free tickets to such hit shows as *Jeopardy!*, MTV's *Loveline*, *Wheel of Fortune*, and the *Roseanne Show*. The search engine leaves a lot to be desired, and there are lots of shows that Television Ticket Co. does not have access to, but if one of your favorite programs is featured here, this Web site will serve you well.

The National Talk Show Guest Registry
www.ourworld.compuserve.com/homepages.ntsgr
Are you absolutely bursting to share all the gory details about your sizzling love affair with your best friend's spouse? Well then make your way to NTSGR, which provides a forum for folks who feel they have a great story to tell on talk TV, but can't muscle their way past surly bodyguards and chilly receptionists. With any luck, you'll be flinging chairs at Jerry Springer before the week is out.

Oscar.com: The Official Academy Awards Site www.oscar.com
The next best thing to strolling down the red carpet, Oscar.com gives Academy Awards fans a peek at the action both onstage and off. In addition to the results of the most recent Oscar night, the Web site also features a fashion review, articles on the various preparation involved, a historical overview of the ceremony, and a trivia game. Some more photos would be nice, especially in the history section, but video coverage of the preshow festivities more than makes up.

Film.com www.film.com
Film.com features video clips of movies and interviews, as well as reviews and listings of film festivals, and recently released home videos. You can search reviews by what's in theaters now or by critics' picks. You're also encouraged to submit your own reviews or slip into the screening room, which features coming attractions. Great content, good design.

film & television

Film Threat Online
www.filmthreat.com
Film Threat Online is the electronic version of a magazine devoted to independent, cult, and underground film. It features much of what you'd expect from such a publication: interviews, reviews, and daily news, with the added bonus of hate mail. The news reports are delightfully biased and scathing, but the archives are limited to subscribers, and the site's design could use some help.

Six Degrees www.sixdegrees.co.uk

This independent film Web site from the United Kingdom has news, interviews, and film, video, and book reviews that are updated on a weekly basis. The monthly competitions offer extremely cool prizes, and the trailers are great viewing fun, provided you have the necessary plug-in.

The I Film Network www.ifilm.net
The I Film Network is one of the slickest sites you'll even find devoted to independent movies. You can search news articles by genre, location, category, or festival, or look up films according to title, subject, or cast. The articles are very well written and the amount of information is excellent. Updated daily.

ReelPreviews.com www.reelpreviews.com

ReelPreviews.com has everything you want to know about the latest movie and video releases, newest soundtracks, and upcoming feature films. There's also a weekly Internet show starring *Diff'rent Strokes* star Gary Coleman. This site prides itself on being completely objective in its reporting, so don't expect to find too much editorializing here. A film site that encourages you to use your own judgment—what a concept!

The Internet Movie Database www.imbd.com
IMDB seeks to provide useful, up-to-date movie information on nearly 200,000 titles; it also has over two million filmography entries that are constantly being updated. Surfers will also find daily news articles, previews of what's opening this week, plot synopses of upcoming movies, and box office rankings. Pretty "vanilla," but impressive in scope nonetheless.

GirlsOn www.girlson.com
The prospect of another super-action sci-fi muscle movie doesn't leave you panting with excitement? Then head for Girls On, "the highly opinionated, completely subjective" guide to entertainment. This site doesn't only feature film, television, book, and music reviews; it's also got updates on "girly" shows like *Ally McBeal*, *Friends*, and *The Real World*. Feels like a big giggling slumber party.

Moviefone.com www.moviefone.com
All the magic of 777-FILM without that horrible man shouting in your ear. Simply enter your zip code and find out which movies are playing in theaters near you. It's also possible to search by movie title. In addition to this directory service, Moviefone.com also allows you to purchase tickets, read reviews by fellow moviegoers, and feast your eyes on clips of coming attractions.

Oh, the Humanity! www.ohthehumanity.com

Fans of Ed Wood and Adrienne Barbeau will clap their hands with delight at this site devoted to the worst movies of all time. Among the gems you'll find here are "The Bad Thoughts Column," "The B-Movie Quiz," the "Crappy Awards," and the ever-popular "Contest for Losers." Great design, even better idea.

Sundance Channel www.sundancechannel.com

Whether you're among the five people who have access to the Sundance Channel or not, you may find this Web site useful. Not only does it offer a monthly schedule of its cable station, but it also has a film store containing videos of festival entries at a 25% discount. The collections packages are especially good buys, and include Grand Jury Prize Winners, Audience Award Winners, Urban Visions, Hong Kong Action, Women We Love, and Celluloid Closet. Occasionally you can apply to enter film contests, too.

Ain't-It-Cool-News www.aint-it-cool-news.com
An initial glance at the headlines on this site makes you think it was created by a psychotic, and upon further investigation your theory would be proved correct. The news and reviews that are posted here have an extremely overzealous cast to them, but their energy is a refreshing alternative to the more staid film sites on the Web. Be sure to check out the Ain't It Cool Museum, which has photos of the 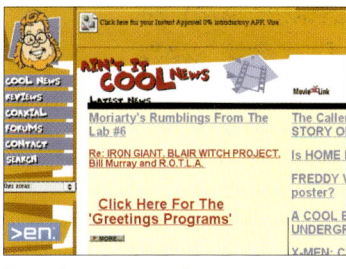 Webmaster's movie memorabilia collection. (Love the Monster's boots from *Abbott and Costello Meet Frankenstein!*)

Fox.com www.fox.com
Featuring programming schedules, video previews, and a Fox store, this site is basically one big advertisement for Rupert Murdoch's television network. Good for updates on favorite shows like *The Simpsons*, *King of the Hill*, and *The X-Files*.

The Cartoon Network www.cartoonnetwork.com
Here's where Space Ghost, Cow and Chicken, and Scooby-Doo hang out when they're not being played in an endless loop on The Cartoon Network. Dial up this site to play games, win prizes, buy cool stuff, and find out exactly when your favorite funny will air. You can also check out series premieres and find out background information on such aging 'toon stars as Elroy Jetson and Pebbles Flintstone.

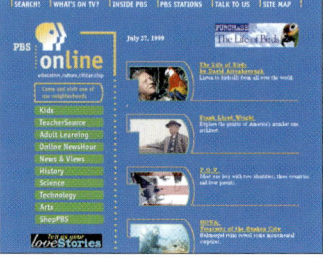

PBS Online www.pbs.org
Hey, it's publicly funded, so we'll forgive the slow loading time of this site. After all, isn't it better that viewers' contributions go toward terrific programs like *Sesame Street*, *Mystery*, and *NOVA*? Programming schedules and synopses are divided into "neighborhoods" that include Kids, Adult Learning, History, Science, Technology, and Arts. Tell 'em Ernie and Bert sent you.

NBC.com www.nbc.com
Notably more sophisticated looking than the other networks' Web sites, NBC.com features program schedules, listings of shows, descriptions of upcoming movies and miniseries, and an overview of past specials. There's also a section spotlighting NBC television stars like Jennifer Aniston, Brooke Shields, and Noah Wylie. Fans of *The Tonight Show* should stop by the "Virtual Jay" page.

Soap Digest www.soapdigest.com
Half an hour to *Guiding Light* and the checkout line was out of copies—save the money and win big on content with Soap Digest's online reservoir of resources on the programs and the stars. In addition to the stories run in the weekly print version, Soap Digest online provides a peek at the week to come, plus message boards, chats, features and interviews, and special Web promotions. For the ardent soap viewer who can't get enough of the tube.

The Ad Critic www.adcritic.com
Ad Critic is a site devoted to dissecting the pesky television commercials that most of us seek to avoid. Feedback on ads is encouraged, so get ready to tell those Madison Avenue executives who should really be doing the laundry in those stupid detergent ads.

Driveways of the Rich and Famous www.driveways.com
This site's got photos of the driveways of your favorite stars, from Ann-Margret to Pia Zadora. OK, maybe they're not your favorite celebrities, but it is inexplicably fascinating to gape at these photos. The best section features interviews with the gardeners, mail carriers, and delivery people to the stars. (Guess Mary Tyler Moore's doorman didn't get a tip last Christmas.) Entertaining and addictive.

TV Guide www.tvguide.com
Addicted to the small screen? Now there's a choice between the TV and the Web—TV Guide online offers all the standard features of the print publication, with the added features that it's free and always at your fingertips. Find out the buzz on the actors, writers, and stars of television and film in the features sections, find weekly listings of what's on, or browse the extensive listings of TV and films past and present in the searchable database of the big and little screen hits and misses.

TVGrid.Com www.tvgrid.com
If you want to know which programs are on what channels and when, dial up TVGrid. The unique remind feature is very helpful indeed; simply enter the shows you want to watch this week, and an e-mail will be sent to you on those days. You'll also find news stories and crossword puzzles here.

Gist TV www.thegist.com
Can't get enough of your favorite television show? Take your habit to the next level with Gist's celebrity photos, downloadable preview clips, and books based on the shows (*Ally! Dawson's Creek! ER!*). Or enter your zip code to see Gist's extensive TV listings viewable by category (movies, soaps), date, and/or time. It's almost as fun as flipping channels!

Seinfeld.com www.seinfeld.com
Featuring video clips, a fortune-telling magic ball, a marble rye toss game, a weekly trivia contest, and downloadable wallpaper, Seinfeld.com is a real treat for fans of the immortal sitcom. The audio clips are especially amusing—George's answering machine is classic.

DEN www.den.net
The television nation will be happy to know that DEN is streaming video shows, online, right now. This innovative Internet TV site pushes a bit further than traditional broadcasting, covering issues, people, power, sex, urbanity, and technology, sometimes all mixed together into one delectable video file. First-time set-up takes some time, but true desk potatoes will take comfort in this refreshingly wise use of Web technology.

The Sync www.thesync.com
This brilliant site features interactive entertainment programs that you can find only here. Programs include *CyberLove* (20-somethings discuss love and sex, *Here and Now* (six college students living in a house...wait— does this sound familiar?, *Snack Boy!* (a five-minute daily comedy show), and the truly weird *Jenni Show*. You'll also find short films here. Innovative and interesting.

Star Wars.com www.starwars.com
The most hyped film of the century (at least), Star Wars clears the air with this official Web site on the films, the founder, and the flurry of products for purchase. Learn about everything from Industrial Light & Magic's special effects to the comic books inspired by the films.

South Park www.comedycentral.com/southpark
The lewdest and best-loved cartoon in America takes full advantage of its 15 minutes of fame with its animated site hosted by Comedy Central. Flash scripts ensure the five rotund kids' entertainment value while the viewer wanders through the download and merchandise offers. For the passive consumer, learn more about the program and its development through the Behind the Scenes with episode storyboards and Q & A with creators Matt Stone and Trey Parker.

77

film & television

finance & investing

The Wall Street Journal www.wsj.com
Expect the same top-flight business news coverage that you get in the print version, with a twist: WSJ online is custom-tailored to your needs and is updated around the clock. This powerful site lets you search the WSJ archives and tailor the news to fit your personal investment portfolio. But it costs: $59 per year, $29 for print subscribers.

Hoover's Online www.hoovers.com
Dubbed "the reigning king of corporate profiles" by *Fortune* magazine, Hoover's is a subscription-based site that provides detailed information and financials on more than 15,000 public and private companies around the world—perfect for investors, executives, and job seekers. The pithy and well-researched profiles sketch out the company's history, ownership, and position within the industry, list officers and their salaries, and provide 10 years of fiscal data (everything from net income in 1990 to current market value). Read the in-depth profiles for $99.95 per year—or access miniversions for free.

Nasdaq-Amex www.nasdaq.com
Just the facts: quick real time quotes on Nasdaq-traded companies, market activity, and news about the stock exchange. Search for stocks or mutual funds that match your personal criteria. Cool feature: direct links to company Web sites.

Company Sleuth www.companysleuth.com
Four beautiful words: legal, inside information, and free! Register with the Sleuth to receive daily e-mail updates on publicly traded companies: new patents and trademarks, insider trades, federal litigation, stock rumors, and other info scoured from Web sources. You name the targets, Sleuth provides the facts. But be warned: Sleuth doesn't guarantee the validity of its tips, so do your homework before acting on the information.

Red Herring www.herring.com
The big fish of technology business news, Red Herring brings you insider info about the big pond of high tech, with a modicum of wit and a razor-sharp eye. Related stories are linked together, allowing you to choose which kind of news is most interesting. Or dive in and write a post to the Herring message boards, which host discussions on all things financial and technological.

CNNfn www.cnnfn.com
Financial news from the Ted Turner empire. Brief, informative articles give you the latest word on the economy, the business world, the latest deals and more in no-nonsense style. Brief summaries let you decide if you want to read corresponding in-depth articles, which are peppered with hyperlinks to related articles and information on companies mentioned in the article.

International Financial Encyclopaedia

www.euro.net/innovation/Finance_Base/Fin_encyc.html
A comprehensive dictionary of financial lingo, this is the place to go for down-and-dirty explanations of unknown terms. These pages ain't the prettiest, but the site's breadth of information more than makes up for its aesthetic awkwardness. Especially worthwhile are definitions of international financial terms (like Gyakubari), knowledge of which is becoming crucial in our burgeoning global economy.

BigCharts www.bigcharts.com

If a picture is worth a thousand words, could a chart be worth a thousand dollars? One thing's for sure: there's no quicker way to absorb so much information, and that speed can make a big difference in your pocketbook. BigCharts is just what it says it is: graphs of various indexes, stocks with extreme behaviors, market overviews, and so on. The interactive charting feature allows charts to be combined to suit your investment and information needs.

ABI World www.abiworld.org
The source for all possible information and news about bankruptcy. It's definitely worth a visit if you're curious (or ultracautious), but calling up this site is mandatory if you're in serious debt. Little life preserver icons direct you to general information and counseling, as well as to resources to keep you afloat once you've decided to take the bankruptcy plunge.

finance & investing

79

Women's Wire MoneyMode
www.womenswire.com/money

One of the Web's most user-friendly personal finance sites (for men, too!), Women's Wire offers information on budgeting and savings, IRA and 401(k) plans, insurance, credit cards, and taxes. There are also chats and expert Q & A's, financial news, calculators, real-time stock quotes, and advice geared especially to women— like how to settle money matters after a divorce.

SocialFunds.com www.socialfunds.com

Learn all about the philosophy and practice of socially responsible investing on this well-designed site. Chock full of strategy advice on all realms of investing, the relevant links to get you started, and advice on how to use your power as a shareholder for good, SocialFunds.com should be the primary resource for investors with a conscience.

Insure.com www.insure.com
A mother lode of insurance info awaits at Insure.com. Read all the latest news related to the insurance industry in its various incarnations. For your own good, check out The Basics section, which gives basic advice on how to select an insurer, as well as all the statistics and tools you'll need to do it right.

Insurance Information Institute www.iii.org
Everyone needs security, but finding out how to get it isn't always the easiest thing to do. III takes the sting out of insurance hunting with its answer guide: insurance categories include auto, accident, home, fire, lighting, storms, and more. Read recent news reports or just browse the insurance companies and associations to find the right security blanket for you and yours.

Federal Deposit Insurance Corporation www.fdic.gov

The primary public resource for information on banking. No one knows the laws better than the lawmakers themselves—on this site, you can wade through the tangle of regulations yourself, or get a handholding guide even a child could understand. You'll also find detailed information about industry trends and history, as well as the skinny on particular institutions—all for the low, low price of a yearly income tax return.

Bankrate.com www.bankrate.com
An independent, objective monitor of the banking industry, Bankrate.com has been collecting data on U.S. banks for 20 years. Interest rates and fees for nearly every imaginable banking service for banks around the country are gathered here to aid your banking decisions. The site also offers general banking tips and news about the industry.

Financenter.com www.financenter.com
Financenter.com is essentially a Web-based financial advice calculator. Ignore the "ClickDeals," which offer human advice through the site for a fee, and instead use the "ClickCalcs" to figure out optimal purchasing, insuring, investing, and saving strategies. Each planning regime contains a calculator designed to help you answer a particular question; results are given numerically, graphically, and in tabular form, attended by relevant facts.

Armchair Millionaire www.armchairmillionaire.com
A financial planning and investment site whose explicit goal is to make you a million dollars? It's worth a shot. Armchair Millionaire is full of great advice for the average Jane who wants financial security (and more) but doesn't know where to start. The greatest asset of the site is the core of devoted members of the Armchair community who participate in the message boards and share their real-life success stories.

MoneyClub.com www.moneyclub.com
Sober advice for all aspects of personal financial planning. Every category is divided into subcategories, under which are collected basic information, advice, tools, and Web links. A great resource for the financial novice, with info on basic financial concepts, from pages culled from all over the Web.

ABCNews.com www.abcnews.go.com/sections/business

For rock-solid financial news and opinion, ABC News.com is as reliable as they come. The well-designed site is information-packed, with top headlines, a daily market overview, real-time quotes, and links to further articles for investors and small business owners. ABC News.com is a great one-shot daily dose for money-minded folk —and makes a great home page.

Motley Fool www.fool.com
If any investment site can be described as jovial, Motley Fool is it. With a mission to "educate, amuse, and enrich," Fool empowers average Joes with the information they need to make any financial decision: buy a house, invest in the stock market, and manage credit cards responsibly. The Fool's liveliness mostly comes from the discussions on everything from stock picks to online investing. But be warned: Fool's contributors aren't necessarily experts, and aren't prohibited from investing in the stocks they discuss. Use what you read as a jumping-off point for further research.

finance & investing 181

The Street.com www.thestreet.com

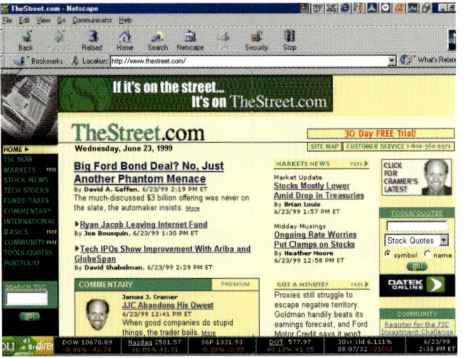

When The Street.com started out in late 1996, there weren't any sites offering comparably intense and thorough coverage of investment news. Since then, a lot more have sprung up, but none quite as hard-core. A site for investors who love to invest, The Street.com offers its members two investment bulletins per day, prepared by writers and analysts who work under what the site claims are "the toughest disclosure rules in the media industry." (None of its reporters may own stock or financial interests in companies, except in mutual funds.) You can't get far without subscribing, but at $99.95 per year, or $9.95 per month, it's a worthy investment.

Quicken.com www.quicken.com
Fans of Quicken's popular personal finance software will be thrilled with its new online component. In addition to providing the full range of online investment and personal finance information, Quicken.com allows users to download checking, savings, ATM, and credit card information directly from their bank into their personal Quicken files. You can even pay your bills online —for less than the cost of a postage stamp.

U.S. Securities and Exchange Commission www.sec.gov
If you stick to online stock trading, you're unlikely to run afoul of the SEC, but anyone who has a hand in the pot should benefit from knowing the rules. The SEC Web page gives you all the facts about what's legal, and its investor section gives impartial info about investing, its pitfalls, and how investors can protect themselves.

FreeEDGAR www.freeedgar.com
Get every single document filed with the SEC by a company of interest, as well as a list of the day's filings on this EDGAR site. Professionals can pay a fee to download filings in a myriad of formats, allowing easy incorporation of the data for whatever your needs. A free e-mail service updates you when a company that you have specified files a new document. The info on this site can be found elsewhere on the Web, but not with the same convenience and ease.

Stanford Securities Class Action Clearinghouse
www.securities.stanford.edu
A compendium of briefs and documents filed in federal and state courts in class action suits against publicly held companies. Find out if a company in which you are contemplating buying shares or already own shares is being sued. If you're more likely to be a member of a class than the subject of a class action, then it pays to know which companies are already in hot water.

finance & investing

IPO.com www.ipo.com
Get in on the ground floor! On IPO.com, investors can read the prospectuses of private companies seeking capital, and arrange to purchase shares before they are available for public trading. A broad range of companies are made available to investors, providing both sides with increased opportunity for cashing in on IPO millions.

E*Trade www.etrade.com
The premier online brokerage site, E*Trade is slick, ultraconvenient, and offers competitive pricing: from $14.95 per trade. Open a cash account and trade stocks, bonds, options, and mutual funds with a few clicks of the mouse. E*Trade's hallmarks are speed (crucial for online investing —a delay in executing a trade can cost you precious dollars) and accessible customer service. For beginners: play E*Trade's risk-free market simulation game, where you can create an imaginary portfolio and see how your stocks fare—each month, the most successful make-believe investor wins $1,000.

DLJdirect www.dljdirect.com
Among the crème de la crème of Web brokers, DLJdirect has numerous awards to prove it. Trading is quick and easy, with real time quotes and extensive trading options. A simple demo lets you see how the trading interface works in a few minutes. DLJ is also one of the only online brokerages that won't charge you for trading over the phone. Useful feature: customizable e-mail alerts tell you instantly when your stocks split, interest is credited to your account, or securities of interest begin trading at a predetermined price.

Datek Online www.datek.com
Datek Online is a superior Web broker, with near-immediate trading, a

user-friendly interface, and access to extensive information, but its real advantage is price: up to 5,000 shares can be traded for only $9.99. Additionally, Datek charges a mere 6.75% APR on loans, allowing you to be up and trading quickly and cheaply.

Morningstar.net www.morningstar.com
The acknowledged king of mutual fund sites, Morningstar.Net gives the most comprehensive information about mutual funds today, including both general strategy tips and up-to-date news. There's also a host of discussion groups, all aimed at particular niches in the world of mutual funds. If you're a little befuddled by the diverse features, check out the articles classified under Funds 101.

The Mutual Fund Café www.mfcafe.com
There is no prettier mutual fund Web page in existence—but if the appearance is delicate, the content is anything but. Designed for mutual fund business and marketing professionals, Mutual Fund Café is not for the novice. Clever and incisive, the articles in these pages analyze the industry from top to bottom. Sit down in this café only if mutual funds are a way of life for you.

GreenJungle www.greenjungle.com

This is the site to visit if you are a novice mutual funds investor. In simple language it walks you through the basics of the game, with bold section headings delineating overviews, descriptions, and explanations. In a similarly lucid style, other pages explain more subtle strategy points. The design is bright and gaudy, but the nuggets of advice are worth your time.

Social Security Online www.ssa.gov
No one really seems to understand how Social Security works, but the official government site is the best resource for trying to figure it out. There's news, research, official information, FAQs, and links to related sites. The Top 10 Services page tells you what features others find useful; among them, a downloadable program that calculates what your benefits will be.

IRS Digital Daily www.irs.urstreas.gov

There's something undeniably annoying about the IRS's attempts of late to become more user-friendly, like a burglar leaving a thank-you card after robbing your house. But this Web site is a welcome addition—you can download forms and read tax regulations in plain English. For true tax mavens: Keep up with changes in collection procedures! Read tax conventions, legislation, and court decisions!

SecureTax.com www.securetax.com
It's 11 p.m. on April 15, and you suddenly realize you haven't filed your taxes and it's too late to get an extension. Without a hint of panic you blithely aim your browser at www.securetax.com, fill out an online form, and have your return electronically filed half an hour after you enter your credit card number. How much would you expect to pay for such a service? Would you believe only $14.95 ($9.95 for 1040EZ)?

CyberInvest.com www.cyberinvest.com
An authoritative and well-organized guide to investing resources on the Web, CyberInvest is worth a visit. Feature-by-feature comparisons of hundreds of different investment sites give you the tools to decide which are right for you. Useful: the Tales, Tools and Tips section, which gives pointers on selecting an online broker and provides a glossary of investment terms.

Taxes4Less.com www.taxes4less.com
For those who aren't quite ready to let a computer program file their return, there's Taxes4Less.com. The site lets you submit your tax information online to a real, live CPA who will quickly prepare your return and file it electronically (or send it to you via snail mail). It's the best of both worlds: the convenience of the Web, and the assurance that your financial information rests in human hands.

QSpace www.qspace.com

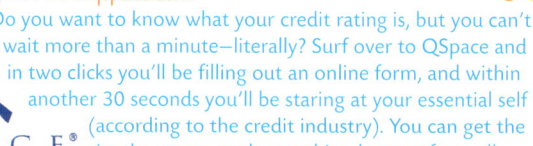

Do you want to know what your credit rating is, but you can't wait more than a minute—literally? Surf over to QSpace and in two clicks you'll be filling out an online form, and within another 30 seconds you'll be staring at your essential self (according to the credit industry). You can get the simple report, or the combined report from all three major agencies. There's also a credit monitoring service that gives you regular updates on that all-important document.

National Foundation for Consumer Credit www.nfcc.org

Went a little overboard with the credit cards last month? A lot overboard? The NFCC is the place to start rebuilding your credit. Its 1,450 offices across the country provide confidential financial counseling and debt repayment plans, and this user-friendly site is also the place to find out how to get a copy of your credit report directly from the credit reporting agencies.

Bloomberg www.bloomberg.com
The big fish in the big pond of financial publications, Bloomberg online is even more than it's print twin. The site is divided into three sections—Markets, with domestic and international news and financial figures; Money, with interviews, advice and personalized mutual fund centers; and Life, covering the finer ways to enjoy money and leisure time. Full access requires a subscription fee, but many sections are available gratis.

food & drink

Epicurious www.epicurious.com

"For people who eat" (that means you), Epicurious is one of the Web's best-known food sites. Over 9,000 recipes, articles from *Bon Appetit* and *Gourmet* magazines, cooking tips, and a food term dictionary with more than 4,000 entries make Epicurious a one-stop resource for foodies. The most delectable tidbits? The Playing with Your Food section, which teaches dining etiquette like how to crack a lobster and where to hide sugar packet wrappers, and the exhaustive wine list.

Cooking Light Online www.cookinglight.com
The print standard for healthy eating and living is online. Food ideas and cooking tips stand alongside recipes with full nutritional information, while the Healthy Living section provides even more tips for eating right and keeping fit. The excellent search feature allows users to hunt for their favorite dishes by such criteria as calories, sodium content, or fat grams per serving.

StarChefs www.starchefs.com
Imagine Julia Child, Jean-Georges Vongerichten, Sheila Lukens, and Emeril Lagasse in one virtual kitchen. At StarChefs, the eager cook can get tips from the masters, visit their restaurants, read bios, order cookbooks, and copy recipes. Culinary hopefuls should check out the links to culinary schools and job listings, or enter their best recipe in the StarChefs contest.

Cooking.com www.cooking.com
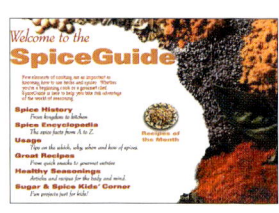
Weekly menu planners, holiday menus at a glance, recipes for international food, and feature articles are just the tip of the iceberg at Cooking.com, which is also a giant kitchen accessory superstore. Find everything from tablecloths to barbeques to cake pans to food processors in the great shopping section, which features searches by product, brand name, or price range. Will inspire even the cooking-impaired to slip on some oven mitts and fire up the grill.

SpiceGuide www.spiceguide.com
The stuff that led to the discovery of the West, spices are a cooking essential. Find everything you ever wanted to know about the history and usage of spices from allspice to vanilla in SpiceGuide's spice encyclopedia which details geographic sources, aroma and flavor, traditional ethnic uses, and history of almost 50 spices both well known and obscure. SpiceGuide also contains a wealth of usage tips including substitution guides and a recipe database for everything from meats to pies to sauces.

CookieRecipe.com www.cookierecipe.com

A cookie monster's mecca, this "all cookies, all the time" site contains over 1,800 recipes and all the equipment and baking hints necessary for the perfect batch. Scan the top 10 recipes, search by ingredient, browse alphabetically, or check out categories like Christmas cookies, No-Bake cookies, Sugar-free cookies, or the classic Chocolate Chip, which alone contains almost 100 recipes. Check out the main page of this offshoot of AllRecipes.com for tens of thousands more recipes and sites like CakeRecipe.com and BreadRecipe.com.

Salt & Pepper www.saltandpepper.com
Straightforward and easy to navigate, Salt & Pepper is simply an extensive list of great recipes culled from public Usenet groups all over the Web. From appetizers to candy and cakes, the recipes range from easy to complex, and the samples include something for every taste.

Gourmet Spot www.gourmetspot.com

A beautifully simple search tool for the wide world of food on the Internet, Gourmet Spot's listings of the Web's best sites in 21 categories makes finding a restaurant, recipe, or rolling pin a breeze. Only the best sites are listed for vegetarian and ethnic cooking, coffee and cocktails, food news, equipment, cookbooks, and restaurant guides. Gourmet Spot also offers site-, tip-, and recipe-of-the-week, as well as its own features on cooking and eating.

Zagat Survey www.zagat.com

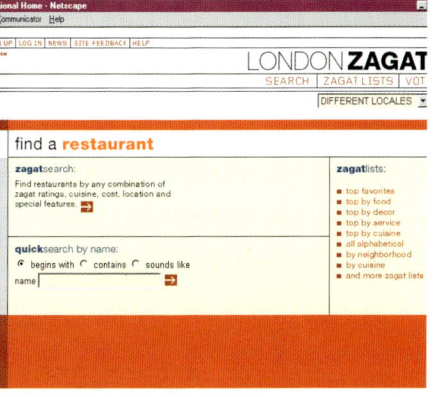

The guide we depend on when dining out is also an easy-to-use Web site featuring 17,000 reviews for restaurants in 20 cities worldwide. Search by location, price, cuisine, decor or food ratings, or using one of the quirky "uniquely Zagat" lists like "Teflons" (restaurants with qualities that keep criticism from sticking). The listings are vast and will make your mouth water as you search: better to choose your dinner venue before your appetite warms up. Be sure to vote on your favorite spots as well; users' critiques are the basis for the reviews.

Food.com www.food.com

Funky '50s graphics, 12,000 participating restaurants, full menus, and delivery to your door when you want it—all reasons Food.com is a tremendously more attractive option for ordering out than searching through take-out menus or the Yellow Pages. Search for restaurants by zip code or city and by cuisine type, then scan the menus, order for take-out or delivery, or locate the perfect spot to dine out without leaving your seat.

Emeril's Homebase www.emerils.com

"Just when you thought you were safe from great food and exciting dining experiences," exuberant chef Emeril Lagasse hits the Web with his Homebase, where one can find the sites of his six restaurants in New Orleans, Las Vegas, and Orlando as well as links to his television haunts, the Food Network and Good Morning America. The restaurant sites feature "restaurant gaze" summaries, which include location info and maps, lunch and dinner menus, hours and services, and recipes for Emeril's famous southern treats.

food & drink

Good Karma Café www.goodkarmacafe.com

As close to a bona fide café as an online community can come, the Good Karma Café offers advice, support and references for vegetarians, almost-vegetarians, friends of vegetarians, and anyone else curious about meatless or healthy diets. Check out meatless recipes for classic dishes like turkey and lasgana, or find a vegetarian restaurant in your area. Way cool feature: a translator that converts the entire site into any of six languages.

Veggie Life www.veggielife.com

Don't let the name mislead you—Veggie Life magazine isn't just for vegetarians. Housed under the same virtual roof as the award-winning lifestyle site Natural Land, Veggie Life has news and living articles on topics from weight loss to gardening to personal care and beauty. Touted as "the only healthy lifestyle magazine that covers natural living from the ground up," Veggie Life offers basics on everything needed to begin or maintain this type of lifestyle.

Gourmet World www.gourmetworld.com

A wonderful, thorough resource for anyone who enjoys cooking and eating, Gourmet World features a bounty of links in 12 categories including catering services and cooking schools, cooking and food chat forums all over the Web, a number of sites dedicated to specific chefs, and recipes for 39 kinds of food from cobblers to puddings. Measurement con-

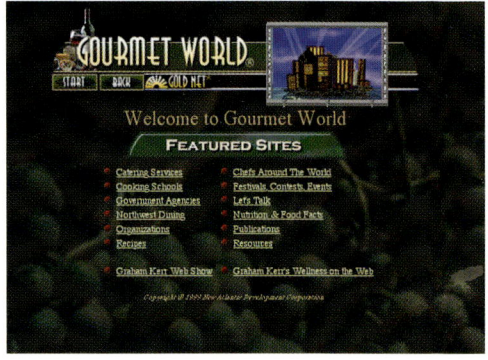

version tables, the National BBQ Association, chef Paul Prudhomme's home page—you'll find it all at Gourmet World.

Ben & Jerry's Online www.benjerry.com

Who can resist a site whose entrance warns "euphoria ahead?" Just as yummy and socially conscious as the real thing, the Ben & Jerry's Web site is the place to find the latest flavors, visit the graveyard of flavors that never made in stores, order ice cream by mail, locate a scoop shop, or read about how bleached paper containers pollute the planet. Irresistibly tempting for visitors with empty stomachs.

Sushi Guide
www.nmd.hyperisland.se/studentzone/crew2/martin_ragnevad
A simple get-to-know-your-sushi online manual sporting a rather Zen design, the Sushi Guide introduces the basics of the etiquette, equipment, ingredients, and preparation of this popular Japanese dish. Recipes for temaki, nigiri, and maki as well as the perfect sushi rice, explanations of the ingredients of sushi (what is wasabi anyway?) and the equipment needed to prepare it (why a bamboo mat?), and step-by-step instructions on how to eat the stuff can make any novice into a sushi guru in no time.

Garlic Festival Foods www.garlicfestival.com

You can almost smell the pungent aroma of the stinking rose at this garlic-lover's paradise. The site of the extravaganza that put the town of Gilroy, California, on the map 20 years ago features more information, recipes, activities, and links about garlic that you ever thought possible. The Garlic Store offers many of the products featured at the festival for sale online (sorry, no garlic ice cream) as well as a list of other garlic-related fairs and events nationwide.

DrinkWine.com www.drinkwine.com
What wine goes with pork? With a very simple menu and links to articles covering the gamut of wine topics, DrinkWine.com has everything for the wine connoisseur from a food and drink pairing guide to travel planners for winery visits. Information on wine growing, sales, labels, clubs, and much more is organized in a straightforward scheme, and anything this site may be missing can be found through its links to other wine sites. A totally complete guide.

Wine Spectator www.winespectator.com
For serious wine buffs, Wine Spectator has the most up-to-date information and releases to keep you in the know. Read the editor's picks, scored and with full description, for the hottest new wines and old favorites (more than 77,000 are listed), keep on top of the most recent wine industry activities, find your nearest fine wine dealer, even visit online wine auctions.

The Republic of Tea www.republicoftea.com

As beautiful and calming as its products' packaging, the Republic of Tea Web site is a virtual teahouse oasis. Tea lovers can purchase teas and accessories here, or read a comprehensive account of the history, mythology, and uses of the ancient beverage. View a map of the Asian tea belt, or have your tea leaves read by Madame Oolong, the Shockwave fortune teller.

The Real Beer Page www.realbeer.com
Much cleaner and a lot less smoky than the local bar, The Real Beer Page has more information about beer than you could ever imagine. News, health information, shopping, games, brewery guides, events, city guides, beer-for-every-occasion lists, book reviews, and even an incredibly extensive online beer library are all documented, linked, and archived here. Join your

local brewer's association, brew your own at home, or select the perfect beer for your barbeque.

food & drink

iDrink: The Drink Mixing Web Site
www.idrink.com
Perfect for a party: Enter all the drink ingredients lying around the house and iDrink will come up with dozens of recipes from its database of almost 5,500 alcoholic and nonalcoholic drinks. The site's 162-ingredient search finds a recipe for any combination. Each recipe is rated by user votes, and the top 10 drinks are listed in their own category. From Atomic Cats to Purple Jesuses, iDrink is almost too much fun.

HotWired Cocktail www.hotwired.com/cocktail
Fabulous, colorful, and cool, just like a cocktail should be. HotWired's Cocktail site has a cocktail of the week (including the history, culture, and proper usage of the drink) and a glossary with entries for everything from maraschino cherry to Ernest Hemingway. The Virtual Blender provides recipes, while the Alchemist teaches bar and drinking etiquette. Bottoms up!

Caffeinated Magazine www.caffmag.com
A cornucopia of clever articles about America's favorite morning buzz, Caffeinated Magazine dares to ask questions such as, Where can I get real cream in the land of skinny health nuts? and What's with the ubiquitous greek-themed paper cups in New York City? Coffee trivia and lore, reviews of cafés in 38 states, and a café-of-the-month index archived back to January of 1997. Caffeine heads, start your engines.

SmellTheCoffee.com www.smellthecoffee.com
Pour a cup and settle in to SmellTheCoffee.com, a full-service coffeehouse featuring today's news, a game of checkers, chat and forums about coffee, a kitchen full of java recipes to share, and much more. Find a coffeehouse or cybercafé across the world (listings for six continents), with over 9,600 listings in the United States alone. Or if you feel like reading, visit the bean for an entertaining history of all things java-related.

Soda Fountain www.sodafountain.com
A virtual museum dedicated to one of the most notable institutions of American social life in the first half of the 20th century. The history of the soda fountain from 1858 on, pictures of fountains and luncheonettes, recipes (including the original Coca-Cola recipe), soda and ice-cream brand links and more are hidden behind the counter of this fascinating piece of pop history.

Quickspice www.quickspice.com
Don't know your pad thai from your kim chi? This elegant site offers a delectable selection of foods and recipes from Asia. Chinese, Japanese, Korean, and Thai dishes are here, as well as chop sticks and bamboo steamers— available for online ordering.

games & gambling

NetBaby www.netbabyworld.com
The "Hello Kitty" of online video games, NetBaby features such adorable offerings as Post Office, Tour de France, Hi-Jump, Ninja Girl, and Ping vs. Pong. Kids will love the cutesy graphics and musical accompaniment, as will adults who are intimidated by Doom.

Macromedia Shockwave www.shockwave.com
Shockwave's got it all: casino games, online sports, arcade favorites and ... peeing etiquette? The offerings are incredibly fast, fun, and visual. Games include Joker Poker, Candystand Baseball, Super Action Bust Out, Letter Mania, Aztec Underworld, Kong Fu, and yes, the Urinal Game. Can Ladies Room Roulette be far behind?

GameCheats.net www.gamecheats.net
Cheaters actually can prosper thanks to this site, which offers more than 18,000 cheats for Gameboy, Playstation, Nintendo, and PC games. The content is comprehensive enough to please even cheaters with the highest standards.

Rolling Good Times Online
www.rgtonline.com
If you like to gamble, be sure to stop by Rolling Good Times Online. It features tips on everything from sports betting to horse racing to casino gambling to Internet wagering. You'll also find information on lotteries, bingo games, blackjack tournaments, and much, much more. There are way too many ads to get through here, but the content is truly impressive.

Pogo www.pogo.net

It could be better organized, but Pogo does feature an exhaustive list of family, professional, and PC games that are easy to play and are, in many cases, free. There's something for everyone here, whether you're playing with a group or going solo, with every conceivable game including solitaire to Quake. The site links to some of the most popular gaming portals online, from Excite Classic Games and The Station@Sony.

Gameland.com www.gameland.com

Gaming junkies will love this site: there are games of skill, chance, and thought, as well as weekly contests. Try your luck at Little Piggy Races, game-land Craps, Basketball Shoot-outs, Hit the Heckler, Concentration, Jumble Sticks, and Caption This! There's a lot more to try here, so be sure to surf around. Great graphics, cool design, and fun games that don't take hours to load.

The Blip www.theblip.com

Touting itself as "an Internet playground," The Blip features neat games like Sumo!, Perambulator GP, Bombardier, and Interactive Chess. The games could be more varied (there are not nearly as many as on Shockrave or Gameland), and not all the offerings even constitute games (witness Spir-O-Matic). Still, what's here is pretty cool and free, for cryin' out loud.

World Opponent Network www.won.net

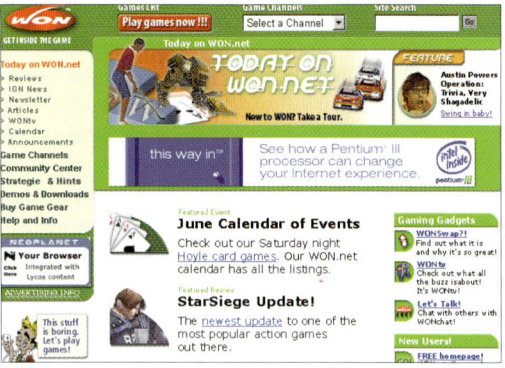

Despite its ominous name, World Opponent network is actually a friendly looking site that features over 50 games that can be played immediately (Leisure Suit Larry's Casino, You Don't Know Jack, PGA Championship Golf, Roach Invaders, and Lords of Magic, among others), as well as hundreds of free video game downloads. (Note: these are only demos, not the actual games.) It's pretty plain-looking for a gaming site, but the respectable content makes up for it.

 Mplayer.com www.mplayer.com
This multiplayer game site promotes itself as a place to meet folks, and it seems to do a fairly good job. In addition to over 80 games, it's also got an audio chat room for members. It's a little difficult to get to the games because of the site's preoccupation with matchmaking, but maybe that's the point. Categories include Action (Extreme Quake, Assault), Classics (Battleship, Hearts), Strategy (Warcraft, Commandos), Simulations (Fighters Anthology, Road Rash), and Sports (ABC College Football, High Heat Baseball). Don't get too excited, though—not everything here is free.

Multi-Player Online Gaming www.mpog.com
Wow, does this site have a lot of stuff on it! In addition to over 250 games, it's got cheats, comics, feature articles, links, news, and reviews. There may even be a little too much here for game purists, because it takes so much time to get to the stuff you want. Rest assured, though, every conceivable kind of game is here. Just be prepared not to leave the house for the next 10 years.

Gamepen www.gamepen.com

Gamepen offers an impressive peek at the countless video games on the market. You'll find previews, reviews, and the top 10 downloads for games designed to prevent you from ever seeing the light of day again. It's remarkably quick and easy to surf, allowing you to devote more time to ... what else? Video games.

GameStorm www.gamestorm.com
Definitely a force to be reckoned with, GameStorm's got free games like Godzilla, Fierce Harmony, and Silent Death, as well as ones you have to pay for, like Air Warrior III and Megastorm. The faint of heart may prefer to stick with with low-key offerings like Chess, Hearts, and Whist, which are anxiety- and fee-free.

Kasparov vs. The World www.zone.com/kasparov/home.asp
This unique site gives chess enthusiasts the rare opportunity to play one of the greatest masters in history: Garry Kasparov. If that prospect is a little daunting, you can always click to learn how to hone your chess skills, find out a new move every day, or simply play online with others who are presumably less proficient than Kasparov himself.

games & gambling

Chess.net www.chessnet.com
Chess enthusiasts will love this no-nonsense site, which features hundreds of games with players of various levels, as well as a chess shop, weekly strategy column, ranking ladder, and photo gallery. There are also constant updates on what's going on in the world of chess, as well as tournament schedules. A welcome change from other gaming sites, which tend to have a bewildering level of content.

Jeopardy! Online www.station.sony.com/jeopardy
The next best thing to seeing Alex Trebek in person, Jeopardy! Online affords you the opportunity to show off your knowledge (or lack thereof) online. You can play others or go solo, and choose from standard Jeopardy!, the sci-fi version, or the college edition. Beware of the audio effects—they can blow you out of your seat!

Trivia World www.triviaworld.com
The folks at Trivia World may be too busy scouring reference books to speed up their Web site, but there are dozens of categories to choose from. It's a little tough to get to the categories you want, though, if your area of interest isn't featured in the weekly spotlight. Good for dedicated trivia lovers—restless surfers will want to move on.

lottery.com www.lottery.com
Which games are offering the highest jackpot? What are the best strategies for playing lotteries? What's it like to be a winner? And most importantly, did your numbers come up last night? The answer to these questions and more can be found on lottery.com, where there are plenty of opportunities to win cool, hard cash.

Lotto World www.lottoworld-magazine.com
Discover the daily numbers in every lottery-playing state, learn where the biggest jackpots are being offered, and pick up some tips on game strategies at this informative Web site. If you need any coaxing to spend your hard-earned dollars on the lottery, simply click on the Lotto Millionaires page, where you'll read glowing accounts of wins from all around the country. There's even an option to play by phone!

Mysteries www.mysteries.com
This irresistible Web site allows mystery lovers a crack at solving cases on their own. Mysteries.com features a different crime each day, along with its solution. If the most recent case proves too easy, you can move on to the database of over 10,000 more crimes to keep busy. There are also numerous message boards that have recommendations of mystery authors and various Web sites devoted to their work.

The Riddler www.riddler.com
The Riddler is pretty sophisticated for a Web site that offers so many free games. Choose among puzzles, crosswords, video games, solitaire, and lots of others for a fun few hours in front of the computer. There are live tournaments every hour, plus free prizes. Membership is free and allows you to access even more games on this site.

Virtual Vegas www.virtualvegas.com
Almost as glitzy as taking a trip to Sin City, Virtual Vegas gives folks the opportunity to squander play money on electronic slots, blackjack, and poker. If you're really lucky, you can win genuine prizes. Considerably safer than some of the other gambling sites on the Net, but if you're looking to cash in real chips, log on elsewhere.

Planet Poker www.planetpoker.com
Feel lucky? Then dial up Planet Poker, where you can download free software and play real folks for either high or low stakes. Nervous novices should check out the simple step-by-step instructions that lead them to the table with a full understanding of how to play and what to expect from the game. A word of caution, though; the money you play with is real and yours, so keep that in mind before betting the farm.

Casino Titanic www.casino-titanic.com
This Web site affords gamblers the opportunity to wager real money on over 25 casino games, sporting events, and horse racing. It's free to download the software, but after that you should know that all the money that's bet is your responsibility. Hopefully there will be no icebergs ahead and you can cash in your trips after having amassed some winnings. Casino games include baccarat, craps, video poker, blackjack, and many others.

Uproar www.uproar.com
An online game show network, Uproar gives people a shot at winning prizes by playing other folks from around the world. Try your luck at such diverse contests as Puzzle A-Go-Go, Bingo Blitz, and Game Scene Arcade. The true test may be your ability to endure the endless stream of pop-up ads that pepper this site. Still, the content is great fun.

Vegas Insider www.vegasinsider.com
Sports betters will love this site, which features expert's picks, free 15-minute odds from Vegas hotels, handicapping tools, weather reports, and lists of injuries. VI covers every sport including horse racing; if you're going to place a bet, stop here first. Not all of the information is free, but a good portion can be accessed without paying a membership fee.

health

Phys.com www.phys.com
Phys.com is physical fitness for women that covers the gamut from weight loss to nutrition and exercise. Lots of advice here on eating healthfully and sculpting your bod into bikini-worthy perfection (whatever happened to being active for fun?). Skip the "Snack Bandit" virtual slot machine and go straight to the Nutritional Rx page for sound advice on how to prevent illness. Cool calculators let you figure out your ideal body weight, body fat percentage (yikes), or daily carbohydrate needs in a couple clicks of the mouse.

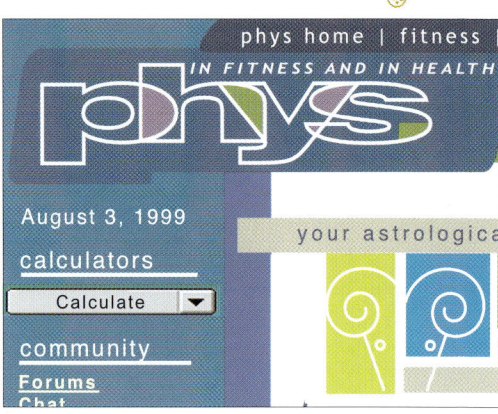

American Heart Association www.americanheart.org
The home of prevention and information dissemination for heart disease, America's number one killer, has a strong online presence dedicated to reducing the risk of this threat through education. The site features invaluable tools such as an A-to-Z guide to heart and stroke-related terms, a risk assessment quiz, a huge store of information on exercise, nutrition, and overall health programs and guides, and even a site for CPR education.

AMA www.amaassn.org
Aimed mainly at health professionals, the American Medical Association's Web site contains information pertaining to the medical trade, but its Journal hosts four information centers for asthma, HIV/AIDS, women's health, and migraines—extremely useful information for the rest of us. Those interested in the latest medical breakthroughs, medical ethics, or current health policy will have more than enough to feast on at this very informative site.

The American Cancer Society www.cancer.org

Clear and thorough explanations of almost 50 types of the disease that affects half of all men and one third of all women in the United States, including risk factors, detection, and treatment information. The site is well organized and easily accessible, with numerous articles, news, and treatment options. A must-see for anyone at risk.

health

Online Medical Dictionary www.graylab.ac.uk/omd
An incredibly complete reference, this site makes up in utility what it lacks in style. Over 65,000 cross-referenced terms include all kinds of medical jargon and acronyms (everything you've heard on *ER* and more!), from Aarskog syndrome to zyxin. Take charge of your medical knowledge with the help of Online Medical Dictionary.

Mayo Health Clinic www.mayohealth.org

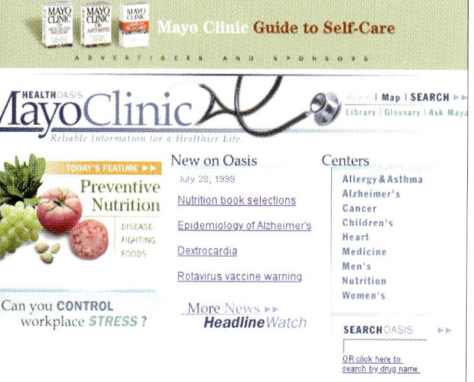

A virtual hospital, the Mayo Health Clinic online has as many departments and services as most clinics with none of the bureaucracy. Find health answers for men, women, children, and seniors for any possible complaint from asthma to thyroid disease.

Go Ask Alice! www.goaskalice.columbia.edu
Am I normal if I ... ? Answers to all varieties of this question come to you from Alice, Columbia University's health education Q & A site. From fitness and nutrition to emotional health to sexuality, Alice has answered more than 1,500 questions and continues to answer more each week. Search the archives to see if your question has been answered, or submit a new inquiry in one of seven categories. This site has been so highly acclaimed that in 1998 Alice published its own source book, which can be ordered from the site.

Drug Free Resource Net www.drugfreeamerica.org
An outstanding effort designed to help parents promote drug awareness and prevention, the Drug Free Resource Net features an informative database of drugs and their slang names, what they look like, and what they do. The site also contains a comprehensive list of advice and contacts for such topics as talking with kids about drugs and helping those who may be addicted. The tips are useful for adults with substance abuse problems as well.

KidsHealth.org www.kidshealth.org
Sponsored by the Nemours Foundation, KidsHealth earns its stripes by providing extensive news and advice for children's physical and emotional health, written in three distinct age-appropriate tones for use by kids, adults, and teens. Parents can turn here to find out more about their child's infection, nutrition, and other health issues, as well as parenting tips. Kids find articles like "Dealing with feelings" and "My body," and teens can get answers to questions about growing up that they're too embarrassed to ask elsewhere.

MedicineNet.com
www.medicinenet.com
A huge anthology of articles written by doctors and scientists for consumers, MedicineNet provides excellent, current medical information in easy-to-understand language on a full range of topics, from diseases and treatments to drug breakthroughs to first aid procedures. More of a guide than a database, MedicineNet doesn't include a search function, so the information provided is often quite general.

MediConsult www.mediconsult.com
As interactive as medical sites come, Mediconsult is almost like visiting your own physician. You'll find medical support groups where users can post and read messages from patients with similar ailments for a wide range of conditions. There are also live events every Tuesday evening hosted by doctors, and a MediXperts function where users can get a complete, specialized health report from a medical expert for a fee.

HealthCentral.com www.healthcentral.com

Featuring America's most popular on-air medical personality, Dr. Dean Edell, Health Central is a complete guide to general health and well-being. Including nontraditional medical topics such as spirituality and divorce and well as information on conventional issues such as disease and drugs, this very consumer-friendly site has tips and trivia on even the most obscure medical questions. Submit your own questions to Dr. Dean, or listen to his radio show over the Net.

Thrive Online www.thriveonline.com
A very cool site dedicated to personal health and happiness, Thrive Online contains a host of ideas and advice in areas such as fitness, sexuality, and serenity to improve physical and emotional wellness. Each area includes self-assessment quizzes complete with advice and explanations of the results, experts to answer questions, boards and chat, news, tips and more. From recipes to exercise programs to tantric sex instruction, Thrive Online is a complete wellness source.

Healthfinder www.healthfinder.gov
The United States Department of Health and Human Services' Healthfinder is an organized pool of information clearinghouses, self-help resources, and government and nonprofit services on a variety of health topics like AIDS, alternative medicine, self-care, and tobacco. With specialized sections on minority health, men, women, infants, seniors, and a large section in Spanish, Healthfinder is a great place to look for Web health resources or contacts in your community.

HealthAtoZ.com

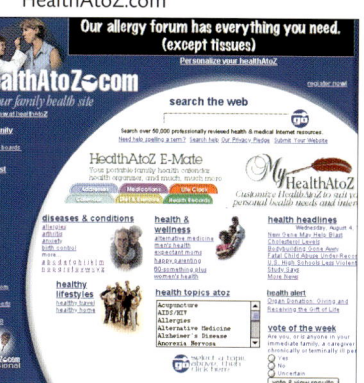

www.healthatoz.com
The most notable feature on this complete health site is the EMate, a personalized calendar, medication schedule, address book, illness record, and more, which can store a family's complete health information and even sends appointment reminders by e-mail. HealthAtoZ also contains a great deal of health and fitness information and news for the whole family.

99

health

Mental HelpNet www.mentalhelp.net
This award-winning guide to mental health and psychology offers news, advice and treatment information for psychological disorders from depression to drug abuse to sleep problems, featuring chat and support forums, a yellow pages of therapists, and a symptoms list. Mental HelpNet also includes a listing of professional resources and services where mental health professionals can find jobs and grants or read up on the latest in psychiatry and the law.

Mental Health.net mentalhealth.net

Weekly journal for both the educated individual interested in mental health issues and the mental health professional. In addition to engaging news stories, MHN offers browsable categories in Disorders and Treatments, complete with online self-help books and counselor locators, professional resources, and a reading room with an experts corner, commentary, and community chats and forums.

At Health www.athealth.com
Straightforward, useful resources about and serving the mental health community. The laundry list design makes locating the information you need as hassle-free as can be—categories include recommended reading and a "medicine cabinet" that describes medications used for different disorders.

Family Village www.familyvillage.wisc.edu
Don't let the 1970s hospital graphics fool you—Family Village is actually a very useful, up-to-date and easy-to-navigate site rich with national and international resources on a full range of physical and mental disabilities. Visit the library to learn about specific conditions and find out where to get help, the coffee shop to participate in community support chat, or the shopping mall for supplies and gear listings around the world.

AEGIS www.aegis.com

"The largest HIV/AIDS database in the world," AEGIS features thousands of articles and references on every aspect of AIDS, social, medical, and legal. Updated hourly, the database includes breaking news on research and incidence around the world, links to an amazing number of publications for patients, professionals, and the general public, law and government libraries, and communities where users can share experiences with others or get information about the disease.

Ask Dr. Weil www.cgi.pathfinder.com/drweil
Perhaps the best-known alternative medicine expert on the Web, Dr. Andrew Weil not only answers all your medical and dietary questions regarding natural and alternative medicine, but also hosts useful healing and self-help features like a personalized vitamin advisor.

Acupuncture.com www.acupuncture.com
Not just needles, Acupuncture.com includes a primer on a number of types of traditional Chinese medicine including herbology and Qi Gong. With information for students, consumers, and professionals (including research news and equipment sales), Acupuncture.com has everything for those already convinced of the virtue of acupuncture and related practices. The Ask the Acupuncturist section answers questions about the efficacy of the treatment for a variety of ailments and includes full explanations for those who aren't so sure.

Alternative Health News Online www.altmedicine.com
Explore alternative health and healing options on Alternative Health News Online, a warehouse of articles and links to the latest health news, diet and nutrition resources, alternative medical systems, and more. The site is updated daily with news and contains a search engine linked to five other medical Web sites for millions of articles on both alternative and conventional medicine. Explanations of various practices such as yoga and naturopathy will help you make informed decisions about your health care options.

Natural Land www.naturalland.com

If you want to live more naturally, but don't know the first thing about soy, organic produce or herb-based eye drops, this is the place to start. Natural Land has a little to say on just about every aspect of your personal care, as well as quizzes to let you see how much you already know. It even has a shop so you can buy your goat's milk soap from the comfort of your desk chair.

MotherNature.com www.mothernature.com/ency
This site is primarily a healthy living products online store, but it boasts a fabulous encyclopedia of natural health that includes a list of appropriate dietary supplements for over 125 common ailments, an overview of 100 common drugs and their possible adverse interactions with dietary supplements, a vitamin and mineral table, an herb chart, and an explanation of homeopathic and alternative remedies and diets. The encyclopedia is produced by a team of physicians and health care specialists, and the products they recommend can also be purchased at the site.

Arbor www.arborcom.com
An award-winning nutrition guide, Arbor is more than a food pyramid or four basic food groups. The guide has links to nutrition and food information pages of governments and organizations worldwide. Broken down into the categories of food science, applied, clinical, and consumer food information, this site has something for anyone seeking information about food, from hospital dietitians to manufacturers to mothers. Find everything from recipes to food history to the chemical makeup of an apple.

Eating Disorders www.aabainc.org
From the American Anorexia Bulimia Association comes this informative site dedicated to anorexia, bulimia, and binge eating disorders, which affect more than five million Americans. Includes information and resources for sufferers, friends and family, and professionals about the diseases' symptoms and medical consequences, causes and risk factors, and a guide to finding help for overcoming the disorders.

Sexual Health InfoCenter www.sexhealth.org/infocenter
While some of the information on this site reads like an issue of *Cosmo* (sex tip of the week!), the Sexual Health InfoCenter also contains loads of serious data and advice on topics such as sex and aging, safe sex, sexual dysfunction, and sexual orientation issues. Guides to the use and effectiveness of a number of birth control methods and the symptoms and health risks of various STDs are two of the more useful features of the site.

American Social Health Association www.ashastd.org

The American Social Health Association, an authority on sexually transmitted diseases, has put together an informational site full of facts and resources to promote education about the diseases that affect one out of every five Americans. Includes program and hotline information, news, an STD fact center and sexual health glossary, and links to other resources.

Male Health Center www.malehealthcenter.com
More than an OB-GYN for men, the Male Health Center is a complete resource for men's health including diet and exercise, medical information, and sexual health. The Health Center includes a guide to symptoms complete with explanations of their causes and advice for achieving relief, a chart for male immunizations and regular tests, and an extensive explanation and guide to impotence.

The American Academy of Allergy, Asthma, and Immunology
www.aaaai.org
What do Loni Anderson, Bob Hope, and Alice Cooper have in common? Allergies. Between 40 and 50 million people, including these three, have an allergy to food, latex, or air born irritants. Luckily, the AAAAI Web site provides comprehensive information on the causes, symptoms, and remedies to all your allergic reactions. Breathe a little easier with the physician referral service and the latest news on allergy-related breakthroughs.

101

health

Women's Health Interactive
www.womens-health.com
An educational site that covers every health concern imaginable, Women's Health Interactive provides women with information on infertility, natural care, midlife concerns, and gynecologic health. Learn about conditions and treatment options, and take a health assessment quiz to evaluate your own health needs.

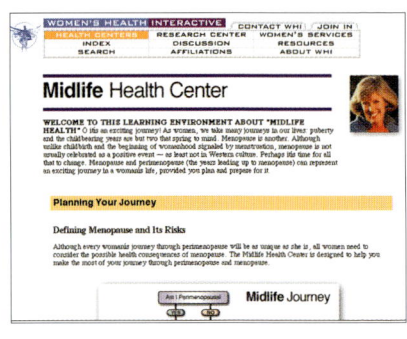

GYN 101 www.gyn101.com
Do you shiver when you imagine those cold metal gyno-gadgets? Ever wonder what they are? GYN 101 offers a complete guide to the most dreaded doctor visit of the year, including the reasons for going, what happens on the table, the patient's rights, and how to find a doctor. The guide includes relaxation techniques, too!

Gay Men's Health Crisis www.gmhc.org

The oldest and largest nonprofit AIDS organization in the country, the Gay Men's Health Crisis has offered support, educational services, and advocacy to men, women, and children since 1981. Its Web site covers the latest news and research on AIDS, medical care, nutrition, financial and legal concerns, and information on testing, volunteering, and much more.

Planned Parenthood www.plannedparenthood.org
A virtual clinic and activist site rolled into one. Planned Parenthood online gives advice on safe sex and sexual health, family planning, pregnancy, parenting, abortion, and more—and the key word is more. Articles on how to talk about sex with children, men's parenting responsibilities, congressional debates on reproductive issues, and the politics of the word "slut" turn this medical insight spot into an interesting and informative news site.

The Daily Apple www.thedailyapple.com
The Daily Apple is devoted to the idea that education and prevention are just as important (or more so) as cures. The articles are penned by medical experts using the latest data and most reputable sources—surfers can feel confident about the advice on this site.

Alcoholics Anonymous www.alcoholics-anonymous.org
The first stop on the road to recovery. AA's site (offered in English, French, and German) presents the facts and signs that can help the concerned friend or family member determine if alcohol has become a problem, as well as the afflicted individual. If AA is the right choice for you, information on their offices and services can be accessed here.

home & living

HomeArts Network www.homearts.com
HomeArts is an excellent resource for people who've turned their home into a hobby. Less manic than Martha Stewart but more exacting than Roseanne, the site invites searchers to discover information on everything from performing heavy-duty repairs to adding the occasional light decorative touch.

EFridge www.efridge.com
No ice cream here—just a virtual refrigerator-inspired calendar and events posting system to share with friends and families online. Post events, keep track of your schedule, and check it from any computer with Internet access. All the convenience of fridge-front magnet notes that travel anywhere.

Traditional Home DesignerFinder www.designerfinder.com
Want to redecorate a room or design it from scratch? Then take advantage of this terrific resource, which can set you up with an interior decorator in your area best suited to your taste and price range. There's an introduction to styles, a directory of designer tours, and a database of decorating resources. Perfect for amateurs.

Bob Vila www.bobvila.com
The household name in home repair and renovation has broken ground online with all the resources and advice he's known for. How-to's, advice, tool guides, and calculation information on indoor and outdoor housework will get you started—any further questions can be directed to the Ask Bob mailbox. Prepare for some minimovies, audio and photo decoration at this do-it-yourself home help site.

Virtual Garden www.vg.com
Are you in zone three or zone eleven? Find out at Virtual Garden. Just type in your zip code, and Virtual Garden gives you advice specifically geared to your climate zone. The site also houses a huge plant database, searchable by plant name or attribute, which makes finding plants for your rocky, partly-sunny garden patch a snap. To get the whole family involved, check out the links for weekend projects and gardening with kids.

Improvenet www.improvenet.com
"Help me do a project," reads a button on the Improvenet homepage, and help is what this site offers in abundance. You can go step by step through your project, from dream to budget to build, getting the information you need at each stage. The site also has a feature called My Project Folder, that records the ideas and items as you gather along the way, making it a fun and invaluable aid for any home improvement.

Martha Stewart Living
www.marthastewart.com
Like Martha herself, this site is practically perfect. It has sneak peaks of her *Weddings* magazine, a tour of her two television studios, an online store, a program guide, a live chat room, plus a biography of the domestic doyenne. Makes you want to move, throw out all of your possessions, and start fresh.

Better Homes & Gardens www.bhg.com

Better Homes & Gardens online is a wonderful resource for anyone devoted to the home arts. It's got tips on gardening, decorating, cooking, and menu planning, as well as feature articles on travel, parenting, and crafts. The Home Repair Encyclopedia is a stroke of genius. Informative, but not as intimidating as Martha Stewart's site.

Living Home www.livinghome.com
This site offers a little of everything for the home in a neat, easily-navigated package. What it lacks in the depth of its archives it makes up for with innovative pages like the Tool Box and Object of Desire. In the former, you enter a room's dimensions to get estimates of how much tile, wallpaper, or paint you need. In the latter, you'll find pictures of new products to fantasize about (designer garage doors?). Definitely worth a browse.

Home & Garden TV www.hgtv.com
In a happy twist of fate for the faithful Web surfer, the Home & Garden TV site actually outdoes the television shows it's based on. The extensive library covers all 40 of the network's shows and allows you to search by episode, week or topic. The Villages section gives you an illustrated site map that zooms in as you hone your search. And, of course, you also get a program guide, though after viewing the site it's doubtful you'll even need to watch the shows.

Benjamin Moore Paints www.benjaminmoore.com
The designers of this site sure knew what they were doing; it's both attractive and easy to search. There are sections devoted to homeowners, designers, architects, and professional contractors, as well as descriptions of industrial coatings.
Everything's broken down into sensible categories and step-by-step instructions. Who would guess there'd be so much to learn about paint?

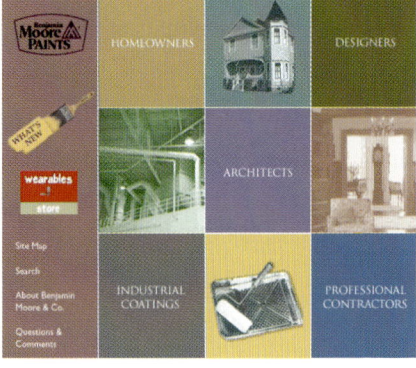

Kitchen-bath.com www.kitchen-bath.com
With pages like "Toiletarium" and "Dishwasherpalooza," this site will make you want to whip out a wrench and start remodeling. Luckily, the site has both a Sweat Equity section (to get you started on a project), and a Doctor in the House (to help you fix it when it goes wrong). You may want to download the crucial "How to Survive a Remodeling" guide, just in case.

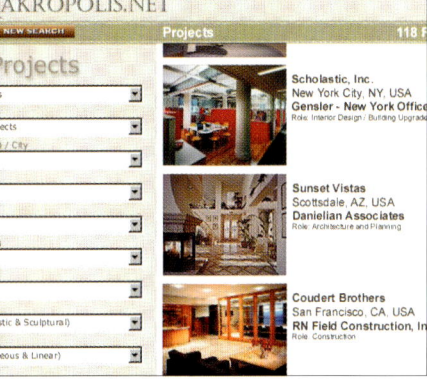

Akropolis.net
www.akropolis.net
An online showcase of designers and builders, Akropolis.net features profiles and portfolios for the most prominent businesses in these industries. Search by project, name of firm or professional, or location. The site is geared toward home and property owners looking for designers, firms seeking employees, professionals wanting to display their portfolios, and students seeking an internship.

Geomancy.net www.geomancy.net
Anyone interested in feng-shui, the ancient art of placement, will love this beautiful site. It is a highly informative reference guide that can help you design your home so that it will look terrific, feel welcoming, and (some say) be more attractive to luck. Learn how to assess the landscape, survey your home, and interpret the intangible forces that affect your living space. You can also buy reports, books, software, or apply for courses here.

Metropolis www.metropolismag.com

This site explores contemporary life through the various design disciplines (architecture, interior design, crafts, planning, preservation). It analyzes why designs evolve the way they do, taking into account the economic, environmental, and cultural conditions surrounding a space. Definitely a high-concept site, but articles like "1001 Ways to Make Your Space Livable" will appeal to almost everyone.

Petstore.com www.petstore.com
Whether your pet is fish, ferret, or foul, keep it healthy, happy, and sans fleas with the help of Petstore.com. You can e-mail questions to the online vet, order all sorts of supplies, and read up on pet care tips from the American Animal Hospital Association. Subscribe to the fantastic Never Run Out Again service to have food and litter delivered to your door on a regular basis.

home & living 105

411 Pets www.411pets.com
"So ya wanna dog, but does he want you?" Find the answer with 411 Pets' SelectADog, a quiz that matches a breed to your lifestyle. Once you've discovered the perfect pup, you can search the site's extensive list of breeders in your area. Cat owners, don't despair: you'll find valuable information on health care, lost pet rescue services, and pet classifieds for all sorts of pets at this site.

Real Estate

LendingTree www.lendingtree.com
LendingTree offers online home loans with a twist: your loan application is submitted to a number of different lenders who compete for your business. Their offers are e-mailed to you within two days, and you can respond and confirm the deal, all without leaving your computer chair.

Homefair.com www.homefair.com
Moving again? Make it easier with Homefair.com, which has home, apartment, and mortgage finders, temporary housing info, furniture rental and storage, and even van and truck rental links. Cool calculators like the Relocation Wizard provide you with a checklist of every little thing you'd otherwise forget to do while moving, and even customizes the timeline to your particular situation.

Housing and Urban Development
www.hud.gov
The word simple isn't usually applied to anything produced by the U.S. government, but it fits this housing info site. Besides offering concise explanations of the home buying and rental processes in easy-to-understand language, HUD gives great advice about common housing abuses and how they can be overcome. Know your rights!

Realtor.com www.realtor.com
A simply awesome number of property listings around the country (1.2 million) separates Realtor.com from the pack of home-buying sites. Once you've entered your search request, you'll see a picture (for most listings), a price, a description of the space, the realtor contact info, and even instant access to stats for your potential new 'hood. You can even search for a particular city neighborhood.

Owners.com www.owners.com
Why pay a realtor when you can check out home listings yourself online? Owners.com makes it a reality. Buyers can use the competent search engine to choose from a surprising number of properties, all without having to pay the standard 7-8% commission.

iOwn.com www.iown.com
Already found a home, but don't know how to pay for it? iOwn.com wants to help you finance it on the cheap. Its premier service is its MortgageCenter, which allows you to apply for a loan online. Boasting low fees and discounted mortages, iOwn.com is one of the quickest ways to get a cheap deal on a home loan.

Homeowners.com www.homeowners.com
Web-based home loans, spiced up with all the information and advice you need to make an informed decision. Homeowners.com is a full-service brokerage, with competitive loans and real brokers for you to talk to. The site's refinancing pages can help you decide if the time is right to trade in your old loan.

Kaktus Productions www.kaktus.com
Simple and to the point, this site lets you get your virtual hands on current, legally accurate real estate forms. All kinds of leases, agreements, and eviction notices can be downloaded by evil landlords for free or for minimal cost. There's also a handy glossary, in case you've been too busy counting your gilt to be able to learn the trade jargon.

Apartment Life www.apartmentlife.com
Far and away the coolest housing site out there, Apartment Life is devoted to educating young hipsters on how to make the most of their first pad. You'll find advice on decorating, storing your stuff, entertaining with style, and making the most of the meager resources you've devoted to spiffing up your lair. Check out the handy Apartment Hunter's Survival Guide, with tips on how to go about getting an apartment in the first place.

Rent.net www.rent.net

Tons of resources for every kind of renter can be found on Rent.net. Corporate and short-term renters, seniors, and vacationers, as well as standard apartment seekers will all love this site. The apartment search feature finds a large number of apartments in your price range, anywhere in the country, and offers pictures when available. The secret surprise is the "360° Virtual Walk-Through," which lets you look all around selected apartments with a few clicks and drags.

kids & teens

Nickelodeon Online www.nick.com
The first television channel just for kids is also a great site complete with news, pictures, and games featuring all of Nickelodeon's popular shows and celebrities. Very kid-friendly, Nick Online includes an Internet safety guide, a "how to help toolkit" designed to get kids involved in community improvement, and a feature created entirely by users, "100% U." Bright graphics, Shockwave games, and links to other Nick sites make this a hot hangout for kids.

Sesame Street.com www.sesamestreet.com

Hosted by Elmo, Big Bird, and the rest of the Sesame Street gang, CTW's site provides fun and empowering "edutainment" for the whole family. Pages for parents, preschoolers, and older kids use Web tools to create a virtual textbook of early childhood education, with games and mind-teasers for young kids and lesson explanations for parents. It's like interactive Sesame Street!

DisneyBlast www.disneyblast.com
Having cracked the code of children's entertainment long ago in film and television, it's no surprise that's Disney's online venture, Club Blast, shimmers and shakes with the same dazzle that kids just love. A 30-day trial membership allows full access to the games, action, and educational stories and activities for kids of all ages. Parents might want to take a look the Parental Control Levels to monitor access for each family member.

Muppets.com www.muppets.com
Don't expect to find any factual info at Muppets.com—they'll tell you DVD stands for Dick Van Dyke. Do expect to be amused by all the old favorites, including Kermit, Miss Piggy, and even those two grumps in the balcony, Statler and Waldorf. Each character hosts a different section in its own zany style, with puns and pictures enough to keep both adults and kids happy.

Sports Illustrated for Kids www.sikids.com
For any Little Leaguer who's ever wanted to draft his own major league team, SI for Kids comes through. The Bat-o-Matic gives kids four million virtual dollars to draft a team, and scores it according to real stats. SI Kids also has advice, sports news, and video clips, making this site a quality junior version of the grown-up magazine.

FreeZone www.freezone.com
A unique community for kids, FreeZone is a completely monitored collection of chat rooms, bulletin boards, personal home pages and other kid-powered forums. FreeZone's strict privacy and safety policy gives parents the assurance that their child's identity remains secure, and since all submissions are screened, the content is safe for kids' perusal. And it's fun!

Crayola FamilyPlay
www.familyplay.com
Build a birdbath, play recipe roulette, or grow a winter kitchen garden—Crayola's online activity resource is an incredible store of offline project ideas for creative parents and kids. Art projects, birthday party ideas, games, bedtime stories, science experiments, and nature adventures are just some of the categories FamilyPlay offers, with databases searchable by age, skill, or location. Parents will love the car trip games and couch potato cures.

Bonus.com www.bonus.com
This colorful online playground includes many standard kids-site features like homework help and pop culture news, but Bonus.com's standout feature is its huge warehouse of Java games and puzzles. From early-Atari lookalikes to interactive board games and more sophisticated strategy challenges, there are enough games here to keep kids of any age occupied for hours.

Yahooligans! www.yahooligans.com

Yahoo! for kids has all the power and breadth of its parent directory, but screens out any material that's inappropriate for kids—a great search tool for younger Web surfers. Like adult Yahoo!, Yahooligans! has other services, like news, sports, and Net events. Search responses are kid-safe as well, so parents can feel secure letting their little ones explore the gentler side of the Web.

eToys www.etoys.com
A kid's fantasy: eToys offers over 750 popular brands of toys, videos, music, video games, and baby products at competitive prices in an easy-to-shop format. Searchable by age group, brand, and toy type, listed under a number of staff-recommended criteria such as "classics" and "under $20," eToys' selection is overwhelming. Online help and personal touches like birthday reminders and wish lists, coupled with 24-hour shopping and the absence of lines, make this site a must-see.

FAO Schwartz www.st2.yahoo.com/faoschwarz
FAO Schwartz online has all of the perks of the store, including a world of toys and that scary, singing clock. However, the site also has something the store lacks, namely an easy way to search for toys by brand, category, or age group. The site also features store locations, a top ten toy list, and fun facts. (Did you know that over 203 billion Lego pieces have been manufactured since 1949?!)

SmarterKids www.smarterkids.com
A parent's fantasy: educational toys, games, books, and software chosen by an expert staff. SmarterKids organizes its offerings by grade level, learning style, and learning goal, and each product is rated according to ease of use, depth, entertainment value, and expert judgment. With a resource newsletter for parents and a low-price guarantee, SmarterKids is a smarter place to shop.

Dr. Toy www.drtoy.com
Toy and education expert Dr. Stevanne Auerbach, aka Dr. Toy, hosts this comprehensive online guide to toy selection. Along with her personal recommendations for the best children's products in 16 categories, Dr. Toy helps parents select gifts, gives play tips and safety advice, and links to related sites.

kids & teens

109

Time for Kids www.timeforkids.com
This online version of the magazine read by 2.2 million kids is actually two magazines: the "News Scoop" edition for grades two to three, and a more content-rich version, "World Report," for grades four through six. The articles, updated weekly and archived from 1995, offer kid-friendly information but don't talk down to readers. Features include Kids' Views on the News, where kids vote on issues such as Puerto Rico's pending statehood and NBA salary caps, and Kids Talk Back, a message board of surprisingly sophisticated young opinions on everything from Kosovo to homework.

Ask Jeeves for Kids www.ajkids.com

Why is the sky blue? Jeeves simplifies the search for answers to kids' common curiosities by providing a huge directory of reference sites. Just type in your question and Ask Jeeves for Kids returns one kid-appropriate site to answer it. The responses aren't always spot-on, but for general information, Ask Jeeves is an excellent and easy resource.

The Yuckiest Site on the Web www.yucky.com
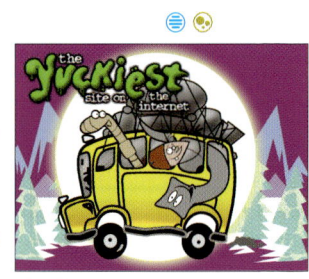
A science education resource cleverly disguised as a catalog of all things gross, the Yuckiest Site is disturbingly fascinating, even for adults. With answers to inquiries such as "What is snot made of?" and "Why do roaches bleed white blood?" this site is loaded with trivia that makes biology fun. While kids enjoy "Yucky Games" and trivia quizzes, parents and teachers will appreciate the tips and links on multimedia education, which include guides for browsing the Net with children of different age levels.

Discovery Kids www.discoverykids.com

An excellent kids' activity site sponsored by the Discovery Channel Online, Discovery Kids promotes curiosity by offering 60 safe adventure ideas, such as growing a salad, building a tree house, and learning a new language. How-to details and new adventures are added weekly. Kids can test their "adventure personality" to find others with similar interests, and check up on the progress of adventure teammates on a monitored bulletin board. Links to other Discovery Channel sites keep kids up-to-date on their favorite science and nature topics.

Spank! www.spankmag.com
The self-billed "voice of youth around the world," Spank! was created by and for teens. It's got articles on entertainment, fashion, education and more. Spank! also hosts five different forums for teens to vent on world events and other issues. You can even post your own reviews of movies and fave albums.

Internet Public Library/Youth
www.ipl.org/youth

The librarians at the first public library on the Internet seek out worthwhile and useful reference sites in the enormous tangle of information on the Internet, and their expertise shows in the youth division. Kid-appropriate links in 12 subdivided categories such as Art & Music and Our World include online reference materials as well as fun links to unusual sites. The equally useful Teen Division of the library can be reached through the IPL home page (www.ipl.org).

Infoplease www.kids.infoplease.com

Adapted from the popular radio quiz show, Infoplease contains an enormous amount of information, updated daily and designed to entertain as well as inform. The ultimate one-stop information guide, Infoplease includes homework tips and hard reference information on a wide variety of subjects, as well as interesting facts on everything from the history of underwear to the difference between a dwarf and an elf. Sleek graphics make learning a pleasure.

Bolt www.bolt.com

If you've long since graduated from high school, you may think Bolt is cute, but if you're still below drinking age, you'll probably think it's amazing. Bolt has a mishmash of information on all things adolescent, from jobs to music to dealing with life. Discussion boards, a calendar, and Bolt Notes messages help techno-savvy teens connect.

Teenhoopla www.ala.org/teenhoopla

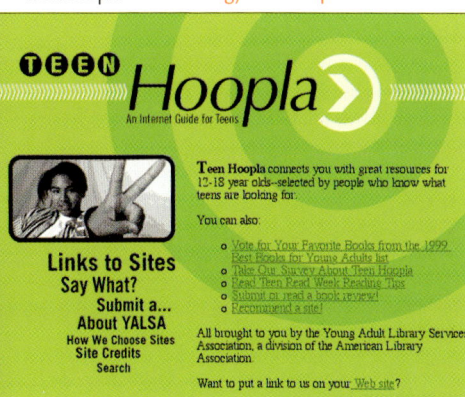

An Internet guide for teens 12-18 provided by the American Library Association's Young Adult Library Services Association, Teenhoopla's primary service is to link teens to sites on such topics as activism, entertainment and life. The YALSA's mission, to ensure young adults quality library service, is reflected in the site selection requirements and high-quality links. The site also features forums on teen violence and other issues of concern.

Doughnet www.doughnet.com

An excellent jumping-off point for the 18-and-under set who want to become more money savvy. The site's investment game lets you invest hypothetical money and watch it gain or lose according to the actual market, and the glossary will help you learn stock lingo from asset to yield. Money news and stock quotes round out the offerings, making it a useful place for of-age surfers as well.

kids & teens

Teen Advice Online www.teenadviceonline.org

Getting through your teens can be tough. At Teen Advice Online, a volunteer staff of counselors in their teens and 20s have the advice you need on issues like dating, social pressure, and even caring for a new tattoo. Hundreds of reader questions are archived and updated every month. Links and information on depression and suicide are here too.

Law

Lawyers.com www.lawyers.com
Featuring profiles of over 400,000 lawyers worldwide, this site also includes pages of consumer-oriented legal information and helpful tips on selecting an attorney. You'll also find an interactive Ask a Lawyer forum, as well as a bank of articles on legal topics and a glossary of 10,000 legal terms. Impressive.

Legal Services Corporation www.ltsi.net/lsc
The Legal Services Corporation is dedicated to improving the provision of civil legal help to those in need. Its Web site includes information on getting LSC's assistance, articles on the organization and a directory of its staff. If you've got legal problems concerning housing, employment, government benefits, or family, you may be able to profit from one of LSC's 267 legal aid programs. Hey, would you rather trust the public defender to take on your case? Didn't think so.

American Bar Association www.abanet.org
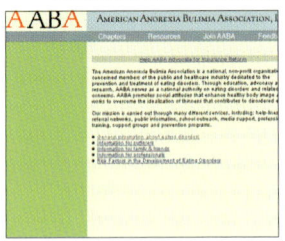
This Web site offers information on all members of the American Bar Association, including associates and law students. Additional draws are the lawyer locator listings of legislative and governmental advocacy groups, and a schedule of ABA meetings. The Public Information section is weak; the featured news articles are far more informative.

FindLaw www.findlaw.com
If you're sweating through first-year law school (or just a glutton for intellectual punishment), FindLaw is for you. This site's got it all: listings of law schools, firms, and attorneys; cases and codes; federal and state resources for the United States; foreign and international legal information; a legal subject index; and much, much more. The astonishing content will be of use to lawyers and the general public. Impressively large and well organized.

Legal Information Institute www.law.cornell.edu
Anyone doing research on the law should drop by this Web site. It features constitutions and codes, court opinions, articles on current affairs, directories of law journals, and listings of international, state, and federal laws. It also gives you access to the American Legal Ethics Library, which contains codes for the professional conduct of lawyers on a state-by-state basis.

The Oyez Project www.oyez.nwu.edu
An absolutely gorgeous site, The Oyez Project of Northwestern University is a multimedia database for the U.S. Supreme Court. You can search cases by title, citation, subject, or date as well as access lists and bios of past and present justices. There's also a virtual tour of the Supreme Court building, and an extensive FAQ page.

Law News Network www.lawnewsnetwork.com
A national daily newspaper about the legal profession, Law News Network is an attractive, well-organized site that features in-depth articles on the latest court decisions. It's also got editorials by prominent attorneys and legal scholars, as well as a discussion section and job listings. The archive of back issues is truly awesome.

NetLitigation www.netlitigation.com
Cutting-edge legal info for citizens of the digital age. NetLitigation provides information about legal issues related to the Internet, such as antitrust legislation, e-commerce, the First Amendment, privacy, and trademarks and copyrights. Headline news articles are also posted on a regular basis.

DivorceNet www.divorcenet.com
A big industry requires a big Web site, and DivorceNet certainly fits the bill. It features a state-by-state resource center, a reading room, links to family law resources, and interactive bulletin boards. In addition, DivorceNet has also got a lawyer on staff who answers one question a day from the surfing audience.

National Partnership for Women and Families
www.nationalpartnership.org
The National Partnership for Women and Families is a nonprofit organization dedicated to promoting fairness in the workplace, quality health care, and policies that help both men and women meet their professional and familial responsibilities. It contains headline news stories, links to work and family resources, and a guide to the Health Insurance Portability and Accountability Act. Extremely informative.

Legaldocs www.legaldocs.com
Create customized legal documents with the help of this Web site. Subjects include wills and trusts, sales, leases, partnerships, employment, business documents, and real estate. Not all documents are free to download, but the fees that are charged are fairly reasonable.

music

All-Music Guide www.allmusic.com
Hands down the most comprehensive source of music information online. Go to All-Music when you need to find out who produced Bob Dylan, which acts have played CBGB, or any other obscure piece of music trivia. All-Music is massive: 339,000 album reviews (even out-of-print favorites), 30,000 bios of musicians, 650,000 audio samples, plus reviews and recommendations—all fully searchable in any of six languages. Tip: Try All-Classical and All-Movie, too.

Ultimate Band List www.ubl.com
Though UBL suffers from an extreme case of overcrowded Web page syndrome (it must be going around), the resources at this site make it more than worth your time. Type in an artist or band name and UBL pulls up just about every Web link, bio, article, review, free MP3 song, or album to be bought (which, of course, can be done here). Sifting and sorting through this morass of information is the user's job—UBL just provides the dirt.

MTV Online www.mtv.com
I want my, I want my, I want my MTV ... online? That's right: fans of the channel will flip for the site. The music news, live chat, and band info are top-notch, but what sets MTV Online apart are hundreds of music video clips (everyone from the Beastie Boys to the Spice Girls), plus live footage of the MTV Music Awards and all the fab shows, from *The Real World* to *House of Style*.

Launch.com www.launch.com
Cleanly organized, updated daily, Launch is the place to go for music news. From reviews, upcoming events, and weekly editorials to the nitty-gritty details—album release info, tour dates, arrests (surprisingly common), marriages, births, and deaths of anyone who's anybody in the music industry— this site knows its stuff. When informational overload sets in, chill with some MP3s, videos, or live chat. By the time you're ready for more news, it's probably been updated anyway.

Wall of Sound www.wallofsound.go.com
In a valiant attempt to cover all genres, Wall of Sound is probably the only music directory that covers Kid Rock, Harry Connick Jr., Jimi Hendrix, and Korn on the same page. News, CD reviews, release dates, and the hype, articles, and pics of the players can be searched or browsed at this comprehensive rock and pop directory.

EMF.org www.emf.org
What is the most important musical innovation of our time? Electronic music, according to EMF.org, the Web site for the Electronic Music Foundation. Their site provides a searchable calendar so you can find classes, concerts, and general happenings in your area. Feature articles and listings of exemplary CDs from all over the globe round out this primer on the cutting edge genre of music.

Rolling Stone Network www.rollingstone.com

Like the magazine, Rolling Stone online is intelligent and well designed—it also links you to CD Now, Webcasts, and MP3 downloads. To get all the articles you'll have to subscribe to the print version, but the site is worth a look for artist bios and discographies, CD reviews, and the excellent photo archive. The browsable gallery of Rolling Stone magazine covers features rock and celebrity icons from John Lennon to Kurt Cobain—practically a visual history of music over the past three decades.

Spin www.spin.com

Spin's super-navigable site leaves no tune unturned. It has the latest music news and reviews, video and audio clips, and even advice on what to wear to that Cyndi Lauper concert. Also included: movie and book reviews, features from the magazine, and an Ask Monkey column that's sure to baffle and amuse.

Vibe www.vibe.com

Hip-hop's number one print rag holds nothing back at this exhaustive Web site of music news and album reviews. The features section covers the stars, the tunes, and the industry that makes, breaks, or bows down to them. Smart, solid writing and a strong grasp of what's happening online and off make Vibe a hit with readers.

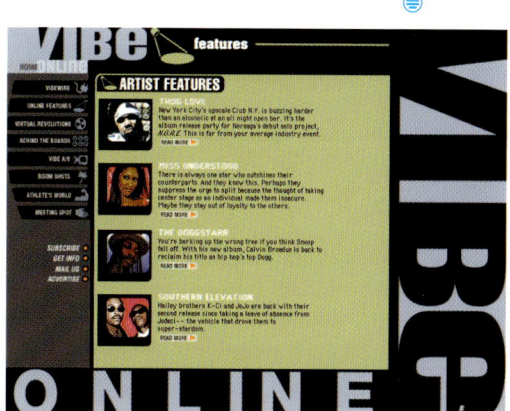

SonicNet www.sonicnet.com

Though many online music channels are just thinly disguised ploys to sell CDs, SonicNet maintains its integrity with top-flight music news coverage, reviews, profiles, and live events. Young and hip, SonicNet is like MTV without the raunchy spring break specials and marathon game shows. The site's alternative music e-zine, Addicted to Noise, covers acts such as punk girl-group Sleater-Kinney, while three live channels provide round-the-clock music videos, animation, and radio feeds.

music 115

NME www.nme.co.uk
With music news, reviews, show dates, chart rankings, and the intriguing "Angst" section, New Music Express may just live up to its claim as the "official" number one music site for England and beyond. Features on artists and their personal scandals are updated daily, so check back often not to miss the beat.

CD Now www.cdnow.com

With over 300,000 CDs, tapes, music videos, T-shirts, and vinyl records (remember those?) on offer, CD Now is the Amazon of music. There are plenty of reasons to buy online instead of in a brick-and-mortar music store: you can listen to sound clips, get recommendations, link to Billboard's Top 100 charts, and create a custom CD. Though CD Now's top picks tend to be pretty mainstream, the selection is substantial, and they will special-order anything they don't have—including rare imports and collector's editions.

EMusic.com www.emusic.com
EMusic.com isn't the only site that bills itself as the source for downloadable music—seems like everyone is scrambling to get on the MP3 bandwagon. Still, it's a respectable source for your online music needs, with rock and pop, jazz, blues, New Age, electronic, and hip-hop tracks available for download as MP3 or Real Audio files. The index of artists is impressively large, but (of course) rather obscure.

Tunes.com www.tunes.com
Tunes.com allows you to listen to MP3s before putting the album into your shopping cart, and gives you countless music search options. Look up albums by genre, time period, compilations, favorites, and recommendations. You can also compile lists of your favorite artists and albums and post music reviews. The site also links to Rolling Stone, Downbeat Jazz, and TheSource.com—you might want to make it your music start site.

Tape Trader Network www.tapetracker.com/traderindex
Fans of live music have a friend in the Tape Trader Network, which provides a forum for folks to swap bootlegged tapes—everything from Dylan to the Doors. Because it's illegal to sell such material anywhere (even on the Net), bootleggers are discouraged from moving their merchandise here.

Ticketmaster Online www.ticketmaster.com
The source for upcoming concert information and tickets is mega-conglomerate Ticketmaster; its Web site is informative and thorough, though the design is a bit clunky. The site also features live broadcasts and chats.

Amazon.com Music www.amazon.com/music
All the selection and service that Amazon brings to books is available for the audiophile at its music site. For massive listings of just about every musical genre buyable online, guaranteed to be delivered to your doorstep within a matter of days, this is among the most reliable and complete music shopping sites on the Web.

House of Blues www.hob.com

Less blues than rock, the House of Blues continues to capture rock, blues, and reggae news with a style all its own. The site succeeds in balancing a wealth of information and good aesthetic values—the scroll through its pages makes the search for what's happening in the cool world a most beatific experience. Complete with album reviews and daily live music cybercasts.

The Virtual Opera House www.opera.co.za
Site guru Dave Leverton is bringing opera to the masses with this irreverent digital romp through opera's past and present. Always informative, never academic, VOH's artist biographies, plot summaries, and historical anecdotes are lovingly described. Hard-to-find audio samples will make even die-hard aficionados hit high C's.

Classical Insites www.classicalinsites.com
The first stop directory for classical music on the Web. This truly comprehensive site leaves no tune untouched, from the masters of centuries past to today's emerging artists. Learn classical fundamentals, genres, and instruments, or delve right into the analysis—sections are custom-tailored to novices or die-hard fans. Exhaustive links round out this most impressive resource.

Country.com www.country.com
Whether you just listen to country or live in your cowboy boots, you'll appreciate this comprehensive country site. Loads of info on the music and the stars, including news, videos, and a hall of fame, plus extensive sections on Motorsports, RollerJam, and The Grand Ole Opry. It even has a schedule of TNN listings, so you won't miss a minute of Shania Twain on the tube.

Sound Market www.countrysong.com
Taking full advantage of technology, Sound Market is the best country music radio station you'll ever hear ... on the Web. Just download a Real Player and you can browse the site to the tunes of Shania Twain or Garth Brooks. Be sure to pick a handful of songs, as browsing the rest of the site's vast collection of news bits, polls, chats, reviews, and artists pages will take some time.

Blue Note www.bluenote.net
This label/club/house of legends feeds the public their rightful beats free of charge online. Wander the site to get the scoop on who's at the club and on the label—even newcomers to the genre will realize that all the heavy hitters did a stint with Blue Note at some point. The real fun is listening to the live audio broadcasts from the club—check the upcoming schedule, then make sure you've got the downloads, dim light, and whisky ready for the performance.

music 117

Great Day in Harlem
www.harlem.org/greatday.html
In August of 1958, a young photographer from *Esquire* gathered 57 jazz greats on a doorstep in Harlem for a group shot that would go down in history. This unique site is designed around that photograph—click on any part of the picture to get detailed information on the artists you see. Nearly every major jazz recording artist from the turn of the century on (Sonny Rollins, Thelonius Monk, Count Basie) is here, along with a savvy bio on the how's and why's of their instruments of choice, style of expression, and role in music history. A must-see for jazz lovers.

Billboard Online www.billboard-online.com
It's no surprise that the biggest name in the charts should overshadow the music news and status of the artist before the rest. A catchall for concert updates, album releases schedules, and behind the scenes artist reports, Billboard Online may take some time to get through, but you'll find out more than you ever thought you wanted to about pop and rock music on the way.

Internet Underground Music Archives www.iuma.com
The name in alternative music online—in the broadest sense of the word alternative. Browse categories ranging from ambient, Christian, dance, hard core, rockabilly, spoken word, and "weird." You can also search by band name, label, or location, from Scotland to Alabama. If it's out there, it will be on the Web, and if not, it might still be here.

Pitchforkmedia.com www.live-wire.com
Four reviews a day ... considering Pitchforkmedia finds some of the most obscure little gems on the banks of the mainstream, it's hard to believe there are even four new albums to write about. But somehow they find them, rate them, and post them online. While the chances are slim that anyone will actually ever hear all the Pitchforkmedia-reviewed albums, this site will let you know who's doing what in alternative (in the truest sense of the word) music ... and knowing is half the battle.

Mixmag Online www.techno.de/mixmag
It comes as no surprise to fans of techno and dance music that the hottest Web sources are British. Based in London, the capital of club culture, Mixmag covers techno, house, and hip-hop in all their varied incarnations, adding in-the-know articles on DJs, drugs, and club life to the mix. Check out techno.de, Mixmag's parent site, for the full range of online electronica.

MP3.com www.mp3.com
Is digital music the wave of the future? MP3 founder Michael Robertson is banking on it. His controversial site lets you download free music from the Internet. It's feared and loathed by music industry execs, who stand to lose millions when you and I start downloading Lauryn Hill tracks and buying MP3's ultracheap $5 CDs. One catch: because of copyright restrictions, the selection is still pretty obscure. (Ever heard of Black Uhuru?) But stay tuned ... MP3 is definitely a site to watch.

Dream-Escape.org www.dream-escape.org
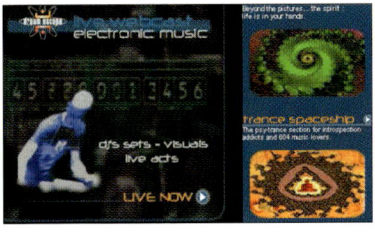
Techno, trance, and all accompanying accoutrements can be found at Dream-Escape's finely stylized site. Download free techno MP3s, listen to live Webcasts, or feast on the eye candy available here with categories such as fractal worlds, virtual reality, and the not so self-explanatory "tekno flash toys" section. Be prepared to spend some serious time swimming in this site's cool colors and tunes.

Auricle www.auricle.cc
An online 'zine of electronic music "aimed at individuals living on the frontiers of the ear." This selective source of articles and tidbits is a bit lacking in organization, but the design is so slick it feels good to get lost. Spend some time wandering the archives for summaries and links to dozens of articles on electronica, or just peruse the sound byte facts on musical goings-on.

Pollstar www.pollstar.com
The poll masters for over 20 years, Pollstar is the place to find out concert and tour information. While the site is primarily geared toward music industry insiders, anyone who wants to find out who is where on the international music scene can benefit from Pollstar's huge database of tour information. Check the side menu for listings of bands or just browse the week's feature concert news story.

Liveconcerts.com www.liveconcerts.com
Be anywhere, anytime, and catch your favorite concerts! Liveconcerts.com lets you choose from a huge archive of shows. Check the upcoming events schedule for the weekly live broadcasts, but if you miss them, they'll be archived soon enough. While the selection is a bit eclectic—everything from Anthrax and Ice-T to Tina Turner and Joshua Redman—it's free, around the clock, and you don't have to find parking.

music

BMI www.bmi.com
Broadcast Music Inc. is for the people who make the music industry a possibility—the songwriters. BMI maintains over three million songs on their online database which can be searched by artist name, title, or publisher. Find the song you need and all the information there is to know about licensing and copyrights, plus articles and photos on featured artists.

International Lyrics Server www.lyrics.ch
Can't get those pesky '70s and 80's tunes out of your head? Want to know what the words really are? Checkout the Lyrics Server, which contains the full texts of 500,000 songs. Search for songs by artist, album, or title, but be aware: when published lyrics weren't available, LS contributors filled in the ditties themselves with mixed results.

Spinner.com www.spinner.com
With over 120 music channels and loads of custom features, Spinner.com is truly addictive Internet radio. Channels range from 90s Rock to New Age to Neo Japan. Song and artist info pops up in your Spinner window while songs are playing (so you never have to wonder who sings that song). Tip for ultrashort attention spans: you can always check out what's playing on other stations and change channels midsong.

Net Radio.com
www.netradio.com
With more channels than cable TV, NetRadio is one of the largest customizable Internet broadcasting sites on the Web. Selection ranges dramatically, from the Burundi Drummers in World Music to Weird Al Yankovic in Pop Hits. Listen to songs online or click through for the option to buy the albums.

news & e-zines

The Wire www.wire.ap.org
The official Web site of the Associated Press, The Wire is a collection of links to member newspapers and broadcasters, searchable by region. Great if you're looking for a quick news fix, but look elsewhere for in-depth coverage.

The Drudge Report www.drudgereport.com
News the old-fashioned way—reporters file their stories however they darn well please. The result? Refreshingly real hard-fact lineups of daily, weekly, and long-running stories. Expect to find links to just about every major news organization on the planet, plus writings from commentators of eminence such as Dave Barry, Maureen Dowd, Larry King, and of course, Matt Drudge.

Time.com Asia www.cgi.pathfinder.com/time/asia
Everything happens half a day ahead in Asia. Read about what's going on their time, with all the convenience and familiarity of *Time* magazine. Updated daily, Time.com Asia reports on the latest in people, politics, economics, and social issues in the East. The site also offers links to additional Asia resources such as weather forecasts from CNN.com and select Asian city guides from Lonely Planet.

U.S. News Online www.usnews.com
Finally: a news site whose front page is simple and manageable. At U.S. News Online, they haven't tried to pack in a gaggle of links and headlines—just the top of the news, plus features on money, health, technology, work, and travel. You can search archived issues dating back to 1997, or check out the popular rankings of top colleges and graduate schools at .Edu.

Time.com www.pathfinder.com
The weekly news standard, Time.com covers personalities and their turmoil, politicians and their turmoil, and everyday folk and their turmoil. Now it's daily and interactive on the Web. Select articles from the print magazine can be viewed online, but you'll have to spend a buck or two for the whole shebang. Fortunately the daily version is quite comprehensive and should suffice for the average news skimmer.

Newsweek www.newsweek.com
The weekly perspective on the state of affairs, domestic and international, in the arts, business, and politics is available for free online. The catch? Well, the pictures aren't as vibrant as in print, the pages won't give you paper cuts, and Web sites aren't easy subway reading, but otherwise, there isn't one. Peruse, be influenced, or conscientiously object to one of America's most widely read opinion makers.

Salon.com www.salon.com
Sleek, intelligent, and addictive. Salon.com is hundreds of commentaries, comics, critiques, snippets, and stories. It's news, book reviews, cultural reporting, and dispatches from the worlds of high tech, pop culture, and the arts. The coolest feature? "Mothers Who Think." Haven't seen it yet? What are you waiting for?

news and e-zines

Smithsonian

Smithsonian
www.smithsonianmag.si.edu
The name is synonymous with some serious cultural and historical stuff. Smithsonian Institution's monthly **magazine online is just as smart, elegant, informative, and entertaining as you'd expect. Unfortunately, you'll have to subscribe to the print edition for total access, but the selected stories covered on the Web are substantial and link to several additional resources on the topic, including archives of past issues.**

Enews www.enews.com
The magazine matchmaker. Browse by title, top 10 list, or interest area for **any of the 750 magazines available** through this site, then register to receive the title delivered to your door. À la 10-CDs-for-a-penny schemes, magazines are free for the first 90 days, after which you'll be billed. Fortunately, the discounts offered through Enews, some up to 80% off the cover price, make the bills more than acceptable. For hard-core magazine junkies: rotate through 90-day free subscriptions for all the magazines you could ever want. For the rest of the world, just enjoy the supercheap deals.

Atlantic Unbound www.theatlantic.com
Culture, arts, and literature captured in liberal form; Atlantic Unbound is *Atlantic Monthly*'s complete print magazine and then some. The extensive archives and search features invite readers to browse through past issues, literary works, poems, columns, and features. This plus a sprinkling of Web-only articles make the Unbound a treasure trove of word, thought, and opinion on the Web.

The Nation www.thenation.org

Founded in 1865, The Nation is one of America's oldest political, social and cultural commentary magazines. The lefty weekly features clean, intelligent writing on everything from the most current trends in popular culture to long-standing debates on the values that shape the nation. Look here for columns by Katha Pollit, Christopher Hitchens, and Patricia J. Williams.

HotWired www.hotwired.com
A daily for the tech inclined, HotWired covers the newest in technology-related news, stories, innovations, and idiosyncrasies. Learn what's happening from WiredNews (the Executive Summary report is especially useful for busy businessfolk), check out how-to guides from the Webmonkey, or peruse the RGB Gallery of interactive multimedia art. The only thing better about this online 'zine than *Wired*'s print mag is that it's online, it's a 'zine, and trees remain intact.

Slate www.slate.com
So much to read, so much useless information to sift through. But wait, there's Slate! Think of it as an online, daily updated colander for the news you need to know. The fearless fluff-fighting Slatesters ferret out the best of the major magazines, domestic and international papers, pundit pontifications, and critical reviews. Skimming the headlines alone will provide even the most current event-challenged with fodder for weeks of cocktail party conversation.

1st Headlines www.1stheadlines.com
Search headline newspaper stories by country with this handy little Web site. Over 100 newspapers are featured here; terrific for news junkies or anyone doing media studies or current events reports. You can also search business, health, and sports headlines.

AJR News Link www.ajr.newslink.org
With 9,000 links to newspapers, magazines, broadcasters, and news services, American Journalism Review is one of the most comprehensive news sites online. There's also inside dirt on the journalism biz, with features and profiles on prominent reporters and columns, in addition to an extensive job bank. An invaluable resource for anyone interested in journalism and the direction it's taking on the Web.

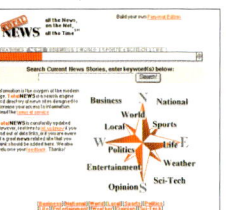

Total News www.totalnews.com
Just can't get enough news? Point your browser to Total News, a search engine and directory of news sites that allows you to look up world, national, business, entertainment, and sports stories posted all over the Web. Links include Fox News, MSNBC, CBS, ABC, NOR, and CNN Interactive.

WorldNews.com www.worldnews.com
Terrific photographs give this news service an edge over the competition; the main draw, however, is the collection of world news stories grouped by country. Other search categories include pollution, population, world ports, and cities.

NewsMaps.com www.newsmaps.com
Featuring vast amounts of news articles, press releases, and discussions, this Web site literally maps news stories onto a visual landscape (you'll need at least a 56k modem to download them). It's a cool concept, especially helpful for people who want a broad view of the issues. Go elsewhere if you need quick access to specific stories.

China News Digest www.cnd.org
Expect solid, balanced coverage of news and historical issues, information databases, and community services. Browse the site's photo library, literature, and historical texts in either Chinese or English for a glimpse of China from anywhere in the world.

news and e-zines

The Paperboy www.thepaperboy.com
Offering over 2,500 links to newspapers around the world, The Paperboy affords folks a more rounded view of news stories that they'd otherwise get from reading local reports. You can look up papers by name, city, or country, and even listen to live radio broadcasts from stations around North America, Europe, and Australia. Great if you're looking for local news from particular countries, from Lithuania to Zimbabwe, but be warned—not all of these papers are in English!

Mylook www.mylook.com

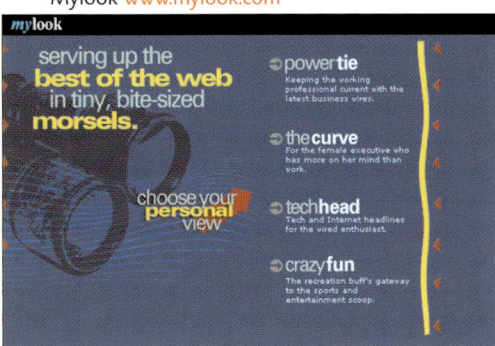

Mylook allows you to design a news Web page according to your interests and aesthetic tastes. Simply choose headlines from whichever categories concern you most: arts, business, entertainment, news, lifestyle, sports, and/or technology, then pick one of the four layouts that suit your personality best. Your page will then give you only the news stories you want on a daily basis. Cool and creative.

Infobeat www.infobeat.com
This terrific Web site will deliver the news stories you want via e-mail. Take your pick of finance, sports, entertainment, news, and weather beats. You can also have a selection of comics, columns, and crosswords sent to your personal account. Absolutely free and eminently time-saving.

CRAYON www.crayon.net
CRAYON—an acronym of sorts for Create Your Own Newspaper—allows you to cut and paste news stories, feature columns, cartoons, and crosswords into a customized web page. Your "paper" will be updated on a daily basis, allowing you to enjoy your favorite features on a timely basis. The number of news links available here is truly staggering—just scrolling through the list makes your mind whirl. Newshounds owe it to themselves to check it out.

Newcity.com www.newcity.com
Alternative news for 20-somethings. Newcity.com is the very definition of cool with edgy political content and a funky design; you'll find stories here that most newspapers wouldn't touch with a 10-foot pole. News categories include top stories, arts and entertainment, pop culture, and service stations.

News of the Weird www.newsoftheweird.com
From sparks flying out of a baby's diaper to the guy who nailed himself to a barstool for an all-night drinking binge, News of the Weird features all those stories that leave the general public scratching their heads. Story topics include police, drunkenness, marriage, and dogs. Texas merits a section unto itself!

The Onion www.theonion.com
Tongue-in-cheek doesn't begin to describe this site. The Onion is a weekly e-zine with a smart-ass perspective on the news—a refreshing alternative to newspapers that take Washington seriously. Think *South Park* meets *Nightline*.

The MoJo Wire www.motherjones.com

The electronic version of *Mother Jones* magazine, MoJo wire has articles for independent thinkers. Recent stories include "Trust Us, We're Spies," "Razing Appalachia," and "Texaco's Crude Legacy." Look here for news that corporate-sponsored papers are too afraid to report.

Reuters www.reuters.com
For up-to-the-minute news, dial up Reuters. Although its commercial orientation is tiresome, there's no denying that this is the best place to go for breaking stories. Particularly good for checking out the stock and securities markets. The photo gallery is also excellent.

Reader's Digest www.readersdigest.com
No longer consigned to be read in doctor's office waiting rooms, Reader's Digest brings all the humor, heroes, and tales of life's adventures to the world online. In addition to print edition favorites, categories at Reader's Digest online include home improvement with "The Family Handyman" and the "Walking" section, to name a few. Browse the international sites as well to see what European readers are digesting.

The New York Times www.nytimes.com
Tired of those musty unread papers piling up in the corner? Then take out a free electronic subscription to The New York Times; it gives you access to the entire paper, including the Sunday edition and the Book Review. Unparalleled news reporting that's absolutely free, with a solid search feature to boot. Archived articles do cost, though.

news & e-zines

Washingtonpost.com www.washingtonpost.com
Not only does Washingtonpost.com feature all the articles found in the print edition, it's also got a tool and resources guide for airfare bargains, school report cards, a medication finder, software downloads, and much, much more. One of the most practical and useful news sites around.

The Christian Science Monitor
www.csmonitor.com
Famous for top-flight reporting, the electronic edition of *The Christian Science Monitor* gives surfers access to its headline stories, archived articles dating back to 1980, and editorials. Be sure to check out CSM's famous interactive crossword puzzle and the weekly news quiz.

Guardian Unlimited www.guardian.co.uk
The decidedly British flavor gives Guardian Unlimited a special place among the countless news sites on the Internet. In addition to headline stories, GU covers football, cricket, and museum exhibits. Impatient Americans may exhibit their patented crude behavior while waiting for these pages to load.

The Independent www.independent.co.uk
The United Kingdom's premiere news source brings you the scoop from England and abroad. Everything in the print edition is here. Browse by section to find out the Independent word on international events, U.K. news, business, sports, education and travel—or skip the dailies and head straight for the Sunday recaps.

Fox News www.foxnews.com
You won't find the footage of wild police chases that made Fox News famous, but you will get a taste of the network's hard-edged and irreverent reporting. Besides headline stories, you'll also find coverage of health, entertainment, and sci-tech news. How could anyone resist a news site that features such stories as, "A Beer in One Hand and a Bible in the Other"?

C-Span.org www.c-span.org
This handsome site features the very best in public affairs reporting. Informative pages include Capitol Questions, a Congressional Votes Library, Historical Oral Arguments, and the C-Span Schoolbus. Invaluable for anyone interested in American politics and history.

BBC Online www.bbc.co.uk
If you're tired of reductive and sound byte-oriented news coverage, stop by BBC Online. It's got all the in-depth political, business, and sports stories you crave without the hysteria of some other papers we know. This site also features links to other top BBC sites (including their Web guide), as well as local stories from all around England.

Electric Telegraph www.telegraph.co.uk
The Electronic Telegraph is a British service that has all the news that's fit to print, plus a business directory, interactive football game, motoring section, and an expatriate network. There are also pages devoted to students, books, and travel.

news & e-zines

Oneworld.net www.oneworld.net
A news service dedicated to promoting human rights, Oneworld.net puts the world back into the World Wide Web. You can search topics by country or issue, or just browse by sections, which include headlines, dispatches, campaigns, big issues, and think tank. Wonderful content, superlative reporting.

CANOE www.canoe.ca
A Canadian news and information site, CANOE has three levels of content: Web-only reports, online editions of daily newspapers, and applications and services. Confirms the rumor that Canada is indeed its own country and not the 51st state.

Intellicast.com www.intellicast.com

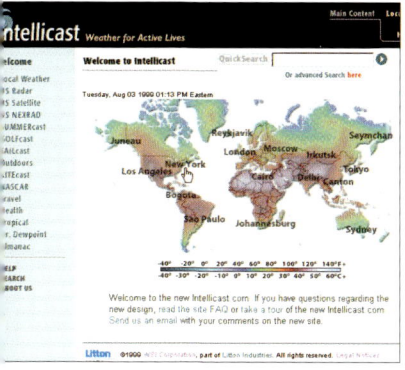

Featuring over 250,000 pages of weather information, Intellicast.com has specific forecasts to help you plan outdoor activities like golfing, sailing, hiking, or skiing. In addition to weather reports, the site has reports on health and how it relates to outdoor conditions, plus a Kitecast for folks who don't want to follow Benjamin Franklin's example.

WeatherLabs www.weatherlabs.com
Search WeatherLabs for forecasts in every continent. Reports include current conditions, monthly averages, and the seasonal outlook. There is also a weather glossary and a list of safety tips. Doppler, satellite, and current conditions maps provide visual interest.

National Climatic Data Center www.ncdc.noaa.gov
The NCDC's got information on the weather as it relates to insurance claims, building contracts, health issues, agriculture, relocation, transportation, and more. It's also got satellite and radar resources. You never knew weather could be so interesting, did you?

Federal Emergency Management Agency www.fema.gov
FEMA is an independent agency of the federal government dedicated to reducing loss of life and property from hazards, particularly natural disasters. Its Web page can direct you to disaster assistance, information for businesses, and a list of regional offices, plus a number of articles on the agency's initiatives.

National Public Radio www.npr.org
NPR is a part of life for many Americans with unfaltering, quality news programs, interviews with figures of cultural interest, plus live jazz, classical, and new music performances. A sure bet for news and entertainment.

Colors www.benetton.com/colors
Life doesn't stop for naps—neither do issues of political, social, and humanitarian import, according to Benetton's print and online 'zine, Colors. The premise? "Diversity is good." The issues? All the goodies that get the blood a boilin'— religion, war, politics, travel, social ills and issues. The elegant design and stunning Shockwave animations are among the best on the Web. Definitely worth a stop.

Suck.com www.suck.com
With a new story every weekday, quotable news information, comic satire, and a healthy appreciation of irony, Suck.com takes the serious sarcastically. No archived stories seem to be available, so check daily to experience this perfect balance between thoughtful analysis and humorous cynicism.

Word www.word.com
A young, cutting edge e-zine of issues and culture. Daily pages cover an eclectic array of topics that simply can't be tucked neatly into a particular category. To wit: our visit turned up articles like "I Was a Caddie at a WASP Country Club" and "My Year of Chastity." Hours of entertainment, information, and time-wasting, plus cool animation and design. A must-see.

Feedmag www.feedmag.com

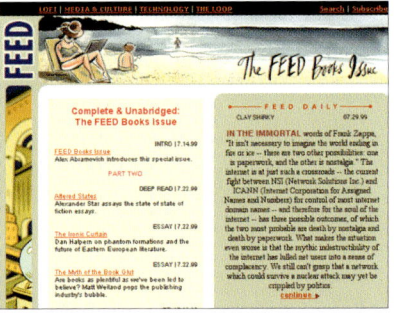

The source for "wisdom from raw information," Feedmag is a virtual reservoir of events, issues, and cultural coverage extracted from sources both online and off. A laissez-faire approach to cultural commentary defines the essays and commentaries on media, culture, and technology—Feed provides the fodder, you form your own opinion.

Rsub www.rsub.com
A collection of the best in e-zines. Links to Literate Smut by Nerve.com, Tips of the Day by Papermag.com, Music News by Sonic Net, Subculture Search from disinformation, and Cultural Eye Candy from The Blue Dot fill out this colorfully designed clearinghouse of 'zine gems.

The Book of Zines www.zinebook.com
For every culture, there are thousands of subcultures—and chances are, there's a 'zine covering each and every one. Find out what's what in any imaginable scene at this catchall clearinghouse of 'zines online and in print. Search the resource guide or just scroll through the "Big List O' Zines" to browse, read, or buy.

Parenting

® Parent Soup www.parentsoup.com

A one-stop parenting community with info on every aspect of raising a child, from grade-by-grade guides, developmental milestones, and curriculum norms, to expert Q & A on breastfeeding, bullying, and sibling rivalry. Check out the Cool Tools section for neat stuff like the baby name finder, or join a parenting community and chat on just about any topic relating to your little bundle of joy.

Dr. Greene's House Calls www.drgreene.com

Pediatrician, author, and father of four, Dr. Alan Greene offers "pediatric wisdom for the information age"—just think of it as an online house call. Dr. Greene gives lengthy and informative answers to a wide variety of health questions ("Is there an at-home tool to check my 11-month-old for ear infections?"), and discusses the causes and treatments of common ailments and more unusual problems. Thorough and easy to understand.

The CyberMom.com www.thecybermom.com

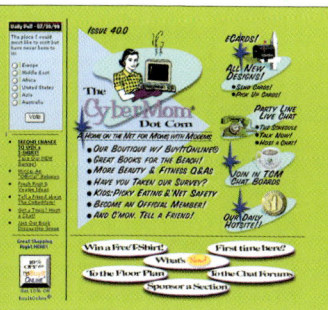

Don't let the retro '50s look fool you: the CyberMom site is as cutting edge as they come. Click through to the site's Floor Plan for the lowdown on parenting books (in the library), health and beauty (in the powder room), or a steamy sex poll (in the bedroom, of course). Geared toward mother care as much as child care, CyberMom.com is a fabulous meeting place for "moms with modems."

Family.com www.family.go.com
Disney does it again. Family.com promotes family bonding with activities that parents and kids can enjoy together: travel tips, kids' cookbooks, and craft projects. There are also tips for parents here: how to help children make friends, what to do with picky eaters. Links to other Disney sites lead kids to safe activities and games on the Web.

Baby Zone www.babyzone.com

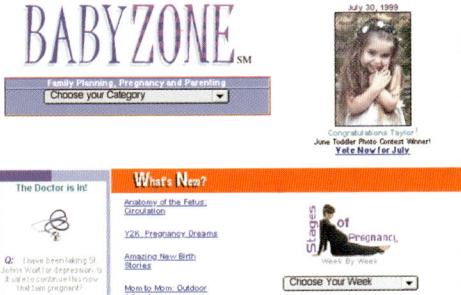

A great site for new and expecting parents, Baby Zone features a week-by-week pregnancy planner to prepare moms- and dads-to-be for each new turn of their first nine months, plus a baby gear shopping guide and loads of tips on everything from birthing to breastfeeding. A special fathering section treats the oft-neglected partner to all the pregnancy info he'll ever need, financial and emotional tips, and fun facts about baby fat and sex during pregnancy.

Making Lemonade www.makinglemonade.com
Making Lemonade offers single parents the resources they need to turn a potentially sour situation into a wonderfully sweet parenting experience. Articles focus on single parents' needs as much as the needs of their children, with bulletin boards, chat and dating advice, financial resources, divorce support, therapy listings, and almost every other helping hand you could hope for.

MamaMoon www.mamamoon.com
The site for this baby source with a conscience is as warm and snuggly as the products it sells—you can almost smell the lavender and almond oil scent of a natural products boutique as you peruse the organic cotton bibs and blankets, hemp diapers, glycerin baby soap, and herbal teething lotion. A great variety for hippie-mamas or for anyone seeking ideas for a classy, alternative shower gift.

HipMama www.hipmama.com

With "entertainment, information, and stimulation for parents who didn't check their personalities at the door when their kids were born," HipMama takes a wry, realistic look at issues ignored by most parenting resources. Feature articles on nursing in public, relationships between kids, and moms with boyfriends, plus the popular HipTalk community discussions on nipple piercing and the sex lives of new parents make HipMama a sophisticated alternative parenting 'zine.

Bedtime-Story www.bedtime-story.com/bedtime-story

Created for "busy business parents," Bedtime-Story contains a massive database of full-text original stories to read to your kids—a fresh alternative to the bedtime book you've read your child a million times. Stories are illustrated, categorized by subject, reviewed, and include suggested age group and reading time. What a cool idea!

AdoptioNetwork www.adoption.org

Services and support groups for birth parents, adoptive parents, and adoptees in every state are just a few of the resources listed on this smart and socially conscious information center for the adoption community. AdoptioNetwork provides federal and international initiatives and laws, state-by-state agency listings, and guidance for the entire adoption process. The design could use improvement, but the resources are worth it.

Fathering Magazine www.fathermag.com

A source for fathers of all kinds, single as well as happily married, this monthly magazine offers news, advice, and even fiction and poetry for the modern dad. As devoted to inspiring strong and dedicated fathers as it is to providing the latest information and advice, Fathering Magazine allocates much of its site to articles about the importance of a father in a child's life.

Fit Pregnancy www.fitpreganacy.com

How much weight should you gain during pregnancy? What nutrients do you and your baby need? Fit Pregnancy has simple, straightforward advice on how to keep healthy during those all-important 9 months. Brought to you by Shape magazine and Fitness Online, the site has articles on exercise, diet, and general health, plus a chat room, advice column, and links to maternity and baby shopping.

CareGuide.com www.careguide.com

Finding child care providers takes a lot less legwork with CareGuide.com. The site provides detailed information on day care centers, preschools, and after school programs across the country. Narrow your search by entering your child's age and desired curriculum, or just search by neighborhood—either way, you'll get a list of care centers in your area, with specifics on the services and requirements for each.

parenting

politics & issues

E-the People www.e-thepeople.com
Change the country without ever getting out of your chair! E-the People is an ingenious solution for the politically lethargic: simply pick an issue from the home page's list of topics, learn a little from the petition initiators' statement, and sign away!

Political Junkie www.politicaljunkie.com
Political Junkie is one of the most comprehensive sites you'll see anywhere on the Net. It provides links to nearly 100 newspapers across the United States and over 20 international sites, as well as various labor organizations, government libraries, legal committees, and political magazines. The sheer scope of this site has to be seen to be believed; a must-bookmark for political scientists.

All Politics www.cnn.com/allpolitics
All politics, all the time. CNN's army of reporters, analysts, and researchers mine the day's political intelligence in D.C. and around the globe with the zest and constancy they're known for. Scroll down to browse headlines from today and yesterday, search the archives, or review the week's featured stories.

Mr. Smith E-mails Washington www.mrsmith.com
This brilliant site gives you instant access to the e-mail accounts of every member of Congress, as wells as the president and the vice president of the United States. There are also links to the White House and various government committees. Easy to use and terrifically helpful, Mr. Smith deserves a standing ovation.

Stateline.org www.stateline.org
This site offers a state-by-state view of political issues ranging from health care to welfare reform, taxes, budgets, education, and utility regulation. The text is well-organized, informative, and easy to read, yet it's not condescending by any means. You'll also find an event calendar, data tables, and an archive of back issues. Stateline.org can even e-mail you any late-breaking news stories.

World Conflicts library.advanced.org
This tremendous site has hours of reading material for anyone interested in learning about world conflicts — their origins, their current status, and the ramifications on local, national, and global levels. You'll be surprised by how much of this stuff goes unreported in the popular media. Search past or present clashes and even ask for research help. A chat room enables folks to contribute their own two cents on these infinitely debatable issues.

EmbassyWeb.com www.embpage.com
This is the place to go for information on embassy locations, ambassadors, diplomatic offices, overseas jobs, and town square meetings with officials. Whether you want to renew your visa or need to know the diplomatic status between various nations, EmbassyWeb.com has the information you're looking for. It may not look like much, but there is a lot of useful information here.

The British Monarchy www.royal.gov.uk
The official Web site for the world's most watched, loved, spurned, and scandalized royal family. Speculate, read the newsstand gossip, and check out the official scoop here, with photos, family history, current goings-on, and info on regal rule throughout history. It's here, it's free, it's royal!

The Democracy Network www.democracynet.org
Although this site takes some time to load, you'll find it worth the wait if you're seeking information on public affairs. There are links to political parties, including "fringe" groups like The Prohibition Party and The Natural Law Party, as well as information on various policies and political races going on all around the country. The information is basic, well explained, and easily accessible. Perfect for students doing current events reports and people who want to brush up on the issues.

The Jefferson Project www.capweb.net/classic/jefferson
This is one of the few Web sites that profiles political personalities as well as providing information on the executive, legislative, and judicial branches of the U.S. government. There are also links to international resources, political watchdog groups, activist organizations, and political humor. Nonpartisan and informative.

THOMAS thomas.loc.gov
In the spirit of Thomas Jefferson's democratic ideals, this Web site was created by Congress to inform the public about past and present legislative goings-on. There are directories to the House and Senate, bill summaries, congressional records, and committee reports. Information can be accessed three ways: by topic, short title, or number. Perfect for researchers or folks who want to be in the know.

Amnesty International www.amnesty.org

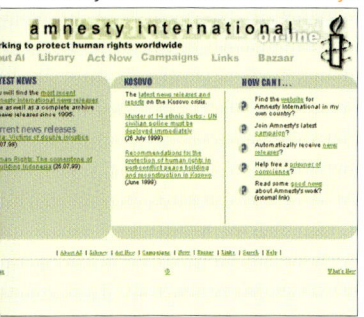

"Working to protect human rights worldwide," Amnesty International's site includes a history of the organization, outlines of its various campaigns, in-depth news articles, and various country and thematic reports. Browse through it for an eye-opening view of human rights violations taking place all over the world—including your very own backyard.

politics & issues

133

The New Republic www.thenewrepublic.com
The electronic version of *The New Republic,* offers the same intelligent Washington-insider news and opinion articles on politics and foreign affairs, plus limited access to its extensive archives. Contrary to popular belief, *The New Republic* isn't just devoted to politics; a sizable portion of the publication is devoted to the arts.

Leadership Conference on Civil Rights
www.civilrights.org
Brush up on civil rights issues at civilrights.org, which covers affirmative action, age discrimination, disability laws, education, fair housing, and religious freedom. Find out the background on bills coming before Congress, as well as which legislators support which initiatives. There's even information on getting personally involved with various issues.

The National Review www.nationalreview.com
With the same quality of reporting as *The New Republic* from a very different perspective, *The National Review* is perhaps the most respected conservative political publication in the United States. The electronic content is stellar; there are articles written exclusively for the Web, as well as town hall chats, movie reviews, and excerpts from the print magazine. The archives are extremely generous: this is one case of conservatives being far less stingy than the liberals.

Fed World www.fedworld.gov
If you've ever searched for a government document, you know it can be a daunting task. Enter Fed World, the catch-all government portal with 20 searchable databases, a huge bulletin board, and individual links to government sites like the EPA, IRS, and Customs. When looking for anything from tax forms to the NOAA Diving Manual, this is the place to start.

Greenpeace International www.greenpeace.org

Who says you can't fight the power? Dial up this site to learn all about what Greenpeace is doing for the environment, including cleaning up the oceans, battling genetic engineering, and preserving our dwindling forests. There are also links to search its archives, become a cyber activist, and join the organization. In case you get really inspired, job listings are also posted here.

Doonesbury Electronic Town Hall www.doonesbury.com
Another brainchild of brilliant cartoonist Gary Trudeau. The site has an archive of strips spanning the past 28 years (you can e-mail favorites to friends), cast biographies, a daily news briefing, and a get involved page, among other delights. It loads fast, looks great, and promises lots of food for thought (along with laughs). What more could you want?

The Library of Congress Home Page www.loc.gov
Believe it or not, the Library of Congress started out as Thomas Jefferson's personal book collection. These days it's a bit bigger, offering over 532 miles of shelved material. The Library's Web site features descriptions of special collections, access to films, interviews, and historical documents, and provides lots and lots of information on copyrights. Oh, yeah: it's a great resource for congressional materials, too.

The White House www.whitehouse.gov

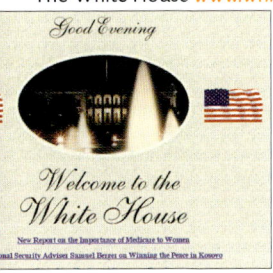

Here's your big chance to tour the First Family's mansion without having to agonize over what to wear. After putting in some time at the Oval Office and taking a nap in the Lincoln Bedroom, take a look at the impressive artwork scattered throughout what Jacqueline Kennedy called "La Maison Blanche," then read about the lives of all the presidents and first ladies. "The First Families" link is a must-see.

The United Nations www.un.org
Despite the rather shoddy design (did somebody forget to pay their dues again?), The United Nations Web site does offer extensive information on its projects, including peace and security initiatives, programs for social development, and outlines on international laws. Do examine the audio-visual services, which offer a fascinating overview of the UN's history.

Federal Bureau of Investigations www.fbi.gov
The layout's not particularly flashy and the photos are a bit unflattering, but the FBI Web site is a mother lode of info on crime in the United States. Needless to say, the biggest draw is the Most Wanted page, but the Reading Room shouldn't be overlooked, either.

Unrepresented Nations and People's Organization
www.unpo.org
The UNPO is an international organization comprised of over 50 countries and peoples currently unrepresented by diplomatic groups like the United Nations. Forget what you learned in geography class; you'll discover people and places that you never knew existed. For instance, do you know where the Mon People live? (Lower Burma.) Can you find Ingria on the map? (Start looking along the southern coast of Finland, right near the Estonian border.) Anyone seeking a broader view of the world must drop by this site. Not simply a "who's who" of indigenous peoples, the UNPO gives the history of their struggles and the political issues facing them today.

WebActive www.webactive.com
Published weekly, WebActive offers progressives a valuable Internet resource for finding other political organizations and individuals who share their concerns and interests. It also features several radio broadcasts from around the country. The content is limited but enlightening.

politics & issues

135

Dumb Laws www.dumblaws.com
Browsing through these pages could actually save you a trip to the pokey: how else would you know that it's against the law to throw a ball at someone's head for fun in New York State? Or that it's illegal to remove bandages in public in Canada? On the other hand, some dumb laws might actually benefit you. For instance, there's no such thing as an age of consent in Japan, while escaping from a Danish jail won't add time to a prisoner's sentence.

Do-It-Yourself Congressional Investigations Kit
www.opensecrets.org/index.htm
Search this site for the skinny on who's been naughty and who's been nice in Congress vis-à-vis issues like the environment, gun control, health care, ATM fees, and a whole lot more. You'll learn what the issues are, where the money's coming from, and who's on the take. A real eye-opener, as well as a valuable resource.

Political Resources on the Net www.agora.stm.it/politic
Extensive political data, links to parties, organizations, media, institutes, and campaign sites from all over the world are a click away. Just select the region or country of your choice. It could be updated more frequently, but Political Resources on the Net is by far the best of the scanty group of Web sites devoted to international politics.

Project Vote Smart www.vote-smart.org
Cut through all the mudslinging, flashy advertisements, and red herrings that normally pervade political campaigns. Here you'll find just the facts on over 13,000 candidates and elected officials. You can look up voting records, campaign positions, campaign contributions, and contact information with a few clicks of the mouse. Best of all, there's not an intern in sight here.

Institute for Global Communications
www.igc.org/igc
PeaceNet, EcoNet, LaborNet, WomensNet, ConflictNet, AntiRacismNet...if there's a social ill, IGC has it covered. Frequently updated alerts on everything from public policy to protests, related news headlines, and an extensive searchable database that pulls up links from around the globe are all available for free.

Policy.com
 www.policy.com
At first glance, Policy.com could pass for any major news site — it's got daily updated headlines on world issues and events, briefings and analysis, and reader polls. With a searchable archive of past articles and links to just about every related political site there is, Policy.com is truly comprehensive coverage of the changing face of world politics and social issues.

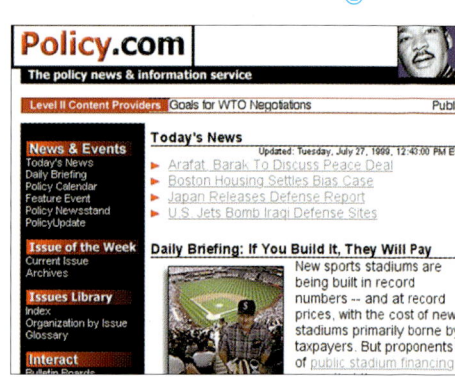

Give.org www.give.org
Sponsored by the National Charities Information Bureau, give.org's Quick Reference Guide links to over 400 charities organized by issue (Relief Agencies or Environmental Organizations, for example) and alphabetically. A useful symbol system shows readers how each of the organizations fare by NCIB's strict standards of philanthropy. A great guide for informed giving online.

Protest.net www.protest.net
The urge for action is there...so where do you go? Protest.net is activism HQ, with a beautifully organized calendar listing for events arranged by date and topic in the area nearest you. Learn about the issues, who stands behind them, how to get involved or make known your own action groups here.

FreeSpeech Internet Television www.freespeech.org

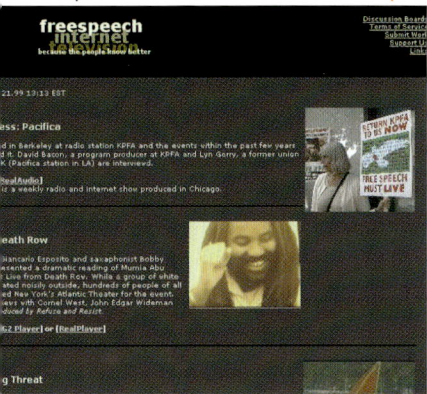

The first and only audio/video Webcasting site that is entirely member created, FreeSpeech Internet Television is high-tech democracy in action. Stories range from Chomsky, Chiapas, and overpopulation to the Gulf War, Cuba, and neoliberalism, all of which are located on the home page or in video archives. Requires Real Player, Real Audio or G2 Player.

Idealist www.idealist.org
Aptly billed "the global clearinghouse of nonprofit and volunteering resources," Idealist is a gold mine for anyone interested in learning more about nonprofit and volunteer organizations, getting involved in ongoing groups, or even starting one yourself. Find organizations, consultants, jobs, and, of course, volunteers at this free resource.

VolunteerMatch www.volunteermatch.com
Concern alone isn't enough — but it's not always easy to find the right opportunity to serve your community. VolunteerMatch offers

a unique site where potential volunteers can browse opportunities by region, skill, and interest, and sign up for e-mail notification when something matches their interests and schedule. Walk-a-thons, tutoring, meal deliveries, and beach day cleanup are just a few examples.

Lambda Legal Defense Fund www.lambdalegal.org
Lambda Legal Defense Fund is an association of lawyers working for the civil rights of gays, lesbians and people with HIV or AIDS. Surfing their site will get you information on the laws in your state that impact these groups of people, as well as what action you can take to change them. You can also read up on past cases and rulings in the site's extensive library.

politics & issues

137

The Electoral Websites www.agora.stm.it/elections/election/index.htm
The majority of the world still struggles for the right to vote — find out where at this site on elections around the world. Search on the world map or alphabetically by country to learn where elections are underway and what they mean for the country. The related links to Parties Around the World, Parliaments Around the World, and Political Resources are unmatched on the WWW.

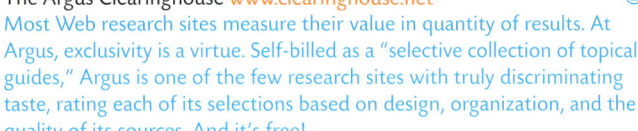

Reference

The Argus Clearinghouse www.clearinghouse.net
Most Web research sites measure their value in quantity of results. At Argus, exclusivity is a virtue. Self-billed as a "selective collection of topical guides," Argus is one of the few research sites with truly discriminating taste, rating each of its selections based on design, organization, and the quality of its sources. And it's free!

Elibrary www.elibrary.com
Research sometimes necessitates scholarly journals. If not, Elibrary is for you. Its research collection includes national and local newspapers, with *USA Today,* the *Los Angeles Times,* and the *Christian Science Monitor* and magazines such as *Time, U.S. News & World Report, Fortune,* and *Sports Illustrated.* Combined with their unique assortment of transcripts from television news programs, Congressional sessions, and NPR's *All Things Considered* and *Fresh Air,* Elibrary is the first stop for media-based research. Try the 30-day free trial.

Encarta Online Library www.iac-on-encarta.com
For reference material you can actually reference, the Online Library is the place to go with over a million articles from scholarly journals, reference books, magazines, and news sources, organized in clean, intuitive subdivisions. Test the waters with their seven-day free trial or pay per article — at a buck a piece, it's cheaper than bus fare to the library.

The Internet Public Library www.ipl.org/ref
In keeping with the spirit of good public libraries, IPL's research collection is vast, its organization fluid, and best of all, it's free. Check out the Ready Reference Collection for an overview of major subdivisions, or use IPL's Pathfinders — "home grown guides to get you started" — on topics ranging from childbirth options to Michigan authors.

CIA World Factbook
www.odci.gov/cia/publications/factbook/index.html
It should come as no surprise that America's information scouts should also be the premiere source of political, economic, and geographic statistics. The WFB is an unparalleled resource for maps, country statistics, concise political histories, and U.S.-foreign relations info. User friendly, well organized, and red tape free, it's easy to forget the site is maintained by a government agency.

Perry–Castaneda Library Map Collection
www.lib.utexas.edu/libs/pcl/map_collection/map_collection.html
Over 2,400 map images are public domain at the PCL—just a small percentage of the library's awesome collection of 230,000 maps, which includes everything from a contemporary map of Yugoslavia to a 1912 map of ancient Jerusalem. The site is navigable, the maps are sharp, and can be viewed, printed, or downloaded at various sizes. Check the links sections for those rare—*really* rare—cases when the PCL does not have the map you need.

Alta Vista: Translations www.babelfish.altavista.digital.com
For anyone who ever read the *Hitchhiker's Guide to the Galaxy,* Alta Vista's translation service is as close as modern technology has gotten to creating Babelfish. Type in a word, a phrase, or even a sentence and in a matter of seconds view your personal translation. You can even translate entire Web sites into English, French, German, Spanish, Portuguese, or Italian—just type in the URL. *C'est magnifique!*

Bartlett's Familiar Quotations
www.columbia.edu/acis/bartleby/bartlett
In comparison with the majority of quotation sites out there, Bartlett's serves as a soothing reminder that things are classics for a reason. Search by topic or browse the authors and works arranged chronologically. If the forefathers of modern literature had a few pearls of wisdom on a subject, you'll find it here.

Merriam Webster Online Dictionary www.m-w.com
This isn't your parents' dictionary: Merriam-Webster Online has all the information in the old standby, plus a search engine and loads of great features. Dictionary and thesaurus search queries work even when you misspell a word, providing a list of close words. In addition to these standards, M-W's Word a Day feature includes example sentences and etymological explanations.

Project Bartleby Archive www.columbia.edu/acis/bartleby
Its mission is to reproduce canonical works online with 100% accuracy. Columbia University's Project Bartleby houses a number of useful reference classics, including *Roget's Thesaurus,* Strunk and White's *Elements of Style,* as well as literary works from Eliot, Keats, Stein, and Wilde.

reference

A Web of Online Dictionaries
www.facstaff.bucknell.edu/rbeard/diction.html
Bucknell University's amazing site links to over 800 dictionaries for every language from Hebrew to Eskimo to Klingon, plus specialized dictionaries and thesauri perusable for academics and laymen alike. Log on to find out the Czech word for computer (*pocitac*), or brush up on French or Esperanto.

All Experts.com www.allexperts.com

Have a pressing question that can only be answered by a gardening expert? Or a cigar expert perhaps? With 4,000 volunteer experts, All Experts is sure to have an online guru on call. Experts everyone needs such as CPAs, doctors, and moms sit alongside the more obscure Amish, bookbinding, and Lipton Tea experts, making any one of this site's 12 categories an adventure in education.

Ask Jeeves www.ask.com

Jeeves isn't your typical butler — no food, no drinks — just facts. Ask Jeeves any question in plain English or check out the example questions posted from other readers, such as "What is Bill Gates worth today?" or "What is the folklore behind a blue moon?" Often Jeeves has answers already prepared as well as a list of similar questions and links. While the value in these trivia bits depends entirely on your research needs, Jeeves provides a refreshingly human-friendly way of "asking" a search engine for information.

How Stuff Works www.howstuffworks.com

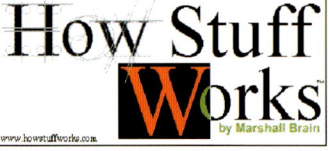
How Stuff Works is paradise for the nerd in all of us, perfect for those who wonder how their remote control functions or how it is that jet airplanes don't just fall out of the sky. Ask a question, browse the list of questions (such as: How DO Pop Rocks candy work?), or search by topic for the mysteries of everyday object science revealed.

Encarta Virtual Globe Online
www.encarta.com/ewa/pages/a/ea_indw.htm
It's safe to say that if there's a town out there with a zip code, you can learn more about it here. Listed alphabetically, each place name is identified by type (country, city, river, municipality, etc.), linking to a variety of sources for maps and weather, travel, and profile information. There are no search features, but with a little patience and the scroll bar, you should find the place you're looking for.

Information Please Almanac www.infoplease.com

Did you know that more people speak Javanese than French? That Denmark is the least corrupt country in the world? That Dr. Seuss originated the word nerd? Information Please is good for quick statistic retrieval, but it's also worth wandering around its 12 categories of almanac, dictionary, and news for interesting trivia bits.

Encyclopedia Britannica www.eb.com
The reference standard, EB online demonstrates exceptional and effective use of hypertext publishing. Both topic and keyword searchable, EB's articles include a healthy supply of links for relevant topics, personages, places, and events. The 30-day free trial offers full access to the online version of the original 32-volume reference set. Once this runs out, subscribe or wait for the door-to-door salesperson.

Lycos Roadmaps www.lycos.com/roadmap.html
The days of accidental origami with road maps are over! Type in the address of any location in the United States (with a street name—"Grand Canyon" won't work), and Lycos presents a zoomable map and driving directions in seconds. While these detailed services are only offered for the United States, you can find general city and area maps for just about every country with pavement. International street maps are available for commonly requested countries in Europe but are still under construction for other regions.

Librarian's Index to the Internet
www.sunsite.berkeley.edu/internetindex
Who better to put information at your fingertips than a trusty librarian? This is indeed the index to the Internet—perhaps the only subjects not included on this page are pet grooming and bread making. A search depot for the smart researcher, and of course, for librarians themselves.

Encarta Encyclopedia www.encarta.msn.com
Microsoft's truly comprehensive and meticulously organized encyclopedia is the information browser's best friend. In good free-market style, MSN offers two freebie samplers: the Concise Encyclopedia, good for fact-checking or Cliff Notes-style summaries on everything from existentialism to the history of the Muppets, and the seven-day free trial to the Deluxe Edition, which is where the site's elaborately cross-referenced organization really shows its stuff.

Compton's Encyclopedia Online www.comptons.com

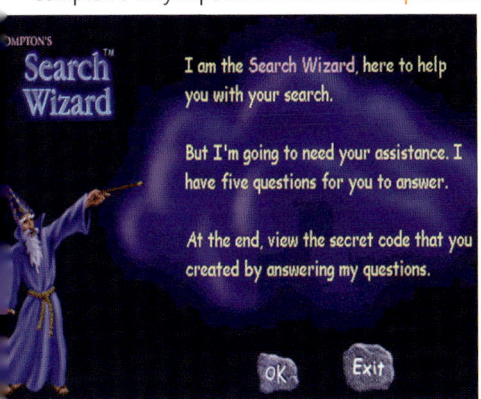

As with other online encyclopedias, Compton's offers search and browse capabilities—its uniqueness is in its aesthetic. Every article is accompanied by an array of links to related images (the Acropolis article features photos, floor plans, and links to a virtual tour), providing the option for visuals without forcing you to wait unnecessarily for images you don't want. Tip: Try the seven-day free trial to see if Compton's whets your appetite before subscribing.

reference

The Blue Book of Grammar and Punctuation

www.grammarbook.com
You've heard of Strunk, White, and MLA — the classics. Yet like Cliff Notes for Shakespeare, sometimes we need something contemporary, easily explained in words we can understand. The Blue Book site is easily navigable, its explanations are straightforward and perfectly logical — it solved our who/whom usage questions forever. Its unabashed promotion of the print version of the book is a bit irksome, but its usefulness redeems.

ResearchPaper.com www.researchpaper.com
While this may look like it's just for students, ResearchPaper.com is a great place for people who need their brains jogged. Its Idea Directory offers fresh angles on possible research paper topics (such as: How has inflation affected the arts?) as well as the standard issues discussed in most subjects in the humanities. Links to both Elibrary (subscription) and Net Info (free) accompany each question so that further research about these topics is only a click away.

PC Webopaedia www.pcwebopedia.com
If you confuse SCSI with SSI or PCI (or have no idea what any of them stand for), this is the place for you. The Webopaedia is a godsend to anyone trying to keep up with ever-changing Internet and computer-related lingo. Search for specific terms or check in for daily features and updates.

Research-it www.itools.com/research-it
The metasearcher of reference material. Research-it's interactive home page includes searchable language, library, geographical, financial, shipping and mailing, and Internet tools. Search results are sometimes too plentiful, but thoughtful keyword entry can solve that.

StudyWeb www.studyweb.com

At first glance, StudyWeb looks like a Yahoo! for homework. Click on one of its subject areas, and you'll see that it gets even better. A Zagat guide to educational Web sites, StudyWeb's reviews and ratings help you locate thousands of research-quality Web sites for all age levels. An ideal resource for anyone sharing the research experience with a child.

Today's Calendar & Clock Page
www.panix.com/~wlinden/calendar.shtml
You won't find bells and whistles and cool graphics here. What you will find is the most thorough and extensive listing of calendar information on the Internet (could 500 visitors a day be wrong?). It is worth scrolling down just to see the all-text depiction of the current moon phase.

The World Wide Holiday and Festival Page www.holidayfestival.com
Whether it's self-education, travel planning, or curiosity that brings you here, you'll probably find what you're looking for. Searchable by country, religion, holiday, or festival, this site offers calendars of public holidays, moveable feasts, and local festivals through the year 2002. Countries are still being posted so check back if yours isn't available.

U.S. Census Bureau www.census.gov
America's population monitors do much more than just count people. Their online repository of statistics is invaluable for anyone seeking facts on demographics, business and economy, and geography. Site navigation can be tricky without a game plan, so for specific statistics, consider multiple search queries and browse through related categories.

Religion

The First Church of Cyberspace www.godweb.org
Organized by the Central Presbyterian Church of Montclair, New Jersey, the First Church of Cyberspace states in its mission a goal to organize within the Web and discover "the presence of the Creator within the creative chaos of the Internet." And Deus ex Machina it is; an ecumenical site, the "church" provides prayers and sermons for every occasion, real-time conversation open to all, and links to articles and sites discussing God and other religious topics.

The Tricycle Hub www.tricycle.com
This online version of the well-known nonprofit Buddhist quarterly is, like many online magazines, sparse in content, saving the full-text articles for the paper version. But Tricycle Hub makes up for this with other features: Buddhist chat, an extensive history and explanation on the ABC's of the faith, a regional source directory, and even a personals section where Buddhists can meet that special person and become one.

The Vatican www.vatican.va
As graphically sparse a site as they come, the Holy See online is nevertheless chock full of news, information, and wisdom about and from the center of Roman Catholicism. Read, listen, or watch the pope deliver speeches in five languages; read or search the letters, constitutions, and exhortations of the last four popes; or browse information about the Vatican libraries and museums. The Holy See also offers comprehensive explanations of the church's hierarchy and offices.

IslamiCity www.islamicity.org
IslamiCity is a vast collection of Internet resources for the worldwide Islamic community, with news from and about Islamic nations including radio and television broadcasts in a number of languages, cultural and economic information, and a huge list of links to Muslim businesses and organizations. The site also includes a large section on the religions tenets and activities involved in Islam, prayers and prayer times, and a searchable Qu'ran.

From Jesus to Christ
www.pbs.org/wgbh/pages/frontline/shows/religion
The site from the PBS program "From Jesus to Christ" presents an easy-to-follow guide to the controversial history of the early Christians. Containing maps, a biblical archaeology collection, and critical articles complete with graphics discussing Jesus' life and the social and political world around him, the site attempts to trace through sociological evaluation why Christianity succeeded and other key issues concerning New Testament historians. A beautiful and interesting site for those curious about religious history.

Secular Web www.infidels.org
The largest and most heavily visited atheist site on the Web, the Secular Web attempts to provide a community for users interested in the existence of a god, science and philosophy of religion, church-state separation, and a number of other religion-related issues. The site contains a library of over 6,000 documents on various aspects of nontheistic and theistic philosophies written by field experts and scholars, and it features a monthly Web scan that scours the Internet to uncover religious claims and schemes.

Judaism FAQ www.shamash.org/trb/judaism.html
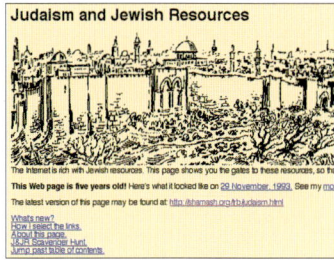
Andrew Tannenbaum's personal project to compile and organize Jewish resources on the Net is a fabulous and comprehensive database of links to Jewish history, culture, and services including news, education, and singles sites. Extensive listings about and from Israel include sites in English as well as in Hebrew and Yiddish, international Jewish museums, and gift shops. Indexes of several large Jewish libraries, and home pages of international Jewish communities round out this exhaustive list.

Christianity.net www.christianity.net
Communities and columns on everything imaginable relating to modern Christian men, women, children, teens, seniors, and singles—from marriage builders to Bible study to Christian music reviews. Christianity.net also features a church finder and ministry guide to help locate Christian communities in any neighborhood.

About.com Religion
www.home.about.com/culture/religion/index.htm
A great guide to an enormous number of topics in 14 religious categories, About.com's religion directory combines the function of a search engine with the specialized information and assistance of a guided tour. Each category is presented with articles by the About.com guides and new links with reviews. Find out more about Wiccan holidays, or read a debate on abortion between pro-life Catholics and pro-choice agnostics.

science & nature

Nine Planets www.seds.org/nineplanets/nineplanets
A small step for mankind, a giant step for the Web. Nine Planets gives complete up-to-date facts and figures on all the known planets and moons of the Milky Way, along with historical and mythological overviews, sound and movie clips, and links to other references. With minimal graphics, the site is quick and easy to navigate; a dip into the vast body of information hidden within this sleek organization reveals an amazing resource for space enthusiasts.

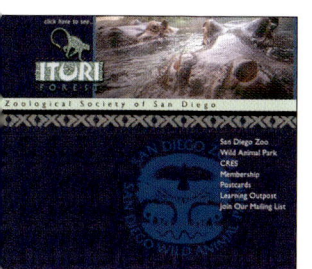

The San Diego Zoo
www.sandiegozoo.org
Meet the world-famous zoo's new babies, take a cybertour of recently opened exhibits, or guess which footprints go with which animal. The San Diego Zoo Web site hosts news, information, and games about the zoo and wildlife park as well as its related research facilities for endangered species. With beautiful photos illustrating its virtual exhibits, the site is almost as vibrant as the zoo itself.

Popular Science www.popsci.com
Science is involved in just about every aspect of our lives; click around Popular Science online to find out just how much. The site brings you serious (and not so serious) science breakthroughs for home, auto, and computer, plus forums and chat boards.

Wired www.wired.com
Wired's comprehensive daily coverage of the business, culture, technology, and politics of the information age makes it the quintessential site for citizens of the digital age. From Microsoft stock quotes to crash courses in Java and Web design, Wired is required reading for everyone from programmers to Sunday Web surfers.

New Scientist Magazine www.newscientist.com

The international weekly of science news boasts much of the magazine's offline content, plus special Web-only sections. An enormous database of science and technology career opportunities, site-of-the-day lists, links to hot science pages, and other features of interest to science lovers around the world.

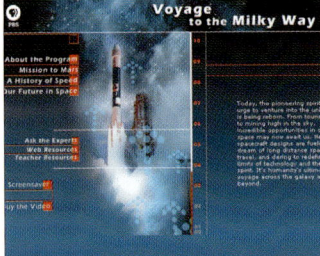

PBS Online Science
www.pbs.org/science
Home of such long-running series as *NOVA, Newton's Apple,* and *Stephen Hawking's Universe,* PBS is the educational source for the natural and physical sciences. PBS Online Science's archives feature articles from 11 different programs. The beautiful graphics and engaging full-text stories are reason enough to visit. The site is well organized and easy enough for kids to use.

Discover Magazine www.discover.com
Covering everything from astrophysics to anthropology, Discover Magazine online offers hundreds of full-text articles on science news in current and archived issues dating back to 1992. The stories include hyperlinks to related articles of interest, and the site features a list of science Web sites in seven fields.

Bill Nye the Science Guy www.nyelabs.kcts.org/flash_go.html
For those who miss their childhood chemistry set: you'll find dozens of at-home experiments and explanations on the Science Guy's site. The virtual Bill Nye turns everyday and obscure scientific phenomena into weird activities and fun facts. The Teacher's Lounge section aims to tutor teachers in the fine art of edutainment.

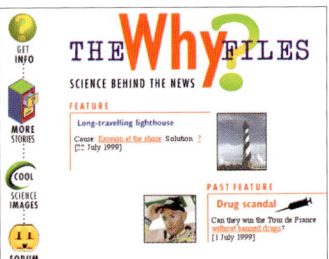

The Why Files
www.whyfiles.news.wisc.edu
Why are so many women giving birth to supertwins these days? Why do kids kill? A layperson-friendly information bank of "the science behind the news," the University of Wisconsin's Why Files explain the biology, physics, chemistry, and psychology behind the day's headlines. In-depth, engaging investigations of stuff you may (or may not) have wondered about, like mad cow disease and global warming.

History of Science, Technology and Medicine Virtual Library
www.asap.unimelb.edu.au/hstm/hstm_ove.htm
From Einstein to ether, this rich compilation of links to scientific history resources on the Web allows users to browse or search in 14 different scientific fields, and by scientist, source, region, and institution. Most of the sites are also rated for depth, content, and design. Extremely useful.

National Parks Service www.nps.gov
Besides the massive listing of national and local parks in the United States, the NPS Web site is a rich educational resource for environmental and geological studies. Articles, photos, and fact sheets as well as tour guides and contact information supplement visits to the parks, while a fascinating historical section highlights the importance of conservation and open space. A great tool for teachers.

NASA www.nasa.gov
Blast off into cyberspace with NASA's awesome site, which links to all the info you could ever want about America's 40-year-old space program, plus the Earth Observatory and the Mars Global Surveyor, where you can view the latest and archived images of Mars. You can even follow status reports of the Mars mission—you'll feel as if you were there with the astronauts.

Lawrence Berkeley National Lab www.lbl.gov

America's oldest national research lab has been revolutionizing the sciences since 1931, and virtually all of its current projects and findings are posted on its home page. With technical reports of the latest research in particle physics and electrochemistry as well as student-friendly articles and projects covering genetics, magnetism, and a "virtual frog dissection," the Department of Energy and U.C. Berkeley host an intelligent site with something for everyone.

Natural Resource Conservation Service www.nrcs.usda.gov
Dial up this site to learn about the environmental state of the Union, from conservation efforts in California to endangered species in your own backyard. The maps, facts, and figures here will keep tree huggers happy for hours.

The Exploratorium www.exploratorium.org
The celebrated museum of "science, art, and human perception" nestled in San Francisco's Palace of Fine Art stretches out online with an impressive collection of exhibits, library files, and Webcasts whose archives include solar eclipses, robot sumo wrestling, and the science of skateboarding in Real Video. Check the searchable digital library by topic, image, or sound.

National Air and Space Museum www.nasm.edu
Pictures of air and spacecraft, planetary exhibitions, and the cool Curator's Choice section make this site worth a stop. It's got detailed explanations of select objects in the museum, like the lunar module (the one Apollo astronauts took to the moon). You can also view past and current museum exhibits and ones specially produced for the Web, complete with Real Audio and Video clips.

National Zoo www.si.edu/natzoo
Keep tabs on your favorite National Zoo animals via a Webcam, a huge photo gallery, and regularly updated news articles on newborns and newly acquired animals like Hsing-Hsing the panda. The virtual tours and interactive exhibits at this site require plug-ins and often load slowly, but make for a fabulously realistic virtual zoo trip.

science & nature

New York Botanical Garden www.nybg.org

Get away from it all: take a virtual walk through one of North America's largest and most beautiful rock gardens, or check out some of the 5,000 types of orchids grown at New York's 250-acre botanical park (you can almost smell them!). The Garden's site will also keep you up to date on the latest research in the botanical sciences as well as flower facts and tips for cultivating any type of plant imaginable.

U.K. Natural History Museum www.nhm.ac.uk
The interactive floor plan takes visitors through dozens of earth and life galleries that showcase 68 million specimens from Britain's 250-year-old Natural History Museum. From meteorites to ancient teapots, the online galleries offer views and explanations of the artifacts of our natural and cultural history. Interactive exhibits include an animated simulation of a dinosaur.

National Geographic.com www.nationalgeographic.com
While the contents of the renowned magazine are available only in excerpt online, the NG network still has plenty of stuff to keep you busy, with incredible photographs and links to National Geographic Television, World Children's magazine, Traveler, and Adventure magazines. Cool animations let you take a virtual swim through a kelp forest, or view a time-lapse weather map of El Niño.

The Tech Museum www.thetech.org

The Tech Museum's virtual presence is as instructional and hands-on as its physical counterpart in the heart of Silicon Valley. Build a satellite, pet a robotic rhino, get an up-close look at DNA, or simply browse articles detailing the technological innovations that got you online in the first place.

Environmental Protection Agency www.epa.gov
Whether you're an activist, an educator, or just a concerned citizen, the EPA's Web site awaits your awareness! Search for projects by natural resource and topic, learn about legislation in the works, or just explore the site for tips on how to be a more environmentally friendly member of the earth.

seniors

ThirdAge.com www.thirdage.com
An all-around community for active older adults, Third Age covers work, technology, family, and romance for those in their "third age of life." Chat, communities, forums, and free home pages for users make for a fun and vibrant community experience.

Senior Living Online www.livon.com

The Senior Living Online network claims to be the world's largest interactive resident referral network, and with over 60,000 senior living facilities and care centers listed, it's tough to argue. Find housing and care for aging adults by searching the database—search criteria include health status, level of care, location, and price. The Senior Living Online network also helps you make sense of the financial ins and outs of assisted living.

American Association of Retired Persons www.aarp.org
The AARP site is partly an advertisement for the services provided by the association, including travel discounts and special insurance rates. But the site also offers info that other senior sites neglect, like legislative coverage and advice for older drivers. With content from its *Modern Maturity* magazine on life transitions, leisure, and health, AARP is a great resource for retired folks.

AgeNet www.agenet.com

Aimed at aging parents and the adult children who care for them, AgeNet offers medical information; financial, legal, and insurance facts; and resources for home care providers. AgeNet also provides an Ask A Pharmacist section for geriatric medical advice, and a caregiver support section.

Health and Age www.healthandage.com
Hosted by the Novartis Foundation for Gerontological Research, Health and Age contains three separate sections for physicians, patients, and other health care professionals. Each one gives information on specific conditions like Alzheimer's and impaired mobility.

Social Security Online www.ssa.gov
Learn more about Social Security benefits, retirement planning, disability, Medicare, and more on the Social Security Administration's home page. A bit bureaucratic but still very useful, the SSA site offers a personal earnings and benefit estimate, guides to understanding Social Security, news, policy information, legal rights, and more, in English and Spanish.

Senior.com www.senior.com
Age 50-plus adults are the fastest-growing group of computer users; Senior.com aims to serve them with forums, chat rooms, and sponsored home pages. Books clubs, travel clubs, tech clubs, forums on news, romance, and entertainment, and additional articles and links in such categories as money matters and health keep users in touch with the issues they care about.

WidowNet www.fortnet.org/widownet
A site dedicated to widows and widowers, WidowNet is an upbeat and supportive community with advice on issues like getting through the holidays without a loved one. Self-help, support groups, and chat boards remind users that they're not alone.

Quicken.com Retirement www.quicken.com/retirement
Where will you be when you retire? If Pebble Beach and Paris top your list, you'd better head to Quicken.com Retirement. All sorts of financial management tips await, including the skinny on IRAs, 401(k)s, and estate planning. There's also a great section for those who want to retire early. With a little luck and a lot of planning, you'll be headed for the greens in no time.

50 Something.net www.50something.net
Bringing the 50-something community together to celebrate its age and energy. There are plenty of resources here, from recipes to travel tips to lifestyle articles. Join the fun!

Alzheimer's Association www.alz.org
This sleek and useful site by the Alzheimer's Association covers the disease that affects over four million Americans and their families. Learn about the causes and symptoms of the disease here, and explore treatment options. A special caregiver section helps the families of Alzheimer patients find the care and support they need.

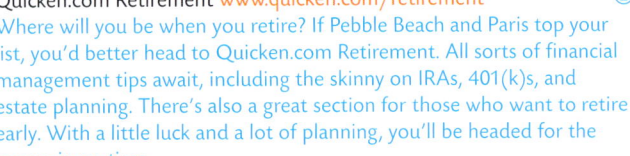

shopping

BottomDollar.com www.bottomdollar.com
A great first stop for new Net shoppers, BottomDollar links to some of the hottest shopping spots on the Web. Enter the item you want, and BottomDollar will tell you which online store offers it for the lowest price. The truly exhaustive list of offerings includes books, electronics, flowers, hardware, movies, software, video games, and more. Searches can be a bit tedious, but the savings potential is terrific.

shopping

Bloomingdale's www.bloomingdales.com

Upscale clothes, electronics, jewelry, appliances, furnishings, and toys for the discriminating shopaholic. Click around, browse, and drop your favorite items into your virtual big brown bag. You can also post a wish list on the site. That way, your loved ones will know exactly what to get you for your birthday. What a concept!

ShopNow.com www.shopnow.com

Think of it as a directory to the giant mall that is the Internet. Whatever you need — clothes, shoes, hair care, *Star Wars* goodies, you name it — ShopNow probably links to a store that sells it. Be sure to check out the ever-changing list of shoppers' favorite sites, as well as the section of hot bargains. Well organized and easy to use.

Macy's www.macys.com

All the variety you get at the store, without the crowds. You'll find everything from clothing to jewelry to accessories to cosmetics to fragrances; you can even buy flowers from the gift shop. Search for gifts by occasion, price, product, or keyword. A phenomenal range of merchandise.

Bluefly www.bluefly.com

Shop with the Fly for discounts on designer fashions (Donna Karan, Tommy Hilfiger), housewares (Mikasa, Ralph Lauren), and gifts. It's practically impossible to surf this site and not find cool, affordable stuff. The My Catalogue option lets you enter your essential stats (gender, size, favorite designers); Bluefly will give you an up-to-date, personalized catalog every time you log on.

NYstyle www.nystyle.com

If you're into labels, be sure to stop by this site. The impressive list of merchandise is grouped by designer names like Fiorucci (women's wear), Alex & Me (baby gear), Tony & Tina (cosmetics), Manhattan Fruitier (gourmet), Dooney & Bourke (handbags and luggage), and Jonathan Adler (home furnishings). Trendy, hot, and (surprise!) expensive.

The Nature Company www.natureco.com

Be prepared to appreciate nature! Whether this means tempting hummingbirds to your garden with a special nectar feeder, stargazing with that high-powered refracting telescope, or gauging the weather with a glass Galileo thermometer, The Nature Company comes through with all the tools you need at a click. Shop online, order the print catalog, or check the store locator for nonvirtual window-shopping.

iQVC Shopping Page www.iqvc.com
Why wait for your desired item to show up on TV when you can order it from the Web site? The amount of merchandise here is awe-inspiring; you'll find everything from collectibles and toys to electronics, apparel, and health and beauty aids, often at terrific prices.

Wal-Mart www.walmart.com
As if the actual store wasn't convenient enough, now you can shop Wal-Mart from the comfort of your own home. Not only can you buy everything from appliances to gourmet food to toys, you can also apply for a store credit card or submit your résumé for a job. The impressive Good Works section will tell you all about the charitable initiatives Wal-Mart is involved with. Who knew?

Shop For Change www.shopforchange.com
A great new way to shop responsibly, this site donates 5% of what you spend at your favorite online vendors to nonprofit organizations. Link from here to sites like Amazon.com, Jcrew.com and Netgrocer to help Greenpeace, Children's Defense Fund and Planned Parenthood, among others. There aren't any additional charges—just an easy way for your buying power to make a difference.

Mercata www.mercata.com
The greater the demand, the lower the prices. Mercata pools online shoppers together and negotiates bulk discounts for them—kind of like an online Price Club. Though the jury's still out on how effective Mercata is at nabbing those discounts, it's certainly a site worth watching. Wander through sections on consumer electronics, power tools, home and kitchen, lawn and garden, sports and fitness and more to see the hot ticket of the moment.

Spree www.spree.com
Another unique Internet shopping scheme. The scoop: sign up to be a SIP (Spree Independent Partner) and earn points for each purchase you make. Refer friends to Spree and receive points for purchases they make. The points equate to cash amounts (10 points = $3) which you can use to shop with. The idea definitely has potential: get paid to shop?!? Makes sense to us.

auctions & classifieds

eBay www.ebay.com
Whether you're looking to buy a solid gold wristwatch or trying to move your old Sonny and Cher dolls, your first stop should be eBay, the site that put online auctions on the map. Buyers are given a limited time period in which to bid on an item; if you pledge the winning amount, you'll be notified via e-mail. Sellers can set minimum bids, too—so no one is forced to give up their merchandise for a song. Really practical and easy to use.

Sotheby's www.sothebys.com
One of the most elegantly designed sites on the Web, Sotheby's makes you want to liquidate your stocks and start bidding for treasures. The site allows surfers to search the revered auction house's catalogs, and buy or sell unique and valuable items. Collections include decorative arts, fine arts, Asian art, jewels, precious objects, and books and manuscripts.

Bidder's Edge www.biddersedge.com
This fabulous Web site allows you to monitor auctions across many sites  at the same time. It will quote market prices for the items you want, and will alert you when something you've been seeking makes it to the auction block. There are over two million items up for sale here, so there's sure to be something you desperately need—that signed poster of Jennifer Love Hewitt, perhaps?

EPage www.ep.com
Featuring over one million ads each day, Ep.com allows you to search its huge database of classifieds with a few clicks of the mouse. Categories include vehicles, collectibles, jobs, computers, personals, and real estate. Well organized and easy to use.

Excite Classifieds & Auctions www.classifieds2000.com
You can find anything from a car to a house to a roommate to a spouse on this Web site. You can also place ads or create a hot list of interesting ads that you'll want to consult after you've finished surfing. A great way to locate bargains, the love of your life, or both, as the case may be.

clothes & accessories

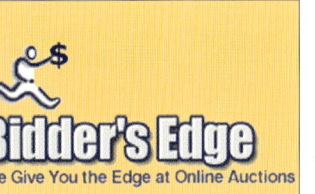 Guess Online Store www.guess.com
Guess Online has got it all: the clothes, the models, the commercials, and even a VIP Lounge decked out in lush leopard prints. The fashion-impaired will dig sections like "What to Wear Now?" and "Style Guide," with nonintimidating tips on how to look *gorgeous, darling.*

Brooks Brothers www.brooksbrothers.com
This elegant Web site has Brooks Brothers written all over it. Items are divided into five categories: shirts and ties, dress clothing, casual clothing, essentials and gifts, and women's clothing. The prices may cause you to break into a cold sweat, but the timeless quality of the merchandise should serve you well into the future.

1 5 3

shopping *clothes & accessories*

Gap Online www.gap.com
Quick—it's your brother-in-law's birthday. Card? Not enough. Flowers? Wrong message. Thanks to Gap Online's thoughtful selection of gift items for men, women, kids, and even newborns, family crisis is averted. Just make sure the plastic's good. And you might as well prepare yourself for dress-down Fridays while you're here. (Did Gap invent those?)

Armani Exchange www.armaniexchange.com
Armani = the sexiest models on the planet. Is it the clothes? This site will help you find the A/X in your neighborhood or purchase select products online. You can even download any one of four steamy screen savers featuring the crème de la Xchange. "From A to X" offers an alphabetical listing of what nourishes the minds and bodies at the greenhouse of style.

L.L. Bean www.llbean.com
L.L. Bean has got the catalog biz down to a science, so it's no surprise that their Web site is such a pleasure to shop. Search sporty gear and apparel with the product guides, or use the handy catalog quickshop option. The Park Search section features breathtaking photos of America's parks that you won't want to miss.

Bebe www.bebe.com
What a fabulous looking site! Not only does Bebe sell must-have basics like sweaters, dresses, and pants; it's also got accessories, lingerie and swimsuits to keep you beautiful 24-7. Beauty tips, a style forecast, accessorizing tips, and a VIP lounge spice things up at this must-see site.

Coolshopping.com
www.coolshopping.com
Aimed at the *Seventeen* magazine crowd, Coolshopping.com offers daily updates on the, um, coolest shopping sites on the Web—and often finds hidden gems that are useful to all age groups. The site also lets you create a personal start page with your favorite shopping links.

dELiAs www.delias.com
A site that could bring out the girly-girl in Sylvester Stallone. Browse the catalog or the discount domain for all things femme: glittery slip dresses, funky jewelry, makeup, and shoes (thigh-high boots!) that will make you wish you were a teen again. Great clothes, great fu

Lands' End www.landsend.com
For a classic, comfortable look, go straight to Lands' End. They've got everything from swimwear to school uniforms to casual clothing to tailored fashions for men, women, and children. The swimsuit finder, bargain page, and a personal virtual model for women are tops. There's even an adventure section with a column called "Wild Planet" and journal entries from polar explorer Will Steger.

JCrew.com www.jcrew.com
For that sporty, oh-so-self-assured look. Take your pick of suits, shirts, sweaters, skirts, dresses, pajamas, underwear, and the like from its extensive catalog. They've even got shoes! Fast, easy, and convenient shopping so you can spend less time at the stores and more time at the club.

Kenneth Cole www.kennethcole.com
Quintessential American cool straight from the New York stylemaker. The clothes and shoes are great, but the site itself is worth exploring for the gallery of Kenneth Cole ads (stylish with a social conscience) and the fascinating article, "Birth of a Shoe Company," where Cole recounts how he set up shop in a fully furnished 40-foot trailer in midtown Manhattan.

Esprit.com www.esprit.com
Fresh, breezy style that won't break the bank. Try out Eprit's way-cool Product Finder, where you can enter your style (party girl, trendsetter, workaholic), your fabric of choice (velvet, cotton, denim), and preferred color and price; Esprit digs up your perfect outfit in seconds.

Fabric8 www.fabric8.com

"Urban designs for open minds." The standard departments simply don't apply at Fabric8: you'll find stylish sundries, modular jewelry, handcrafted everyday wear, music, and interactive art from indie designers. If you can't be seen without the latest cell-phone holder or mod leisure shirt, this site's for you.

LondonWide www.londonwide.co.uk
Designer street and clubwear for the terminally hip. LondonWide sells decidedly utilitarian duds from London designers like Nicki Pumpkin, Mickey Brazil, and Cinema X. The clothes are handpicked by the LondonWide's team of "fashion addicts"—definitely stop in for a browse.

DesignerOutlet.com www.designeroutlet.com
Imagine: the heavy hitters of fashion—Prada,

Calvin Klein, Dolce & Gabanna, DKNY—at outlet prices. Designer Outlet has some great finds in first-name fashion at discounts from 30-70% off the retail price (keep in mind that retail price for a Prada bag is almost the same as a PC). Women's, men's, and children's apparel, plus accessories.

shopping clothes & accessories

1 5 5

Style Shop www.styleshop.com
When in Rome, shop as the Romans do: Style Shop's got city guides that tell you where to shop and what's on sale in over 200 cities across the country. Become a member (for free!) and get e-mail bulletins on sales in your area; for a customizable My Style page, you'll have your own frequently-updated personal sale bulletin board on the Web. Sign up — it's a steal.

Insider Shopping www.inshop.com
It's like hiring your own personal shopper, but better: 24 hours a day, 7 days a week, Inshop.com is on call to keep you posted on the sales at all your favorite stores, from Barney's to Bloomies. Loads of great deals await — just select a city and the product, designer, or store you want (everything from furniture to Frederic Fekkai is here); InShop gives you the lowdown on where and when to buy at discounts of up to 50%.

Victoria's Secret
www.victoriassecret.com
The honeymoon ain't over yet. Victoria's Secret sells all the luxurious lingerie you love at this highly surfable site. For the ladies: the bra salon, the glam lounge, sleepwear, bedding, perfume, and lotions. For the guys: all the pictures from the catalog for you to drool over.

Fashion Mall www.fashionmall.com
You're trapped deep in suburbia and all you want are...Skechers. Well, if there's a computer around, you'll find them available for purchase at this one-stop fashion shop. It may take a few months for all the graphics to load up, but once they do, have your credit card ready. The men's collection offers the best selection for brand, but there are some ladies' finds here too, as well as wedding guides and boutiques. Brands include Brooks Brothers, Fortunoff, and Dolce & Gabanna.

Piece Unique www.pieceunique.com
Ever wonder where to get the clothes and accessories worn by runway mega-models? Try Piece Unique, where you can buy Chanel, Versace, and Gaultier hand-me-downs (to name a few) at up to half price. We're still talking a major dent in your credit card bill: a Chanel suit will probably run you about $1,000. Still, it's great fun to look.

Shades.com www.shades.com
Protect your peepers and keep your wallet happy with stylish sunblockers from Shades.com. Aviators, wraparounds, clip-ons, sports shields and cat-eyes from Rayban, Gucci, Swiss Army, Guess?, and others are always on sale. Browse through the brands or cut to the chase with the quick sunglass finder, where you can search by brand, style, color, material, and activity.

Dooney & Bourke www.dooney.com
Stop here for leather bags with that signature Dooney flair. You'll also find business and travel essentials (like a gorgeous leather Palm Pilot case) and men's and women's accessories. Well organized, with detailed descriptions of the goodies. Too bad that wonderful leather smell can't be downloaded!

Bestswimwear.com www.bestswimwear.com
Save yourself the agony of trying on teensy swimsuits in the unflattering glare of fitting room lights—dial up Bestswimwear.com. Tops and bottoms can be sized separately, thank heaven. The suits also seem to be made of more substantial material than dental floss.

Underneath.com www.underneath.com
Everyone wears it—so why are there so few places to buy it online? That's right, we're talking about underwear. Lots of it. Calvin Klein, Joe Boxer, Champion, Vanity Fair, and Wonderbra—all sold at Underneath.com. For the adventurous, there's always the "Fun Wear" option, with picks such as Glow in the Dark Skivvies and Scratch & Sniff Undies.

SunglassSite www.sunglasssite.com
Simply put, SunglassSite is 400 models of designer sunglasses (Calvin Klein, Ray Ban, DKNY) at competitive prices. Tip: if you find a pair of sunglasses elsewhere at a lower price than the one posted here, SunglassSite will give you an additional 10% off.

Wristwatch.com www.wristwatch.com
We love the concept: one item, thousands of brands. Browse by manufacturer, activity, function, or type. Very well organized and handsomely designed, this site should serve as an example to other shopping pages on the Net.

Ties.com www.ties.com
Despairing souls searching for the last-minute gift should make a stop at Ties.com—they'll ship you a perfectly respectable Father's Day present overnight for a cool $6. Be sure to surf the Tie Museum, where you can view notable ties by decade— the Japanese '70s tie, made of real feathers, is sure to pique your interest, as is the section on how to tie a tie.

consumer guides & price comparisons

CompareNet www.comparenet.com
The ultimate consumer guide, CompareNet provides product information, merchandise comparisons, reviews, and discussion lists so you can get exactly what you're looking for at the best price possible. Product categories include electronics, automotive, baby care, computing, home appliances, and sports and leisure.

shopping *consumer guides*

WebMarket www.webmarket.com
WebMarket is an excellent choice for online price comparisons, with a simple, easy-to-use interface (pull-down menus let you customize searches) and all the shopping options you could ask for: movies, videos, office supplies, vacation packages, and more. Click through to BizRate's consumer guide for a roundup of best-bet retailers all over the Net.

BizRate.com www.bizrate.com
Bizrate.com is a continual survey of online buyers that compiles its findings into Consumer Certified Report Cards. These reports feature ratings on product selection, pricing, and delivery policies. You can conduct business searches through the merchant directory or find the best values with the shopping guide. Feel free to submit your own shopping triumphs or horror stories.

WorldSpy www.worldspy.com
The comparison shopper's best friend online. WorldSpy collects the brands, the prices, and the consumer reviews on the best buys out there. Several products are sold directly through WorldSpy, though consumer information is not limited to these. For anyone interested in making an informed purchase.

The Better Business Bureau www.bbb.org
Want the real story on those envelope-stuffing businesses, or just feel like blowing the whistle on your boss? Then step right up to The Better Business Bureau Web site, which has alerts and news stories about questionable organizations, a database of company reports, a list of charity reports and standards, and a section devoted to dispute resolution. The search engine is a little convoluted, so don't expect to get a report on a particular business in one click.

Consumer Information Center pueblo.gsa.gov
This Web site has hundreds of federal consumer publications, some that are free to view and others that will cost you. Report subjects include cars, money, food, education, health, and travel. Includes such informative publications as "How to File a Claim for Your Employment Benefits" and "Nontraditional Education: Alternative Ways to Earn Your Credentials." Really quite useful.

Consumer Reports Online www.consumerreports.org
Shopping online can be really bewildering at times; it's hard to know about the potential pitfalls unless you've read up on the subject. If you'd like to fill in the gaps in your knowledge, then check out Consumer Reports Online. It has helpful information on the pros and cons of online shopping and safety tips. This site also features CR's exceptional reporting on vehicles, appliances, electronics, and more.

electronics

zZounds www.zzounds.com
zZounds is on a mission to give you "every tool possible to unleash your musical creativity," and it looks like they just may accomplish their goal, thanks to an extensive inventory of keyboards and modules, electric guitars, studio recording devices, drums, and karaoke equipment. zZounds guarantees the best prices, and vows to refund you twice the difference of a better bargain for up to 30 days after the date of purchase.

Crutchfield www.crutchfield.com
The standard-bearer in consumer electronics on the Net. Crutchfield shines with great customer service (like their toll-free technical support line and order status page), product information, low shipping costs, and all the name brand electronics you could ever want. Check out their list of 16 reasons to shop Crutchfield—or just take our word for it.

800 dot com www.800.com
This neat site has got an excellent selection of audio components, portable electronics, camcorders, phones, music, and movies. The best reason to shop here is the Infozone, which contains a "Before You Buy" fact-checking feature, a lesson in home theater 101, consumer reviews, expert advice, and an electronics glossary.

The Sharper Image www.sharperimage.com
Everything you've ever needed (but didn't know existed) is right here at Sharper Image: an ionic pet bath brush, a wearable air conditioner, a heart soother, and an electric tongue cleaner are among the many incredible and, frankly, sometimes bizarre products here. (We're dying to try the ionic hair wand!) Some useful stuff is here as well.

electronics.net www.electronics.net

Featuring hundreds of brands and thousands of electronics, this Web site has got everything from camcorders to computers to refrigerators to air conditioners to microwaves. The products could certainly stand some more detailed descriptions, but this is an easy and convenient way to shop nonetheless.

Appliances.com www.appliances.com
Blenders, bread makers, juicers, and microwaves—you can go to the local department store for them, or you can order them online at Appliances.com. They've got all the brands you know (Cuisinart, KitchenAid) and a selection that's just the right size—not so mind-boggling that you don't know where to begin.

erotica

Toys in Babeland www.babeland.com
Babeland is not for the faint of heart: if great sex means the standard fare over restraint devices, this probably isn't the place for you. For the slightly more adventurous, curious, or serious sensation aficionados, Babeland offers everything from toys to videos to books and just about everything in between. Order online in blissful discretion, or find out about the Toys store nearest you.

Nerve Boutique www.nerve.com/boutique
Ideal for folks who want their boudoir to scream "Austin Powers," with mood-enhancing accessories like sheepskin rugs, leopard candles, and embroidered pillows. Just be careful with that high-cut silk thong.

shopping erotica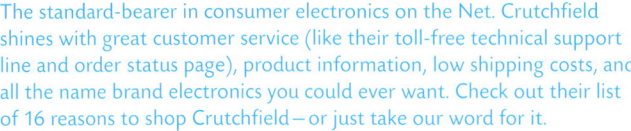

Good Vibrations www.goodvibes.com
More than a shopping site, this sexual accessory standard offers news articles, sex trivia, books and reviews, and the totally unique Antique Vibrator Museum, with some truly medieval looking blender-type devices. Fortunately, Good Vibes offers the modern, user-friendly version of these and scores of other products guaranteed to please.

Condomania www.condomania.com
If there's a shape, size, or flavor of condom out there, you can buy it here. Browse the catalog to get the full selection, search by brand and style, and learn a thing or two at the Safer Sex section, where educational materials including statistics, related links, news stories, and manuals await your perusal. Quick, easy, embarrassment-free shopping for all your condom needs.

food & drink

NetGrocer.com www.netgrocer.com

If you're seeking sanctuary from grocery stores teeming with screaming kids and harried adults, dial up NetGrocer.com. This site has everything you need as far as dry goods are concerned, often at a better price than you'd find at the supermarket. Best of all, some sections of the store are devoted to shoppers with special needs (food for diabetics, baby care products, and contraceptives, among others). Purchases are shipped within two to four business days.

Harry & David www.harryanddavid.com
A gourmand's delight, Harry & David offers beautifully packaged desserts, pastries, dried fruit, nuts, and candy, in addition to fresh meat, seafood, vegetables, and fruit. They even have flowering plants for sale. The merchandise is a little pricey compared to similar services, but the quality of the food and the beauty of the packaging make any purchase worth the extra bucks.

Dean & Deluca www.dean-deluca.com

Westphalian ham, TerraBiance chestnut flower honey, sevruga caviar, Italian truffle butter — the foodstuff of luxury from SoHo's ritziest corner grocery store is now available nationwide thanks to Dean & Deluca online. Truffles and foie gras, fruit and nuts, international cheeses, and everything else for the discriminating tongue, as well as barware like a Hungarian crystal wine cooler can be ordered and shipped anywhere in the country.

Great Food www.greatfood.com
There is something very alluring about having a Chocolate Thunder and White Lightening Torte delivered to your door. Of course, the site offers many other types of gourmet food, and is searchable by category and special occasion. The gift finder is another great feature, showing you what you can get from $15 to over $100, and the corporate gift service will find you the right item and even help you write the card.

Godiva Online www.godiva.com

Gain 10 pounds just visiting —the Godiva Online chocolatier is so decadent you'll feel guilty just browsing. Order products or browse the extensive recipe database, searchable by difficulty level, for gems like chocolate crème brûlée with chocolate hazelnut crunch and mocha anglais. Chocolate reference glossaries and trivia (875,000 chocolate chips can fuel an around-the-world walk) fill out this lavish chocoholic paradise.

Wild Oats Markets www.wildoats.com
Everything you ever wanted in a health food store and more is at Wild Oats online. The country's second-largest health food chain, Wild Oats has stores in 19 states and in Canada which can be located on their virtual map and are listed complete with contact info. Or, shop online and have a huge variety of organic and natural products delivered to your door. The Web site also includes a number of glossaries of health and nutrition terms, a wellness center, and listings of local and national activist organizations.

ThaiGrocer www.thaigrocer.com
Wouldn't it be great to be able to cook the same delicious Thai dishes served in restaurants? ThaiGrocer has everything needed to become a fabulous Thai chef. A fully stocked Thai grocery store complete with fresh produce and equipment that can be shipped around the world, ThaiGrocer also has its own cooking school with a wide array of recipes, how-to advice, and even an Ask The Chef forum where ThaiGrocer's chef answers all cooking questions posted.

Calwine www.calwine.com

Let's face it: Calwine can't compare to touring the Napa Valley, but it can provide you with some sublime wines. You can search for vintages by winery, region, or variety (sauvignon, blanc, pinot noir, dessert wines, etc.). In addition, this site offers gift baskets, a wine finder, and an Ask the Pros service. Shopping by price range is also an option.

shopping food & drink

Winezone www.winezone.com
This lovely Web site allows surfers to take in the sights of vineyards via photographs while reading up on various wineries and vintages. If you've never wanted to tour Wine Country, you will after surfing this site. Strictly for folks who appreciate the finer things in life!

Caviar Assouline www.caviarassouline.com
Anyone who loves caviar will appreciate this Web site, which features an extensive catalog of beluga, ossetra, and sevruga caviar, as well as foie gras, truffles, smoked salmon, and Valrhona chocolates. You can also sign up for cooking classes and newsletters, as well as learn recipes and serving tips.

Atlantic Live Lobsters Delivered www.thelobsternet.com
If you've got a hankering for lobsters, cast your net at this Web site, which sends the crustaceans from Maine to your door within 24 hours. You can also buy lobster tails, Dungeness crabs, steamer clams, shrimp, and freshly caught salmon here, as well as gift packages and cooking equipment.

free stuff & coupons

CoolSavings.com www.coolsavings.com
No more clipping coupons—CoolSavings.com has thousands of printable money savers on its site. The coupons are all free and good at national chains like Kmart and Radio Shack, as well as Web retailers such as eToys and CD Now. CoolSavings also contains freebie offers and e-mail updates on new savings opportunities.

Free Forum Network www.freeforum.com
Unlike most freebie sites, which offer little more than trial magazine subscriptions and coupons for product samples, the Free Forum has hundreds of links to useful products and services. Insurance information, travel discounts, long-distance phone savings, and more, sorted into categories like health and fitness, gardening, and sports. A great find.

Free Shop www.freeshop.com
Free free free—don't you love the sound of that word? The Free Shop has free offers, free samples, free demos, free catalogs, and free product information. There are also 204 free magazine offers in over 30 categories.

#1 Free Stuff www.1freestuff.com
This search engine of freebie offers is huge and comprehensive, including everything from free screen savers to contests and games to pet supplies, credit cards, MP3s, clothes, and movie tickets. Don't overlook the contests either—you'll find all sorts of opportunities to test your luck.

gifts & cards

FTD.com www.ftd.com
Now, honestly, who doesn't love to receive flowers? Whether you're surprising your sweetheart or begging her for forgiveness, FTD.com is here. Search floral arrangements and gift baskets by holiday, product, occasion, or price. Guaranteed to get you in good with your honey.

GreatFlowers www.greatflowers.com
So you missed you mother's birthday? A FedEx'd greeting card might not smooth this one over. At GreatFlowers, order a bouquet with a few clicks and that magic plastic card. Quick convenient delivery.

Violet www.violet.com
This wonderfully creative site invites you to buy gifts by personality, interest, price, or department. Choose some bejeweled barrettes for that femme fatale in your life or an elegant fountain pen for your sophisticate boss. If you're still not sure what to get, try the Psychic Search feature.

GiftPoint.com www.giftpoint.com
A clever concept: GiftPoint.com lets you purchase gift certificates from over 150 national and local retailers; take your pick of book, music, department, and toy stores, among others. You can even purchase credit toward personal services like manicures, massages, and haircuts. A great idea backed up by a wonderful organization.

RedEnvelope.com www.redenvelope.com

Haven't got a clue what to get your neighbor's daughter for graduation? Then stop by RedEnvelope.com. It allows you to search for presents according to recipient (girlfriend, grandfather, nephew, etc.), occasion (birthday, anniversary, retirement, get well soon), department (bath & body, fun & games, healthy living, romantic gifts), or price. If you're still stumped for ideas, you can always submit a query to the GiftExpert and get an e-mailed response within 24 hours. There's also a handy GiftAlert option that will e-mail you a reminder a few days in advance of a special event.

Hallmark www.hallmarkreminder.com
Now keep in touch more easily than ever with electronic greeting cards from Hallmark, the masters of verbal magic in 25 words or less. Hallmark's site offers thousands of gifts and cards to purchase online, but the real fun is with the free electronic greetings; choose the old standby poems for grandma or something spicier from the Shoebox collection.

Sparks.com
www.sparks.com
The fabulous selection of paper cards here should spark your attention. Sparks.com will ship blank greeting cards to you, or handwrite them (with a personalized message) and send them to your wife/friend/ Valentine/ boss/pet/ etc. Wow. If only they could mimic your handwriting it'd be foolproof.

shopping gifts & cards

1 6 3

health & beauty

Drugstore.com www.drugstore.com
If there's a consumer heaven, Drugstore.com may be it. This Web site has everything from prescription medications to vitamin pills, beauty aids, and family planning devices. The prices are incredible and the quick lists cut down your shopping time considerably. Simply put, a fabulous place to shop.

Mybasics.com www.mybasics.com
Health and beauty staples online. If you've already established your beauty regimen, you can create a personal profile here; all your favorite products will be swept into one lump credit card order in seconds. Or just browse through the reasonably priced selection for men, women, and children. Let the beautification begin!

Eve.com www.eve.com
Face it: clothes aren't the only thing that makes the look. Rediscover your "original beauty" with Eve.com's selection of makeup, fragrances, bath, body, and skin care products. Browse by brand favorites (that's right, Ahava online!) or try out Eve's suggestions from bath beads to sleep soothers.

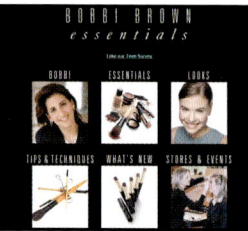

Bobbi Brown
www.bobbibrowncosmetics.com
Bobbi Brown brings it home, online, for free. Find out how to create dozens of looks for teens, brides, black tie events, women of color, over 50, and more, or browse makeup application techniques you need to know. Then click over to the online store and go crazy!

Urban Decay www.urbandecay.com
When "Acid Rain" is a good thing, you know you're dealing with Urban Decay. The site's got over-the-top makeup and advice for spies, vamps, and the terminally cool. Looking for some shimmery body powder? Take your pick of shades like Exhaust, Smog, and Uzi. Need some gooey iridescent lip gloss? Try Gash, Roach, or Litter. The tips page lets you pick a look and make it yours.

Fragrance Counter www.fragrancecounter.com
Looking great and smelling like mothballs won't get you very far on that first date. Fragrance Counter's got tons of scents to tickle the senses. Shop by product name, gender, the "gift selector" for featured products, or the Calvin Klein section. Each product comes with description, associated mood, and, where applicable, celebrity wearer.

Clinique www.clinique.com
Clinique.com does more than sell makeup; the site helps you put your best face forward with a virtual library of beauty advice. Men, don't feel excluded—the Men Only section links to an archive full of articles on all things manly, from having more productive workouts to "de-fuzzing" your fridge.

PlanetRx.com www.planetrx.com
This attractive site affords consumers some relief from the staggering cost of prescription drugs. You'll also find over-the-counter medications here, as well as vitamin supplements, medical supplies, and skin, oral, and hair care products. Amazing content and savings.

home & garden

Smith & Hawken.com www.smithandhawken.com
This lovely site caters to folks seeking to cultivate beauty in their home and yard. It's got flower bulbs, garden ornaments, lighting, statuary, tools, kitchen items, furniture...everything. Elegant merchandise articulately described.

Crate & Barrel www.crateandbarrel.com
You would expect a store as classic as Crate & Barrel to have an equally elegant web site, and it does. The product images are simple and clear. Browsing is effortless; you can easily view everything from flatware to furniture. The site also features access to the store's popular gift registry, and a gift planner that can e-mail you reminders of all those occasions you usually forget.

GreenMarketplace.com www.greenmarketplace.com
It's not just about recycled paper: did you know that cleaning products, beauty supplies, and even regular old cotton clothing can contain harmful chemicals? Shop worry-free at The Green Marketplace, where you'll find a slew of eco-friendly products for you and your home from proven brands like Seventh Generation. The site's For the Mind section contains information and FAQs on the ins and outs of green shopping.

Garden.com www.garden.com
Planning and planting just got a whole lot easier for gardeners who surf the Web. This site's Design a Garden program helps you choose the right plants for your garden, perfect your plant placement, and order what you need from Garden.com's supply of 16,000 gardening products—everything from bulbs to fertilizer to outdoor furniture.

Art.com www.art.com
Warm up your office, bedroom, hallway, or bath with prints from the greats: Chagall, Monet, even Vargas pinup girls. Art.com will frame it and deliver it to your door. Search by artist, category, or the unique online galleries—most of the art is pretty mainstream, but the variety of selection makes it worth a look.

office supplies

Office Depot Online www.officedepot.com
Talk about comprehensive...this site's got it all: software, planners, maintenance supplies, office machines, labels, paper, pens, and more! There are even free downloadable business forms and full-service postal mailing envelopes. Fast, easy, and convenient.

OnlineOfficeSupplies.com www.onlineofficesupplies.com

"The future of office supplies." A bold claim, but judging from this simply designed and straightforward site's features, ease of use, and personalization options, it might just be true. In addition to the standard category search, browse the list of 100 most commonly ordered supplies, or set up a personal profile of commonly requested items. Next time the printer runs out of ink, just click on the Quick Shopping icon and voila! The usual is ready to be delivered within 24 hours (in the continental United States).

shoes

NineWest www.ninewest.com
NineWest has more than just shoes—it's got handbags, belts, jewelry, hair accessories, watches, tights, jackets, sunglasses, and sweaters. The items are elegant and well priced; for especially good bargains, check out the Great Buys page (good if you've got a popular shoe size that tends to sell out a lot).

Onlineshoes.com www.onlineshoes.com
If there could only be one shoe store on the Web, it would have to serve everyone. Onlineshoes may well be it—walking or working, athletic and dress shoes for male and female feet (little kids will have some growing to do first) can be purchased quickly and conveniently at this site, often at impressive discount prices. Search by brand or style, or head straight to the clearance bin and go nuts.

Foot Locker www.footlocker.com
All the selection of the brick-and-mortar store is here, minus the salespeople clad in referee gear. Over 10,000 products in 150 brands (Nike, Reebok, Adidas) are photographed and described. If you need to return something, you can go to the store or mail it in to get your refund. Easy!

Airwalk.com www.airwalk.com

You've got to give Airwalk credit for constructing an ultracool-looking (and sounding) site. Search for shoes by such diverse categories as snow, bike, skate, or couture. It's not especially easy to find what you want here, but you get the feeling that the Web designer wants you to check out each and every page before heading to the checkout counter.

SteveMadden.com www.stevemadden.com

An awful lot of cute dress shoes, boots, sandals, and sneakers here (platforms galore), as well as clothing and accessories. Be advised that it takes a lot of clicks to find the shoes and accessories you want, but what it lacks in organization it makes up for in style. For women only, unless you've got a fetish of some sort.

sporting goods

Fogdog Sports www.fogdog.com

It's pretty difficult to conceive of any piece of sports equipment that wouldn't be available at Fogdog. You can search for what you need by sport, brand, or department. Shipping and handling fees are reasonable, and the amount of merchandise is huge. A wonderful alternative to shopping in chaotic, understaffed sporting goods stores.

Big Deal Worldwide www.bigdeal.com

If you're in the market for a snow, skate, or wake board, check out Big Deal Worldwide. Despite its annoying pop-up ads, it does have a great variety of equipment, accessories, and clothing. There are definitely easier sites to shop at — this one requires a lot of clicks to get what you want — but Big Deal is a good resource simply because its stock is so specialized.

Overtons.com www.overtons.com

Yes, we've officially entered an age in which you can order a boat over the Internet and have it delivered to your door just a few days later. Featuring a catalog of over 14,000 items, Overtons.com has virtually everything you need in the way of boating and water sports needs. You can even create a wish list of items to send friends and relatives who want the privilege of buying you a present.

Campmor www.campmor.com

Anyone who loves camping will breathe a sigh of delight upon dialing up this Web site. It's got a huge amount of merchandise (everything from bicycles to compasses to kitchenware to water filtration supplies), as well as an excellent search engine (look for what you want according to product name, popularity, category, and price). There's also a section of hot deals that you won't want to miss.

SportingAuction.com www.sportingauction.com
Sporting Auction.com offers incredible prices on sporting equipment by putting items up for auction. While this method of shopping probably won't be convenient for a person needing equipment immediately, it is a good place for people who can anticipate their shopping needs and map out a strategy for buying everything from baseball bats to fishing rods to Rollerblades.

REI.com www.rei.com
Listed as *Fortune* magazine's "Top 100 Best Companies to Work" for two years running, Recreational Equipment Incorporated is a business cooperative that has an overwhelming amount of quality merchandise. Anyone can shop here for sporting goods, but becoming a member will snag you some terrific discounts on camping, climbing, and cycling items, among others.

Online Sports www.onlinesports.com
If you have very specific sporting goods needs, then Online Sports is probably for you. It organizes its merchandise by sports, teams, items, suppliers, players, and departments. You can also find unique sports memorabilia here, as well as a listing of sports-related careers.

Gear.com www.gear.com

Gear.com has got great prices on sporting equipment. Search merchandise from a list of 30 activities or look up items by brand, price, or keyword. This site's got a real warehouse feel to it, but it goes well with the rock-bottom prices. For especially good bargains, check out the Closeout Deals section.

tickets

Tixx.com www.st4.yahoo.com/tixx
Whether you want concert, theater, or sports tickets, you can find them at this Yahoo!-linked ticket clearinghouse. If you're looking for a bargain, be sure to check out the special page, which features last-minute openings that are sometimes less their original price. Gift certificates are also available.

Ticketmaster Online www.ticketmaster.com
So Eddie Vedder may not shop here, but that doesn't mean you have to follow every single rock star fad, does it? Ticketmaster has the biggest selection of tickets you can find on the Web: take your pick from rock concerts, baseball games, the ballet, museums, the circus, and more.

Soldout.com www.soldout.com
Pssst...looking for Springsteen tickets? Well, stop skulking around the stadium and head for Soldout.com, where you can buy tickets to the hottest shows in town for outrageously inflated prices. You won't find many bargains here, but when your kid wants to see the Backstreet Boys, what are you gonna do?

Videos

Reel.com www.reel.com
Reel.com is to home videos what the Gap is to clothing; if you're in the market to buy a video, take advantage of their great prices. There's also a list of used videos you can score at a discounted price, as well as a section devoted solely to children's movies. DVD buyers won't be disappointed, either—these are some of the best prices you'll ever see for digital films. Reel.com is definitely limited when it comes to foreign, art, or far-out films, but will satisfy the majority of your mainstream needs. Great search engine, too, as befits a comprehensive site like this.

BigStar.com 3D www.bigstar.com
BigStar.com is an electronic movie superstore that has thousands of videos and DVDs to choose from. In addition to its wide selection of movies for purchase, you'll also find film news that's updated daily, as well as box office results, contests, and gift certificate packages. Nothing terribly original, but the content is solid.

Best Video www.bestvideo.com
Whether you're looking to buy or rent videos, laserdiscs, or DVDs, Best Video has probably got what you want. If you're not sure what you're looking for but are desperate to spend some cash anyway, drop by Hank's Corner, which has film reviews and top picks for independent movies, film noir features, romantic pictures, and more.

Tower Records www.towerrecords.com
The video department of Tower Records is really quite impressive: you can search for films by category (action/adventure, documentary, drama, horror, science fiction, etc.), actor, or director. The trivia challenges are great fun, as well as the picks lists. Great prices, huge catalog.

TLA Video www.tlavideo.com
A cinemaphile's paradise, TLA video invites shoppers to search its catalog according to decade, category, and price range. The selection is far more varied and palatable than that of the big chains (most of the titles fall in the foreign, independent, or alternative genres), and the prices can't be beat. The "Top 25" lists are compulsively surfable.

The on-line leaders in independent, international, alternative, gay/lesbian and adult video sales.

www.tlavideo.com

Acses www.acses.com
If you want to find the very best price for a video, laserdisc, or DVD, head for Acses. This Web site will tell you which movie dealer is offering your desired item for the best price. Search items by title, director, star, or keyword, or browse by genre; the search results are well-organized, with information on shipping costs and delivery times included as well. Acses can find bargains on books on CDs, too.

sports

CNNsi.com www.cnnsi.com
Brought to you by a partnership of CNN and Sports Illustrated, this site spotlights sports, bathing suits, sports, and...more bathing suits. But seriously, CNNsi's coverage is global in scope, with plenty of multimedia features. There's an extensive fun and games section, and some great pages for kids, too.

NFL.com www.nfl.com
NFL.com breaks down the professional football season week by week so you can relish each and every step of the climb to the Super Bowl. Fans can also buy tickets to upcoming games, brush up on stats, look over the career highlights of favorite players, and drop in on the Coaches Club page. There's even a kids page for pint-sized pigskin enthusiasts.

ESPN.com
www.espn.go.com
Hey sports fans: bookmark this site. It's hard to imagine a sports site more comprehensive. In addition to standard coverage of professional and college teams, ESPN takes an in-depth look at careers in sports, drugs and sports, training tips, and video reviews.

GoSki www.goski.com
There isn't any aspect of skiing that's not covered by this informative, easy-to-surf site. Whether you're looking for an overseas resort, wondering about the weather in Aspen, or want to sport the latest in snow gear, check GoSki first. Any site that urges, "Quit the Day Job, Call in Sick" is definitely onto something!

Runner's World www.runnersworld.com
With Runnersworld.com, the only thing you have to do is pick up your legs. The site has great pages on motivation, nutrition, and weight loss, and a training log to track your personal progress.

Explore www.explore.mag

A cool primer on the adventure sports scene, covering rough-and-tumble activities like hiking, kayaking, and snowboarding. There are also guides to sporting gear, adventurous travel spots, and various athletic competitions taking place around the world. Folks worried about mussing their hair need not stop by.

Rock n Road www.rocknroad.com
Rock n Road should be your first foothold for rock climbing info. You can search climbing sites by state, rock type, height, quantity of rock, and much more. Really informative and peppered with beautiful photographs, Rock n Road may be enticing enough to move cyberslugs from behind their computers and into the great outdoors.

Dirtworld.com www.dirtworld.com
The mountain biker's all-inclusive community on the Net. Dirtworld's got trail guides for the United States and Canada, equipment reviews, biking news, and chat groups, plus a useful classified section where you can buy or sell used bikes and accessories.

Pete's Bikindex www.bikindex.com
A no-nonsense cycling resource that's packed with lists of training groups, places to buy bike equipment online, and info for folks looking for riding partners. Not the most visually exciting spot on the Web, Petes Bikindex makes up in content what it lacks in aesthetics.

Women's Sports Network www.wspn.net

This site is strictly devoted to women's sports; while the scope is somewhat limited, what's here is informative and useful. Among the best pages are the backpacking checklist and heart monitor log. The section devoted to high school-aged athletes is a great idea, but could stand to be expanded.

Active USA www.activeusa.com
Arranged by region, Active USA has information on sporting events and competitions taking place around the country. Practically every sport conceivable is listed, from fencing to snowshoeing to water-skiing. Events for disabled athletes are listed as well. If nothing exciting is going on in your area, you can always check out the feature stories, which you can search by sport.

Tune in Sports www.tuneinsports.com
The font size could be raised a point or two, but considering the scope of this site, it's understandable why the creators wanted to save space. There are over 1,800 sports schedules listed here on a daily basis, as well as hometown pages and message boards. Timely and comprehensive.

Charged: Extreme Leisure www.charged.com
Search your favorite way to goof off by clicking on the leisure, action, sin, or adventure buttons at this kooky e-zine. Its definition of "sports" is pretty broad (cross country skate boarding, nude sunbathing, and tree climbing are profiled), but the articles are fun and well written. If you're a jock of the old school variety, there are plenty of other sites from which to get a macho sports fix; leave Charged to the weirdos on the jungle gym.

sports

International Sports Museums and Halls of Fame
www.sportshalls.com
Where can an up-and-comer go for a little inspiration? How about the International Swimming Hall of Fame, located in Fort Lauderdale, Florida? Sports enthusiasts passing through New York will be pleased to know that there are no less than eight athletic museums in that state. And fans of women's basketball may just want to plan a trip to Knoxville, Tennessee, where that Hall of Fame is located. The site isn't merely a databank of addresses; it also has detailed descriptions of the museums it lists. A handy resource.

Cricket Unlimited www.cricketunlimited.co.uk
Sick of watching baseball players dribbling tobacco juice and scratching themselves? Then check out Cricket Unlimited, where the competition is just as fierce but not nearly as vulgar. All kidding aside, this is a great resource for cricket fans who want breaking news, live scores, and players' stats. There's also extensive coverage of the World Cup, as well as articles and interviews with the players.

Everest Mountain Zone www.everest.mountainzone.com
One of the toughest climbs on the planet, Mount Everest has captivated climbers and adventurers for years. Everest Mountain Zone brings together all the stories, facts, and fantastical tales surrounding expeditions over the past 50 years. Includes live cybercasts of actual climbs, interviews with the climbers, and scientific information about the region.

Great Sports www.greatsports.com
If you're interested in a sport that doesn't receive a lot of coverage in the mainstream media, look no further than Great Sports. It has links to sites devoted to such diverse sports as arm wrestling, darts, squash, swimming, and rugby. There's plenty offered in the way of popular sports like tennis, football, and boxing, too. Pretty overwhelming if you're just surfing, but a great resource for people who know what kinds of information they want to access.

Fantasy Sports Guide www.fantasysportsguide.com

If you've ever wanted to compile a sports dream team, here's your big chance. This Web site features links to fantasy sports software, electronic games, statistic services, newsletters, cheat sheets, and ranking lists for everything from auto racing to football to hockey. A great resource for wannabe team owners and coaches (and maybe actual ones, too!)

Sports Jones Magazine www.sportsjones.com
Updated daily, Sports Jones will give you a fix on all things athletic. Sections include books, culture and politics, humor, stats and analysis, and interviews. It's definitely more quirky than most sports sites, but that's part of this magazine's appeal. There's lots to explore, but it may be wasted on folks who don't have a sense of humor.

House of Boxing www.houseofboxing.com
Nifty to look at and easy to search, House of Boxing gives fans everything they need to know about rankings, weigh-ins, fight schedules, and spotlight matches. There are also interviews with an impressive list of fighters and some great video footage.

The International Olympic Committee www.olympic.org
This is the official site of the Olympics, which can be accessed in either French or English. Surprisingly, most of the information is geared toward future games; there's very little mention of past victories and defeats which make the Olympics so fascinating. Still, if you're looking for news about the actual organization of the games, this is the place to go. For information on specific contests and athletes, look elsewhere.

Worldsport.com www.worldsport.com
Wow! There are sports on this site that you've probably never heard of: bandy, korfball, pelota vasca, sambo, and wushu are just some of the selections you can choose from on its lengthy table of contents. No fear, though; sports like football, baseball, and hockey are included, too. The content is simply breathtaking, and the sleek, simple design makes Worldsport.com a pleasure to search.

NBA.com www.nba.com
NBA.com offers the latest news about the league, team features, game highlights, sound clips and photos, chats and mailboxes, and a history section. Stop by the "All Access" section to view the action around the court and in the locker room — it's the next best thing to being there yourself.

Freebord www.freebord.com
Featuring some of the best graphics and videos around, Freebord is really one big advertisement for a snowboard that is designed to execute the heart stopping turns, slides, and flips that strike terror in the hearts of skiers. Be sure to check out the videos, which will give you newfound respect for the death-defying practitioners of this sport.

Harlem Globetrotters
www.harlemglobetrotters.com
Like the Globetrotters themselves, this site features a lot of compelling action. The graphics and sound effects are great, as is the extensive history lesson on the team. This site is very dedicated to promoting the many cultural, economic, and social contributions of the team, both past and present. Highly entertaining, but not as fun as attending an actual game.

The Daily Soccer www.dailysoccer.com
Stay out of trouble (and the stadium) and log on to The Daily Soccer, where can follow your favorite teams without getting mauled by fellow fans. Read game coverage from around the world or get the scoop on new players — most all the info is for European leagues.

Sports Hits www.sportshits.com
A sports ticker tape of sorts, Sports Hits features news, daily odds, trivia, TV schedules, tickets, and more. It's also got links to over 60 sports sections from newspapers across the country. There are even gambling tips and horse racing results. The design is a bit lurid, but is nevertheless a must-bookmark for sports fans seeking a content-rich Web site.

The Yoga Site www.yogasite.com
The Yoga Site seeks to promote fitness, flexibility, and stress relief through this time-honored discipline. Practically all of your questions about yoga will be answered on the FAQ page, and those that aren't can be submitted via e-mail. Seasoned practitioners and novices alike will appreciate the teacher directory, style guide, and organization listings. A retreat directory is also here.

Federation Internationale de Football Association www.fifa.com
That's soccer to you, Yank. Dial up this page to discover (or revel) in the depths with which this sport is revered—every place but the United States, that is. FIFA features articles, interviews, regulations, laws of the game, lists of competitions, a calendar of events, and much, much more. There's also extensive coverage of the women's leg of this sport.

Golf Online www.golfonline.com
If spending hours on the greens isn't enough for you, then head to Golf Online for the golf fix you need. It's got feature stories, course guides, games, contests, a list of rules, tips for all levels of players, and a section devoted to women's golf. Easy to search, loaded with information, and best of all, no stuffy country club restrictions!

In the Crease www.inthecrease.com
In addition to headline hockey news and coverage of all 8 leagues, this site has tons of great editorial columns. Features include Slapshots, A Year in the Life, The House of Ill Repute, Future Watch, Echoes from the Past, and Score Card.

WNBA.com www.wnba.com
The most successful women's basketball league around is here to stay (finally). WNBA.com gives you all the stats, trades, injuries, scores, and schedules you need to cheer the ladies on. There's also a photo gallery and daily video clip for your viewing pleasure.

Tennis.com www.tennis.com
Get the scoop on all the top-seeded players at this tennis megasite. In addition
to news headlines and athlete interviews, Tennis.com also has sections devoted to instruction, equipment, fitness, and travel.

Black Baseball www.blackbaseball.com
This page offers a full-fledged history lesson on the Negro Baseball Leagues. It's a collection of articles, book reviews, interviews, player and team profiles, sound clips, and photo galleries that are informative and fascinating. If your knowledge of baseball is limited to the major leagues, you owe it to yourself to look up this site. Attractively organized and simple to search.

College Hoops Insider www.collegeinsider.com
Whether you want to know which coach will be leading your favorite team, who's being recruited by which school, or what a player's stats and standings are, you can find out at College Hoops Insider. Articles can be searched by conference or school, and there are links to columns from around the country. Great content, easy searching.

John Skilton's Baseball Links www.baseball-links.com
The home page of John Skilton's Baseball Links proclaims, "If you can't find what you're looking for here, then it probably doesn't exist," and that's probably true. It provides over 5,000 links to baseball sites around the Web, and the selections aren't limited to the major leagues, either. There are also sites devoted to the minors, international leagues, high school and college ball, and cards and collectibles. Extremely well organized and tremendous in scope.

NCAA Online www.ncaa.org
Fans of college sports will find all the need-to-know info right here, for fencing, skiing, track, and wrestling as well as baseball, basketball, and football. Exhaustive coverage and quality reporting make NCAA Online one of the hottest sports sites around.

SportsParents www.sportsparents.com
Keep your tots out of trouble: get them into a league! SportsParents features advice on coaching, nutrition, sportsmanship, and equipment. A children's commentary page helps to round out the picture. If you've got any questions, you can always ask a member of the expert panel that's comprised of a sports doctor, nutritionist, and psychologist.

Sports Illustrated for Women www.siforwomen.com
For the latest news on women's sports, stop by SI for Women. You can search such categories as basketball, books, feature articles and training, or hang out in one of the chat rooms. Health and fitness info make SI for Women a sure bet for players and fans.

The Official Site of Major League Baseball
www.majorleaguebaseball.com
This exhaustive site features audio of live games in progress, videos that change each day, scoreboards, player profiles, fan forums, and the scoop on the latest draft picks. You can also find out how various hitters have done against different pitchers, and a statistical breakdown of any two players in the league. If you love major league baseball, bookmark this site.

Kick! www.kicksports.com
Kick! is a slight misnomer; it's really a site devoted to running, jogging, and racing, none of which involve kicking (if memory serves correctly). However, if you are looking for tips on getting motivated, setting rhythms, or training for a big race, you're sure to find what you need at this site. There are even suggestions for dealing with such annoyances as mad dogs (respect their boundaries, act nuts if attacked) and crazy drivers (same advice).

Just Sports for Women www.justwomen.com
For the latest news on women's sports, stop by Just Sports for Women. You can search such categories as basketball, books, feature articles and training, or hang out in one of the chat rooms. Gets props for its no-nonsense coverage, but could stand to cover a lot more sports.

travel

Preview Travel www.previewtravel.com
The one-stop directory for travel planning and research. While Preview offers several services for the traveler, including fare finders, cruise reviews, and travel news, the Destination Guides, nestled right next to the Hotel, Car & Airfare reservation section, make this site a must see. Offering "the same information that travel agents use," Preview Travel shares the tips and tricks from the inside with freewheeling customers for free!

Concierge.com
www.concierge.com
The online home for *Condé Nast Traveler*, Concierge.com is solid, standard travel information. While budget advice crops up here and there and some pricier options can be found, this site is geared towards the basic, comfortable, but not too high maintenance traveler. Check destinations, hotels, airfares, books, and special sections on romantic getaways, and beaches and islands.

Council on International Educational Exchange www.ciee.org
The umbrella for study, work, volunteer, and travel abroad opportunities, CIEE is the heart of international educational exchange. For language and academic programs abroad, check the home page. For cheap airfares, destination advice, and short and long-term employment options, see the Council Travel section. Though the site is geared toward students, fares are often open to anyone or available at a slightly higher rate.

Salon Travel www.salon.com/travel
Among the finest travel writing on the Web. Engaging, intelligent writing on new weekly topics that range from guides to exotic wedding locales to tales of turbulence woes. Salon finds the humor and wit in almost any travel mishap or miracle.

LastMinute.com www.lastminute.com
Romantic notion meets cool execution in LastMinute.com, a sleek site that encourages „spontaneous, romantic, and sometimes adventurous behavior" by providing unbeatable prices on airfare, vacation packages, gifts, and more. The site also features a cool selection of services from dog walkers to grocery delivery, and guarantees that if you find the same offer for less elsewhere, LastMinute.com will refund the difference and then some. A superior service.

PlanetRider www.planetrider.com
It might as well be called WebTravelSiteFinder. This Zagat's of travel Web sites covers travel advice for every lifestyle; business, adventure, budget, and high-end travelers will find expansive reviews and ratings of Web sites tailored to their specific needs.

Travel Channel www.travelchannel.com

Television's trusty travel pros bring their documentary-style stories to the Web. From featured exhibitions (with 360-degree photo walking tours) to live video footage, news briefs, weather updates, currency converters, and maps, the Travel Channel is the first stop for practical education on hospitable destinations around the globe.

SmarTraveler www.smartraveler.com
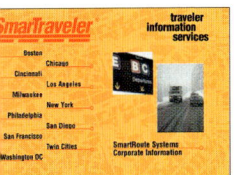
When planning a trip by car, dial up SmarTraveler first. It's got traffic and transit information, up-to-date weather conditions, specific street directions, and listings of where to get food and lodging. The site is somewhat limited in scope; it only has travel information on 11 cities and their surrounding areas. Still, if you're headed to or away from one of these places, you can probably benefit from SmarTraveler's clear, simple directions.

CDC Traveler's Health Information www.cdc.gov/travel
Need to know what vaccinations are required for your trip to Bali? The Department of Health's Centers for Disease Control and Prevention have the hard facts on shots, vaccines, and common travel-related maladies. Check the graphical travel map to find out what's recommended for your destination—and travel safe.

Travel Warnings & Advisories www.travel.state.gov
Wars don't stop for tourists. But with the Web, there's no reason to accidentally wander into rebel fighting on your honeymoon. The State Department maintains an informative and well-organized site with travel advisories and political profiles on countries around the world. Find out what's going on, where not to go, and how to travel safely in less than secure areas.

Foreign Languages for Travelers www.travlang.com/languages
The jackpot for language learning online. This amazingly useful and mind-bogglingly vast site offers over 60 languages. Select the language you speak, the language you want to learn, and the kind of information you want—basic words, numbers, shopping terms, directions, or times and dates. Then read the translations or click on the words to hear them pronounced in Real Audio. The design could use some help, but the site more than redeems itself in helpfulness and ease of use.

Universal Currency Converter www.xe.net/ucc
Moneymaking is a universal fact of life. Don't get caught confused at the counter next vacation—plug in the laptop, type in the money amount you need converted, select the currencies, and in seconds find the exact exchange amount. The UCC can't pick out souvenirs, but it can make the cost make sense in just about every currency on the globe.

transportation

Travelocity www.travelocity.com
While the chances of actually purchasing any of the supercheap tickets at Travelocity are slimmer than you'd expect, the prices make persistence well worth it. More than any other airfare search site, Travelocity often turns up hard-to-find deals, making it a gem for the flexible traveler. Be sure to check out the Faretracker service, an e-mail notification agent that reports fare hikes and dips for your specified destinations.

Priceline www.priceline.com
One of the few too-good-to-be-true sites that actually is. Priceline lets you name the price you want to pay for airline tickets, hotel rooms, and more; you enter your bid, and Priceline notifies you within an hour if it's a go. If your bid is rejected, you can try again, but you'll have to adjust either the date, fare, or the destination airport. If you must leave at a certain time or on a certain airline Priceline isn't for you; but for flexible flyers, coast-to-coast flights for $200 or less aren't unheard of.

Expedia www.expedia.com
The most reliable airline ticket purchase site on the Web. What Microsoft's cyber travel agency lacks in cheap deals it makes up for in rock-solid consistency; punch in the dates and credit card numbers, and fear not—an electronic ticket will be waiting at the gate. It's worth it to try a number of different possibilities before booking your flight, as fares often vary wildly by day and time of departure.

Lowestfare.com www.lowestfare.com
While the veracity of its title is debatable, this site's fairly comprehensive range of package deals are worth taking a look at. The fares themselves are often comparable to other travel search sites, but frequently updated specials, often in combination with hotels, car rentals, or cruises, keep this site true to its name.

Webflyer www.webflyer.com
Managing frequent flyer miles can be complicated for the business or leisure traveler— Webflyer to the rescue with travel deals, live chat, and advice on how to make the elusive airfare currency work for you. You can research and register for a number of different frequent flyer programs at this site, or link directly to your online accounts with dozens of different airlines. A super resource.

RV Link
www.rvlink.com
Why travel in a cramped minivan when you could go in a luxury vehicle? If you've ever considered renting an RV, check out this Web site. It will tell you how to make online reservations, where to camp, and fun places to stop along the way to your ultimate destination. This site could definitely be developed a bit more, but it is a great starting point for anyone interested in this mode of travel.

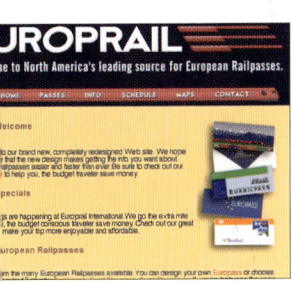

Europrail International
www.europrail.on.ca
You may have to fly to get to it, but once in Europe, take advantage of one of the world's most scenic and accessible railways. Europrail's web site offers information on the rail passes, searchable schedules, and downloadable maps of rail lines across Europe. Presently tickets cannot be purchased online, but telephone and fax reference is provided.

Amtrak www.amtrak.com
So there's only one rail service in the United States—at least it's organized. Schedules, destination guides, fares, and specials are all at Amtrak online. It takes a few clicks to get the station codes of arrival and departure points, but once you have them it's fairly easy to find out schedules, check on arrival status, and purchase tickets online.

travel guides

Fodor's www.fodors.com

An elegant, easily navigable Web site from one of the first names in travel. In addition to the usual resources on travel planning, Fodor's lets you custom-tailor a "mini guide" for your trip. First pick your destination, then click through the checklist of options to choose your budget, dining preferences, hotel, and nighttime activities. Print out the results and go to town—easy!

Frommer's www.frommers.com
Despite the glaring "Budget Travel" logos, Frommer's online is not just for the rugged traveler. Updated seven days a week, the articles and editorials cover breaking news on special deals and hot vacation spots, in addition to sharing perennial insider advice on how to make traveling a little less taxing on the mind and the wallet.

Fielding's Worldwide www.fieldingtravel.com

 Rather standard travel guides for hundreds of destinations around the world, with a healthy dose of humor and adventure to boot. The truly unique side of Fieldings' can be glimpsed at the Danger Finders and Black Flag sections of the site, for the "hard core adventurer." Whether you are or not, the guides are entertaining, bold, and at the very least can provide a sense of where not to go.

Rough Guides www.travel.roughguides.com
Not every traveler wants a lazy vacation—for hands-on, rough-and-tumble adventurers, the Rough Guides travel series leads the way. Browse through their featured destinations or take a look at the often-obscure cities listed in their exhaustive database (Acapulco to Cairo to Zurich). With historical background and practical information on lodging, food, customs, and nightlife, the Rough Guides online offer comforting introductions for those traveling less familiar terrain.

Lonely Planet www.lonelyplanet.com

 The classic backpacker travel guide. Lonely Planet has practically peopled the earth with its scouts, writers, faithful followers, and intrepid travelers—now it's staking a claim on the Web with this information-packed site. While the site lacks the play-by-play details on local restaurants and hostels that you find in the book, it does cover each country in the series with historical and cultural profiles, slide shows, getting there and away tips, and valuable information on visas, money, and climate, both political and meteorological.

destinations

Timeout Worldwide www.timeout.com
The long-standing champion of insider entertainment information spans the globe with this cultural HQ online. From Barcelona to Budapest, Timeout has the scoop on what's going on, when, where, and what's best. Prepare for trips or just explore the virtual scene to find out what's happening elsewhere in the world.

CitySearch.com www.citysearch.com
So many cities, so much to do! CitySearch gives you the hottest restaurant, shopping, arts, and entertainment listings for over 30 cities in the United States and abroad—each city has its own massive site. There's info for locals as well as out-of-towners here, loads of columns and interactive boards, and the kind of writing that's savvy without being snotty. A must-see.

National Park Service www.nps.gov
America may not bristle with as many majestic purple mountains as it used to, but with 376 parks spanning over eight million acres under the protection of the National Park Service, there's still a heck of a lot to explore. Search NPS's online directory of parks, battlefields, monuments, scenic trails, and historic sites by state, theme, or detailed regional maps.

EuroTrip www.eurotrip.com
That America's not-so-distant relative Europe remains one of the most popular backpacking destinations should come as no surprise—but finding those out-of-the-way hostel gems is more difficult than ever these days. Head to EuroTrip for help: it offers the latest information on hostels, restaurants, arts, and entertainment, plus special features on how to pack (light!) and what to read while you're there.

London Net www.londonnet.co.uk
Once you've seen Big Ben and Buckingham, get out and really see the town! London Net has the tips you need, with listings for theater, art, music, films, and events, plus daily updated news and gossip. For planning your vacation or your evening, London Net gives you everything but the tea and cakes.

The Paris Pages www.paris.org
The world capital for romance, red wine, and rude waiters. Though the site is none-too-easy on the eyes, the resources it provides are undeniably vast. Take some time to read about the city's history, culture, and countless monuments, or head right for the sites, accommodations, and eateries. It might take some time to find your bearings, but better in the comfort of home than with an unwieldy map on the streets of Pa-ree.

Roadside America www.roadsideamerica.com

The road trip seems to be a patriotic requirement—it's more fun than taxes, and more entertaining and offbeat than you'd think. Roadside America ferrets out the obscure, bizarre, curious, and creepy to share with the rest of the world at its Sight of the Week section (archives available). From the town atop a burning mine in Centralia, PA to the Fremont Troll of Seattle, see the best of what the country has to offer, by car, or online.

The Village Voice www.villagevoice.com
For the opinionated, anti-p.c. interpretation of what's going on in America's cultural capital, check the Voice. The free paper that loves to complain (and people love to complain about) actually keeps its finger on the pulse of New York politics and culture. Always a fun read, online or off.

Microsoft Sidewalk www.sidewalk.com
Surviving in an unfamiliar city is a snap with Microsoft's Sidewalk.com. Simply type in your zip code and the site locates everything from pediatricians to local lumber stores—it even provides driving directions. You'll also find restaurant reviews and tourist tips on this super-navigable site. A great tool for newbies or natives.

Africa Online www.africaonline.com
Arguably the most diverse and least-understood continent on the planet. Browse Africa Online to find out what's going on today in politics, education, health, culture, and the natural world. Less a travel site than an all-around portal, Africa Online should be your first stop for news, resources, and features direct from the source.

travel destinations

TravelAsia.Net www.travelasianet.com

The name says it all. Geared toward both business and leisure travelers, the site includes event listings and historical and cultural spots of interest in the fast-changing East. Asia is a big place, so more specific research on your destination is advisable, but this travel hub for the Eastern Hemisphere is a good starting place. (For Hong Kong travelers, check the Hong Kong Tourist Association at www.hkta.org. For Beijing, see the Scene at www.beijingscene.com.)

France.com www.france.com

Ooh la la! they say. Actually, it is doubtful this is said anywhere other than in Pepe LePew cartoons and on this Web site. But, say what it will, the site is a valuable resource for anyone planning a trip to the land of fine wine and smoke-friendly restaurants. Book hotels, buy tickets, reserve cars, even check the classifieds in case the country of l'amour just won't let you go.

lodging

All Hotels www.all-hotels.com

All is a bit of a stretch, but the number of hotels, bed and breakfasts, and discount lodgings on this online directory is certainly impressive. Use All Hotels to check out the options before you get to the taxi stand. You can even make reservations online for major hotels and chains planetwide.

Hotel Discount Reservations www.hoteldiscount.com
The most efficient hotel reservation site online. Pick a city, select criteria for number of persons, dates, and nights desired and all available hotels pop up with location information, maps, the exact price, and the option to book instantly. Prices are among the lowest we've seen on the Web.

International Bed & Breakfast Pages
www.ibbp.com

For those vacations where you never get out of bed, you might as well find a friendly and/or romantic place to rest your weary self. International Bed & Breakfast Pages is devoted to the quaint, the cute, and the cozy around the globe, for all those discriminating travelers who appreciate the little things like clean, quiet lodging away from the crowds.

Cyber Rentals www.cyberrentals.com
Find a home away from home without ever leaving the computer. Cyber Rentals offers pictures, descriptions, rental rates, and contact information for thousands of homes around the world. While most of them are currently in the United States, Cyber Rentals is a great resource to post your own lodging to rent or find a vacation home for that week, month, or year away from it all.

Places to Stay www.placestostay.com
Book online, in advance from hundreds of choices of hotels, bed and breakfasts, inns, and resorts around the country — Places to Stay even lets you know when you're getting a deal. While the lodging included per city is far from comprehensive, there is enough range in price, size, location and availability to make this site worthwhile. Check back often for special deals, fare changes, and availability.

Hostels.com www.hostels.com

For the budget-, adventure-, or just plain people-lovin' traveler. Hostels range in price and quality from town to town, but the idea is the same — check out what's available, for how much, and what you might expect at this web hub for communal travel options.

wacky

Dancing Megababy Site www.megababy.com
As the name suggests, you will find a dancing baby here. Not simply the animated dancing baby that made waves on the Net and on *Ally McBeal;* a whole cottage industry seems to have sprung up around the strange little guy, with hundreds of new baby animations, styles, and grooves popping up daily. Contests, movies, and dancing babies await!

Find A Grave www.findagrave.com
Not even death can keep dedicated fans from the object of their idolatry: Now they can set flowers at the celebrity headstone of their choice with Find A Grave. Search graves by name, location, or claim to fame — Jim Morrison to the Habsburg monarchs. Check back often for new listings — you never know whose gonna go tomorrow!

The Hamster Dance www.hamsterdance.com
What does it mean?? Hundreds of hamsters of all shapes and sizes (well, only three but some of them are turned around) boppin' all over the place in perfect unison. Take a look and see if it doesn't make you smile.

Virtual Dog www.virtualdog.com
It's just like it sounds — go to the virtual pound and pick your virtual pup! There's plenty to keep you and your mutt occupied at Virtual Dog's ongoing adventure story, where owner and pooch compete with other players based on their dogs' wealth and health. In Tamagachi style, the virtual dog needs to be attended to daily — the better you care for it/him/her, the more likely you are to win!

Deathclock www.deathclock.com
Time is running out — find out exactly how much you have left at this sadistic but somehow fascinating site. Type in your birth date and year to find out your Personal Day of Death (in seconds!)—you can choose the optimistic, pessimistic, or sadistic forecast. Special features include celebrity predictions, a write-your-own-obit section, and, for the truly obsessed, download your personal deathclock screen saver for a second-by-second countdown to the big, bad day.

Superbad www.superbad.com
Ten minutes to spare? Just browsing? Superbad is a page clicker's dream. To figure out what it is, just keep clicking. Amazingly entertaining considering it provides absolutely no information or guidance.

women

Oxygen www.oxygen.com
A sleek but accessible, informative, and entertaining body for women's health, humor, and happiness. Branching out from Oxygen's sharply designed homepage are the Ladies' Room, a collection of stories, advice and venting grounds, and links to stories from the equally solid women's magazines ThriveOnline, MomsOnline, Electra, kaChing, and Oprah. Check "the lab" for daily stories, quotes, and excerpts audio enhanced and with an eye on the future of technology.

Women.com
www.women.com
If you need answers but don't have the time to browse several sites, Women.com was made for you. The site includes insider info on careers, selected articles from popular magazines, a recipe finder, a party planner, and just about everything else a busy woman needs. Fun, extensive content.

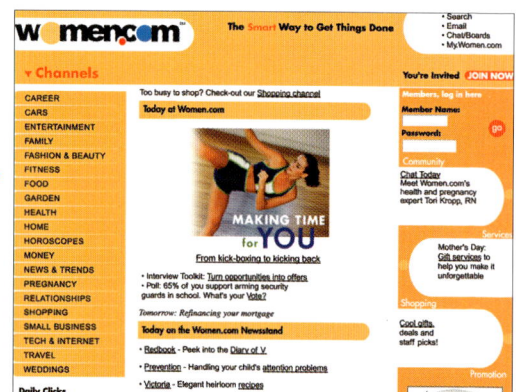

ChickClick www.chickclick.com
This site has attitude, but that's not all. It's also got links to a big bunch of awesome, women-oriented sites like Breakup Girl and Maxi that perk up the brain and get the estrogen flowing. It's also got hilarious e-postcards, classifieds, auctions and free e-mail and home pages. Just like the logo says, these girl sites don't fake it.

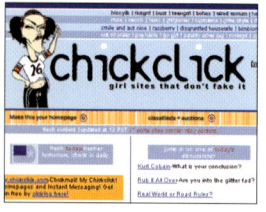

iVillage.com www.ivillage.com

You have fifteen errands to run on your lunch hour — where should you go first? iVillage.com. Now, tasks like buying stamps, getting advice on money management, and finding computing answers can be completed all with a few clicks. This family of sites has interesting quizzes to explore (Should you switch careers?), a book club, parenting help, and even a pet name finder to streamline your life.

gURL Mag/zine www.gurl.com
A fantastic 'zine devoted to all things femme: pages include "Looks Aren't Everything," "Dead Women You Should Know About," "The Sexuality Series," "Those Sucky Emotions," "Splitsville," and "Street Hassle." There are also reading lists, interviews with famous authors (Judy Blume, Francesca Lia Block), and articles on such topics as blending in with the crowd and body piercing. Smart, subversive, and visually dazzling.

Her Health Online www.herhealth.com
Don't let the holistic slant of this site mislead you: yes, there's the typical information on vitamins, animal testing, and yoga, but there are also articles on sexuality, body image, and strength training. A valuable look at health practices that exist outside the traditional approaches of Western medicine, Her Health Online is definitely worth your precious time.

A Celebration of Women Writers
www.cs.cmu.edu/afs/cs.cmu.edu/user/mmbt/www/women/writers.html
This incredibly exhaustive site celebrates the contribution of women writers throughout history — and when they say history, they're talking 3000 B.C. and beyond, everyone from Sappho to Anne Sexton. Browse the list by century, country, or author name; many of the listings have links to other sites devoted exclusively to a particular writer.

Bust Magazine www.bust.com
Find the fashion mags in the checkout line — for slick, savvy, stories, chats and links lists written by, for, and about women at their most badass, go to Bust. A member of the ever growing front of women online who aren't afraid of technology, Bust puts out its online version of the print zine with the same raw force.

1805 women

Women's Health Interactive www.womens-health.com

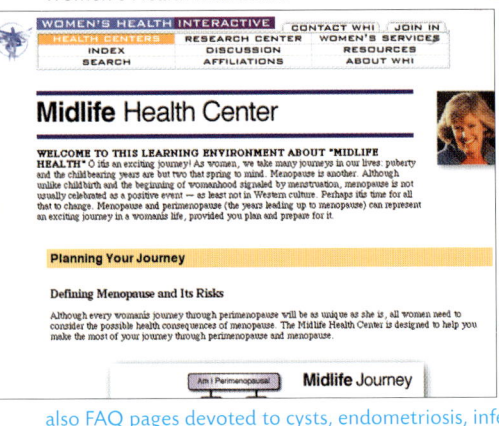

Women's Health Interactive is dedicated to promoting an open exchange of information on women's health. Topics include midlife sexuality, menstrual disorders, an overview of the reproductive system, preparing for pregnancy, and pathways to parenthood. There are also FAQ pages devoted to cysts, endometriosis, infertility, and other health problems. Well organized and very educational.

Go, Girl! Magazine www.gogirlmag.com
Go, Girl Magazine is dedicated to getting girls and women of all ages involved in sports. Founder Melissa Joulwan decided to launch the e-zine after discovering that most fitness publications are really just fashion mags in disguise. Her publication offers feature articles on women's involvement in various sports, editorial rants, and a list of "what's hot/what's not" for women. (Hot: a coffee table book on a woman's solo trek across the Australian outback; Not: The Joey Buttafuoco Show.)

Hues www.hues.net
A women's magazine without the sex polls, makeup protocols, and diet regimes; just good old down-to-earth writing about women as they are. HUES—Hear Us Emerging Sisters—is a bimonthly multi-cultural print and now online publication focused on feminism, music, race, gender, and culture with refreshingly solid writing by for and about empowering the new breed of woman.

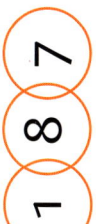

index

#1 Free Stuff 162
1st Headlines 123
4anything 48
4freequotes.com 41
7thonSixth 68
24 Hour Museum 26
50Something.net 150
411 Pets 106
555-1212.com 56
800 dot com 159

A
AAAAI 101
AAA.com 42
AARP 149
ABCNews.com 81
ABI World 79
About.com 49
About.com Fashion 67
About.com Religion 144
accessories 153
Acses 169
Active USA 171
Acupuncture.com 100
Adbusters 26
Ad Critic 76
AdoptioNetwork 131
Advanced Book Exchange 28
AEGis 100
AFL-CIO 33
Africa Online 181
AgeNet 149
Ain't It Cool News 75
airline tickets 176, 178
Airwalk.com 167
AJR News Link 123
Akropolis.net 105
Alcoholics Anonymous 102
All Experts.com 140
All Hotels 182
All-Music Guide 114
All Politics 132
All Things Automotive 39
Alta Vista Translations 139
alt.culture 26
alternative health 100
Alternative Health News Online 100
Alzheimer's Association 150
Amazon.com 27
Amazon.com Music 116
American Association of Retired Persons 149
American Ballet Theater 24
American Bar Association 112
American Booksellers Association 28
American Cancer Society 96
American Heart Association 96
American Journalism Review News Link 123
American Medical Association 96
American School Director 62
American Social Health Association 101
Amnesty International 133
Amtrak 179
Ancestry.com 56
AnyWho 55
Apartment Life 107
Appliances.com 159
Arbor 101
Architecture 25
Argus Clearinghouse 138
Armani Exchange 154
Armchair Millionaire 81
Artchive, The 22
Art.com 165
ArtMuseum.net 22
art museums 22, 23, 26 52
artnet.com 25
Art Resources 22
arts and culture 22
Ask Dr. Weil 100
Ask Jeeves 140
Ask Jeeves for Kids 110
Astrology Zone 66
At Health 99
Atlantic Live Lobsters Delivered 162
Atlantic Unbound 122
ATM Locator 32
AtomFilms 70
auctions 152
Auricle 119
autobytel.com 38
Auto.com 39
automobiles 36
Autoshop-Online 37

B
Baby Zone 130
Back2College 59
Ballroom Dance Resource 24
banking 31, 32, 80, 177
Bankrate.com 80
bankruptcy 79
BarnesandNoble.com 27
Bartlett's Familiar Quotations 139
Bazaar 69
BBC Online 71
beauty 67
BeautyNet 69
Bebe 154
Bedtime-Story 131
Ben & Jerry's Online 88
Benjamin Moore Paints 104
Berlitz 61
Bestswimwear.com 157
Best Video 169
Better Business Bureau 158
Better Homes & Gardens 104

Beyond.com 45
Bidder's Edge 153
BigCharts 79
Big Deal Worldwide 167
BigStar.com 169
Billboard Online 118
Bill Nye the Science Guy 146
Biography.com 57
BizRate 158
Black Baseball 174
Blackhawk Automotive Museum 42
Blip, The 92
Bliss! 53
Bloomberg 85
Bloomingdale's 151
Blue Book of Grammar and Punctuation 142
Bluefly.com 151
Blue Note 117
BMI 120
Bobbi Brown 164
Bob Vila 103
Body Politic 52
Bolt 111
Bonus.com 109
Book of Zines 128
books 27
BottomDollar.com 150
Breakup Girl 50
BreezeNet's Guide to Rental Cars 40
Britannica Internet Guide 48
British Monarchy 133
British Vogue 69
Brooks Brothers 153
Budget Rent A Car 40
business 29
BusinessWeek Online 30
Bust Magazine 187
Busy Teachers' Website K-12 59
Buy.co.uk 30

C

Caffeinated Magazine 90
Calwine 161
Campmor 167
Campus Tours 61
Car And Driver Online 39
car dealers 37, 38, 39, 41
cards 162
CareerBuilder 36
CareerMosaic 34
CareerPath.com 33
careers 33
CareGuide.com 131
CarPoolers.com 40
car rental 40
cars 36
Cars.com 37
CarsDirect.com 38
Car Talk 38
Cartoon Network 75
Casino Titanic 95
Caviar Assouline 162
CDC Traveler's Health Information 177
CD Now 116
celebrities 57, 63, 64, 76
Census Bureau 143

Charged: Extreme Leisure 171
Chess.net 94
ChickClick 184
China News Digest 123
Christianity.net 144
Christian Science Monitor 126
Chumbo.com 43
CIA World Factbook 139
city guides 180, 181
Classical Insites 117
classifieds 152
Clinique 164
clothes 153
CNET 46
CNNfn 79
CNN Interactive 127
CNNsi.com 170
CNN Style 69
Coalition for Positive Sexuality 53
Collector's Universe.com 66
college 58, 59, 60, 61
CollegeDates.com 51
College Hoops Insiders 174
CollegeNET 60
Colors 128
comedy 66, 72, 77
Comedy Central.com 72
Comedy.com 66
comics 64, 65, 75
Comics.com 65
Common Reader, A 28
Company Sleuth 78
CompareNet 157
Compton's Encyclopedia Online 141
computers 43
Concierge.com 176
Condomania 160
consumer guides 157
Consumer Information Center 158
Consumer Reports Online 158
CookieRecipe.com 86
cooking 85, 86, 87, 90
Cooking.com 86
CoolSavings.com 162
Coolshopping.com 154
Cool Site of the Day 49
Cool Works 34
Costume Site 69
Council on International Educational Exchange 176
Country.com 117
coupons 162
Crate & Barrel 165
Crayola FamilyPlay 108
CRAYON 124
Cricket Unlimited 172
Crutchfield 159
CSKAuto.com 37
C-Span.org 126
CultureFinder 22
Culturekiosque.com 25
Currency Converter 177
CyberInvest 84
CyberMatch Worldwide 51
CyberMom.com 129
Cyber Rentals 182

D

Daily Apple 102
Daily Soccer 173
Daily.WAV 66
dance 24, 27
Dancebot 24
Dancing Megababy Site 183
Datek Online 83
dating 50
DaveCentral 45
DC Comics 64
Dean & Deluca 160
Deathclock 184
Deja 42
dELiAs 154
Dell 44
Democracy Network 133
DEN 77
DesignerFinder 103
DesignerOutlet.com 155
dictionaries 97, 139, 140
Dinner and a Movie 71
directories 54
Dirtworld.com 171
Discover Magazine 146
Discovery Channel Online 57
Discovery Kids 110
disinformation 26
DisneyBlast 108
Disney Internet Guide 62
DivorceNet 113
DLJdirect 83
doctors 98, 100, 129
Do-It-Yourself Congressional Investigations Kit 136
Doonesbury Electronic Town Hall 134
Dooney & Bourke 157
DoubleTake Magazine 25
Doughnet 111
Dow Jones Business Directory 31
Dream-Escape.org 119
Drew's Script-o-Rama 71
Dr. Greene's House Calls 129
DrinkWine.com 89
Driveways of the Rich and Famous 76
Dr. Ruth 52
Dr. Toy 109
Drudge Report 121
Drug Free Resource Net 97
Drugstore.com 164
Dumb Laws 136

E

Eating Disorders 101
eBay 152
Edmund's Automobile Buyer's Guide 38
EDSITEment 59
education 56
Educational Resources Information Center 58
Educational Testing Service 61
Education World 57
EFridge 103
Egghead 46
Electoral Websites 138
Electra.com 69
Electric Telegraph 126
Electric Vehicle Association of the Americas 42

electronics 158
electronics.net 159
Elibrary 138
Elle Online 69
EmbassyWeb.com 133
Emeril's Homebase 87
EMF 114
EMusic.com 116
Encarta Encyclopedia 141
Encarta Online Library 138
Encarta Virtual Globe Online 140
Encyclopedia Britannica 141
encyclopedias 141, 142
Enews 122
English Server, The 58
entertainment 62
Entertainment Weekly 64
Environmental Protection Agency 148
E! Online 64
EPage 153
Epicurious 85
EpisodeGuides 72
erotica 52, 159
EscapeArtist 34
ESPN.com 170
Esprit.com 155
E-the People 132
eTour 49
eToys 109
E*Trade 83
Europcar 42
EuropeOnTrack 179
EuroTrip 181
Eve.com 164
Everest Mountain Zone 172
Excite 48
Excite Classifieds & Auctions 153
Expedia 178
Exploratorium 147
Explore 170
e-zines 29, 121, 122, 123, 185

F

F1Racing.net 36
Fabric8 155
Family.com 130
Family Education Network 58
FamilyPlay 108
FamilyTreeMaker 56
Family Village 99
Famous Birthdays 64
Fantasy Sports Guide 172
FAO Schwartz 109
fashion 67
Fashion Angel 67
Fashion Dish 70
Fashion Live 68
Fashion Mall 156
Fashion Net 67
Fashion Planet 70
Fast Company 30
Fathering Magazine 131
Federal Bureau of Investigations 135
Federal Deposit Insurance Corporation 80
Federal Emergency Management Agency 127

Federation Internationale de Football Association 174
FedEx 32
Fed World 134
Feedmag 128
Feelin' Groovy 63
Feminist Majority Foundation Online 186
Ferrari North America 41
Fielding's Worldwide 180
film 70
Film 100 71
Film.com 71
Film Threat Online 74
FinAid 61
finance 78
Financenter 81
Find A Grave 183
FindLaw 112
First Church of Cyberspace 143
fitness 96, 98, 170, 171, 168, 186
Fit Pregnancy 131
flirt.com 50
flowers 162
Fodor's 179
Fogdog Sports 167
food and drink 85
Food.com 87
Foot Locker 166
Foreign Languages for Travelers 177
Fortune.com 30
Fox.com 75
Fox News 126
Fragrance Counter 164
France.com 182
FreeAgent.com 36
Freebord 173
FreeEDGAR 82
FreeForum 162
Free Forum Network 162
FreeSpeech Internet Television 137
free stuff 162
FreeZone 108
FreSch! 61
From Jesus to Christ 144
Frommer's 179
FTD.com 162
Fundsnet 32
furniture 103, 104, 106, 165

G
gambling 91
GameCheats.net 91
Gameland.com 92
Gamepen 93
games 91
GameStorm 93
Gap Online 154
Garden.com 165
gardening 103, 104, 148, 165
Garlic Festival Foods 89
Gas-Money.com 41
Gateway to Educational Materials Project 58
Gay Men's Health Crisis 102
Gear.com 168
genealogy 56
GeoCities 47

Geomancy.net 105
Giant Sponge 65
GiftPoint.com 163
gifts 162
Giggo.com 40
GirlsOn 74
Gist TV 77
give.org 137
glassdog.net 49
Globewide Network Academy 62
Go Ask Alice! 97
Godiva Online 161
Go, Girl! Magazine 186
Golf Online 174
Good Karma Cafe 88
Good Vibrations 160
goracing.com 36
GoSki 170
Gourmet Spot 87
Gourmet World 88
government 26, 32, 33, 84, 98, 106, 109, 127, 134, 135, 143, 146, 147, 148, 149, 177
Great Day in Harlem 118
Greatest Films 71
GreatFlowers 163
Great Food 161
Great Sports 172
GreenJungle 84
GreenMarketplace.com 165
Greenpeace International 134
greeting cards 163
Guardian Unlimited 126
Guerrilla Girls 25
Guess Online Store 153
gURL Mag/zine 185
GYN 101 102

H
Hallmark 163
Hamster Dance 183
Harlem Globetrotters 173
Harley-Davidson 41
Harry & David 160
Headhunter.net 35
health 96
Health and Age 149
healthAtoZ.com 99
HealthCentral.com 98
Healthfinder 98
Hecklers Online 67
Hemmings Motor News 37
Her Health Online 185
Herotica 52
hipMama 130
History Channel 56
History Net 57
History of Science, Technology and Medicine Virtual Library 146
Hollywood Reporter 72
Hollywood Stock Exchange 63
Home & Garden TV 104
home and living 103
HomeArts Network 103
Homefair.com 106
Homeowners.com 107
Homestead 47

Hoover's Online 78
Hostels.com 183
HotBot 48
Hotel Discount Reservations 182
hotels 182
HotWired 122
HotWired Cocktail 90
House of Blues 117
House of Boxing 172
housewares 104, 165
Housing and Urban Development 106
How Stuff Works 140
HUD 106
Hues 186
Hyper History 57

I
ICQ 43
Idealist 137
iDrink 90
I Film Network 74
Improvenet 103
Independent 126
Infobeat 124
Infoplease for Kids 111
Information Please Almanac 140
InfoSpace 54
InfoUSA 55
Insider Shopping 156
Insight 45
Institute for Global Communications 136
insurance 41, 80
Insurance Information Institute 80
Insure.com 80
Intellicast.com 127
International Bed & Breakfast Pages 182
International Financial Encyclopaedia 79
International Lyrics Server 120
International Olympic Committee 173
International Sports Museums and Halls of Fame 172
internet 43
Internet Art Resources 22
Internet Bookshop 27
internet guides 48, 49, 62, 111, 138
Internet Movie Database 74
Internet Public Library 138
Internet Public Library/Youth 111
Internet Shipping Center 32
Internet Shopping Outlet 44
Internet Underground Music Archives 118
In the Crease 174
iOwn.com 106
IPO.com 83
iQVC 152
IRS Digital Daily 84
IslamiCity 143
iVillage.com 185
iVillage.com Astrology 66
iVillage.com Relationships 51

J
JCrew.com 155
Jefferson Project 133
Jeopardy! Online 94
Jewish Museum 23

job search 33, 34, 35, 36
Jobtrak.com 34
JobWeb 34
John Skilton's Baseball Links 175
Judaism FAQ 144
Jumbo! Download Network 47
Jump! 31
Just Sports for Women 175

K
Kaktus Productions 107
Kaplan 60
Kasparov vs. The World 93
Kelley Blue Book 38
Kenneth Cole 155
Kick! 175
kids 107
KidsHealth.org 97
Kitchen-bath.com 105
KnowX Public Records 56

L
LA County Museum of Art 22
Lambda Legal Defense Fund 137
Land's End 154
LastMinute.com 176
Launch.com 114
law 112
Law News Network 113
Lawrence Berkeley National Lab 147
Lawyers.com 112
Leadership Conference on Civil Rights 134
Learn2.com 57
LearnPlus Online Language 61
Learn the Net 46
LeaseSource 39
Legaldocs 113
Legal Information Institute 113
Legal Services Corporation 112
LendingTree 106
Librarian's Index to the Internet 141
libraries 58, 138, 139, 141
Library of Congress Home Page 135
literary reviews 28, 29
Liveconcerts.com 119
Living Home 104
L.L. Bean 154
lodging 182
London Net 181
LondonWide 155
Lonely Planet 180
lottery.com 94
Lotto World 94
Lowestfare.com 178
Lumiere 68
Lycos Roadmaps 141

M
Macromedia Shockwave 91
Macy's 151
Macy's Bridal 54
magazines 25, 30, 39, 64, 69, 86, 90, 104, 105, 110, 118, 121, 122, 125, 126, 128, 131, 134, 143, 145, 146, 148, 158, 175, 187
Magellan 49
Making Lemonade 130

Male Health Center 101
MamaMoon 130
Manpower 35
maps 141
Martha Stewart Living 104
Marvel Comics 65
Match.com 50
Mayo Health Clinic 97
MedicineNet.com 98
MediConsult 98
Mental Health.net 99
Mental HelpNet 99
Mercata 152
Merriam Webster Online Dictionary 139
Meta-Searchers Librarian's Index to the Internet 141
Metropolis 105
Metropolitan Museum of Art 23
Microsoft CarPoint 38
Microsoft Sidewalk 181
Microsoft Smallbiz 29
Micro Warehouse 45
Mississippi Review 29
Mixmag Online 118
Models.com 68
Modern Bride 53
Mojo Wire 125
MoneyClub.com 81
Monster.com 33
Morningstar 83
MotherNature.com 100
Motion Picture Association of America 73
Motley Fool 81
MotoDirectory.com 40
Moviefone.com 75
Movie Juice 71
Movieline Online 70
MP3.com 119
Mplayer.com 93
Mr. Showbiz 63
Mr. Smith E-mails Washington 132
MTV Online 114
Multi-Player Online Gaming 93
Muppets.com 108
Museum of Modern Art 23
museums 22, 23, 26, 52, 148
music 114
Mutual Fund Cafe 83
Mybasics.com 164
Mylook 124
Mysteries 94

N
NASA 147
NASCAR Online 36
NASDAQ-Amex 78
National Air and Space Museum 147
National Charities Information Bureau 137
National Climatic Data Center 127
National Enquirer 64
National Foundation for Consumer Credit 85
National Geographic 148
National Parent Teacher Association 58
National Park Service 146
National Partnership for Women and Families 113
National Public Radio 127
National Review 134

National Talk Show Guest Registry 73
National Zoo 147
Natural Land 100
Natural Resource Conservation Service 147
Nature Company 151
n. b. 28
NBA.com 173
NBC.com 76
NCAA Online 175
NCIB 137
Nearly-Wed Handbook 54
NECX Global Electronics Exchange 44
Nerve Boutique 159
Nerve.com 52
NetBaby 91
NetGrocer.com 160
NetLitigation 113
Net Radio.com 120
Newcity.com 124
New Republic, The 134
news 120
New Scientist Magazine 145
newsgroups 42
NewsMaps.com 123
News of the Weird 125
newspapers 123, 124, 125, 126, 181
Newsweek 121
New York Botanical Garden 148
New York Review of Books 28
New York Times 125
New York Times Current Theater 24
NFL.com 170
Nick at Nite & TV Land 72
Nickelodeon Online 107
Nine Planets 145
NineWest 166
NME 116
Northern Light 48
NPR Online 127
nutrition 100, 101, 102
NYstyle 151

O
Office Depot Online 166
office supplies 166
Official Site of Major League Baseball 175
Off-road.com 41
Oh, the Humanity! 75
Oneworld.net 127
Online Books 28
Online Medical Dictionary 97
OnlineOfficeSupplies.com 166
Onlineshoes.com 166
Online Sports 168
Onsale 46
organizers 31, 44, 103
Oscar.com 73
Outpost.com 43
Overseas Jobs Express 34
Overtons.com 167
Owners.com 106
Oxygen 184
Oyez Project 113

P

PalmGear HQ 44
parenting 129
Parent Soup 129
Paris Pages 181
Partners Task Force for Gay & Lesbian Couples 52
PBS Adult Learning Service Online 60
PBS Online 76
PBS Online Science 146
PBS Technology 46
PC Webopaedia 142
Perry Castaneda Library Map Collection 139
Peterson's 60
Pete's Bikindex 171
pets 105, 106
Petstore.com 105
Phone Numbers.net 55
photography 22, 25, 26, 165
Photography in New York International 25
Phys.com 96
Piece Unique 156
Pitchforkmedia.com 118
Places to Stay 183
Planet Poker 95
PlanetRecruit 36
PlanetRider 177
PlanetRx.com 165
Planned Parenthood 102
Playbill Online 24
Pogo 91
Pointcast 47
Policy.com 136
Political Junkie 132
Political Resources on the Net 136
politics and issues 132
Pollstar 119
Pop Culture Corn 65
Pop History Now 65
Popular Science 145
Powell's Books 27
Preview Travel 176
price comparisons 157
Priceline 178
Pricewatch 45
Project Bartleby Archive 139
Project Vote Smart 136
Protest.net 137
Pulitzer Prizes 29

Q

QSpace 85
Quicken.com 82
Quicken.com Retirement 150
Quickspice 90

R

Reader's Digest 125
Real Beer Page 89
real estate 106
Realtor.com 106
recipes 85, 86, 87
RedEnvolope.com 163
Red Herring 78
Reel.com 169
ReelPreviews.com 74
reference 138
regional 180, 181, 182
REI.com 168
religion 143
Rent.net 107
Republic of Tea 89
Research-it 142
ResearchPaper.com 142
restaurants 71, 86, 87
Reuters 125
Revue 26
Riddler 95
Rides Online 40
Road & Track Online 39
Roadside America 181
Rock n Road 171
Rolling Good Times Online 91
Rolling Stone Network 115
Rough Guides 180
Runner's World 170
rsub 128
RV Link 179

S

Salon.com 121
Salon Travel 176
Salt & Pepper 86
San Diego Zoo 145
science and nature 145
ScreenIt! 72
Script-o-rama 71
SearchShark 55
SecretAdmirer.com 51
Secular Web 144
SecureTax.com 84
Seeing Ear Theater 66
Seinfeld.com 77
Senior.com 150
Senior Living Online 149
seniors 149
Sesame Street.com 108
Sexual Health InfoCenter 101
Shades.com 156
Sharper Image 159
shipping 32
shoes 166
Shop For Change 152
ShopNow.com 151
shopping 150
Six Degrees 74
Slate 123
SmarterKids 109
SmartMoney.com 31
SmarTraveler 177
SmellTheCoffee.com 90
Smith & Hawken.com 165
Smithsonian Institution 26
Smithsonian Magazine 122
Soap Digest 76
SocialFunds.com 80
Social Security Online 149
Soda Fountain 90
software 33, 34, 35, 36, 44, 45, 46, 47
Soldout.com 169
SonicNet 115
Sotheby's 153
Sound Market 117

South Park 77
space 145, 147
Spank! 110
Sparks.com 163
SpiceGuide 86
Spin 115
Spinner.com 120
Sport Hits 173
SportingAuction.com 168
sporting goods 167
sports 170
Sports Illustrated for Kids 108
Sports Illustrated for Women 175
Sports Jones Magazine 172
SportsParents 175
Spree 152
StampsOnline 32
Stanford Securities Class Action
Clearinghouse 82
Starbuzz 64
StarChefs 86
Star Wars.com 77
Stateline.org 132
SteveMadden.com 167
StudyAbroad.com 62
StudyWeb 142
Style Experts 67
Style Shop 156
Style Wire 69
Stylin' 68
Suck.com 128
Sundance Channel 75
SunglassSite 157
Superbad 184
Supercars—Past and Present 39
SupportHelp.com 47
Sushi Guide 88
Switchboard.com 55
Swoon 50

T
Talk City 42
Tape Trader Network 116
Taxes4Less.com 84
Teachers.net 59
Tech Museum, The 148
Teen Advice Online 112
Teenhoopla 111
teens 107
television stations 57, 71, 72, 75, 76, 126
Television Ticket Co. 73
Tennis.com 174
Terraserver 57
ThaiGrocer 161
The Artchive 22
theater 22, 24, 27
The Blip 92
The English Server 58
The Gap Online 154
The Guggenheim Museums 23
The Industry Standard 45
The Knot 53
The Louvre 23
The Nation 122
The Onion 125
The Paperboy 124

The Phantom of the Opera 24
The Street.com 82
The Sync 77
The Why Files 146
The Wire 120
ThirdAge.com 149
THOMAS 133
Thomas Historical Documents 58
Thrive Online 98
Ticketmaster Online 168
tickets 22, 75, 168, 169
Ties.com 157
Time.com 121
Time.com Asia 121
Time for Kids 110
Timeout Worldwide 180
Tixx.com 168
TLA Video 169
Today's Calendar and Clock Page 142
Total News 123
tourism 146, 180, 181, 182
Tower Records 169
Toyota USA 41
toys 109
Toys In Babeland 159
Traditional Home DesignerFinder 103
Trailerpage.com 73
transportation 40, 178, 179
travel 176
TravelAsia.Net 182
Travel Channel 177
travel destinations 180
travel guides 179
Travelocity 178
Travel Warnings & Advisories 177
Tricycle Hub 143
Tripod Resume Builder 35
Trivia World 94
Tune in Sports 171
Tunes.com 116
TV 70
TV Grid 77
TV Guide 76

U
UCAS 62
Ucopia 53
U.K. Natural History Museum 148
Ultimate Band List 114
Ultimate Chat List, The 43
Underneath.com 157
UnGroomed 54
United Nations 135
United States Department of Labor 33
United States Postal Service 32
Universal Currency Converter 177
Unrepresented Nations and
People's Organization 135
Uproar 95
Urban Decay 164
US News.edu 60
US News Online 121
U. S. Patent & Trademark Office 33
US Public Info 55
US Securities and Exchange Commission 82

V

Variety.com 63
Vatican, The 143
VaultReports.com 35
Vegas Insider 95
vegetarian 87, 88, 161
Veggie Life 88
Vibe 115
Victoria's Secret 156
videos 169
Village Voice 181
Violet 163
Virtual Dog 183
Virtual Garden 103
Virtual Job Fair 35
Virtual Opera House 117
Virtual SchoolHouse 59
Virtual Vegas 95
VolunteerMatch 137

W

wacky sites 183
Wall of Sound 114
Wall Street Journal 78
Wall Street Journal's Careers 35
Wal-Mart 152
Washington Post Chapter One 29
Washingtonpost.com 126
WBS 43
weather 127
WeatherLabs 127
Web100 49
WebActive 135
WebComics 65
Webflyer 178
WebMarket 158
Web of Online Dictionaries 140
web page hosting 47
Webpersonals 51
Wedding Channel 54
weddings 53
Weekend Mechanics Club 37
whatis.com 44
Whatsonstage.com 27
When.com 31
White House 135
Whitney Museum of American Art 23
Who2 63
WhoWhere 55
Why Files 146
WidowNet 150
Wild Oats Markets 161
wine 89, 161, 162
Wine Spectator 89
Winezone 162
Wired 145
WNBA.com 174
Women.com 184
Women's Health Interactive 186
women's sites 184
Women's Sports Network 171
Women's Wire MoneyMode 80
Word 128
Wordsworth Books 27
World Conflicts 132
World Museum of Erotic Art 52

WorldNews.com 123
World Opponent Network 92
Worldsport.com 173
WorldSpy 158
World Wide Holiday and Festival Page 142
Wristwatch.com 157
WWW Speedtrap Registry 40

Y

Yahoo! Chat 43
Yahooligans! 109
Yahoo! Store 30
Yoga Site 174
Youth for Understanding 62
Yuckiest Site on the Web 110

Z

Zagat Survey 87
ZDNet 44
zZounds 158

Editor-in-Chief Rula Razek
Design Tika Buchanan and James Tung
of Eric Baker Design Associates, NY
Sales Associate Diana Swartz
Picture Editor Danielle Goodyear
Assistant Editor Krista Prestek
Writer-Researchers Becca Burns, Stephanie Dempsey, Eithne Richardson, Alexis Wichowski, Zanja Yudell
Copy Editor Elaine Luthy
Intern Anna Nordberg

Project Advisor Nan Richardson

Internet Cool Guide
© 1999 te Neues Publishing Company
16 West 22nd Street, New York, NY 10010
www.teneues.com

All rights reserved. No part of this book may be reproduced without written permission of te Neues Publishing Company except in the case of brief quotations for review.

All Web sites reproduced herein copyright © their respective owners.
Certain Web site information, selections, or material contained in Internet Cool Guide may no longer be current at the time of publication because the sites in question are updated and revised on a regular and continuing basis.

While we strive for utmost precision in every detail, we cannot be held responsible for any inaccuracies, neither for any subsequent loss or damage arising.

ISBN 3-8238-0997-0

First Edition

Printed in Germany

notes

notes